WAITING FOR WESTMORELAND

Waiting for Westmoreland

A Memoir

John Maberry

Eagle Peak Press

Published in 2007 by
Eagle Peak Press
P.O. Box 151922
Alexandria, VA 22315-1922
www.eaglepeakpress.com

Cover by Gary Ross, www.graphicdesignfx.com

Note to the reader: *This work depicts actual events in the life of the author as truthfully as recollection permits and/or can be verified by research. Occasionally, dialogue consistent with the character or nature of the person speaking has been supplemented. All persons within are actual individuals; there are no composite characters. The names of some individuals have been changed to respect their privacy.*

ISBN: 978-0-6151-6045-0

Library of Congress Control Number: 2007906359

Printed in the United States of America

For Juanita, the love of my life
and for
Daisaku Ikeda, my mentor in life

— · — · — · — · — ·

and to
George and Jackie:
See you in another lifetime

Acknowledgements

Thank you, Leslie, for putting me on the right path. Thanks to the SGI members or leaders that helped keep me there with their encouragement, inspiration and assistance. There are too many to list all of you, so in naming only a few, I hope those I don't mention here won't feel slighted. Although I don't see you as often anymore, I must thank Bob Tansey, Jeff and Joanie Kaye, Gene and Charlotte Hurdle and John Benson. I must thank Masami Hussey, a co-leader from long ago. Also some fellow members I once led who now lead me: Tony Goodlette, Mike Gauer and Rich Winkler. For reviewing this book for adherence to Buddhist doctrine and otherwise counseling me, I thank Greg Martin.

Thanks much to Marj Watson, Kathleen Kelly, Frances Grande, Kim Olson, Lin Booth and Mike Stringer—writing class and writing group members for your critiques and suggestions from the early stages onward. Thanks especially to Vonnie Schmitt who critiqued a draft of the entire book. Thanks to Joanne Glenn, for instruction in the writing trade. Thank you especially to Jeanette Ritzenthaler, who passed away several years ago, without hearing from me how much her 12-grade English class meant to me.

Thank you to Jackie who kept me company while I worked on this. You won't remember it in your next life, but thank you anyway. Thank you to Bill and Lorraine who tolerated the two years I spent with them and who must endure my commentary about those days. Most of all, I thank Juanita for encouraging and supporting me in writing this, as well as having the grace to accept the publication of all the personal details that other persons might wish were kept private. But if they were, I could neither write this book nor could we sincerely encourage others about the power of our faith.

Prologue — The Threat, the Opportunity

"IF THE TWO OF THEM get married or I find the two of them together, I'll kill the both of them." It was the week before Thanksgiving, 1979, when a shaky-voiced Juanita called to pass along her father's plans for us. At least that is what she overheard him telling her brother.

"He's just saying that, right?"

"Maybe, but we need to take this seriously—he has a gun in a safe at home," she said, a tremble of fear in her voice.

"But he wouldn't really do that, would he?" *No way,* I thought.

"You don't know my father. He has a very angry nature. There are things he's done that…well, things I can't tell you about. But believe me, he is perfectly capable of it."

"So what are we going to do?" I asked, my disbelief finally fading.

"I don't know. I just want you to be careful. He might be following me."

"Well, maybe you shouldn't come here to my place for a while."

"We could still see each other at activities," she added, hopefully.

"Unless he followed you. What kind of car does he drive?"

"A '78 Caprice wagon. It's black."

"OK. Let's lay low for a few days, just to be safe. We need to think about this."

"We need to chant about it!"

"Uh, yeah, I guess so."

I had first met Juanita at a Buddhist meeting in the spring of 1977. Four years of college and three years of law school were soon ending. Now what would I do? Paralyzed by indecision about my future, I was still grasping at straws as graduation approached. If Buddhism would enable me to move, I would try it. What I wasn't interested in was getting intimately involved with someone right then. At age 30, I had already been twice married, with the second marriage well on its way to the same end as the first—a divorce. Marriage had been a refuge I sought, a safe harbor to which I could retreat, protection from whatever storms or stress might trouble my existence. In the end, my twice-mistaken monogamy brought me misery, not security.

So, instead of looking for lasting love, beginning the summer of 1977 I went looking for the social life I had never had. Over a 15-month span, I went out with more people than I had in the previous 15 years. I wasn't out for casual sex, just for social interaction. Juanita was not among those I went out with at first, but near the end of that period, following a Halloween party in 1978, we began dating. She had the same powerful life force I found typical among women who practiced Buddhism. But she had something more as well. She shared my passions for science fiction, waterfalls in the woods and more. When we got serious a year later, I figured I had defeated my relationship demons. I no longer needed someone else to make me happy. Instead of an escape into dependence, marriage would be a place to share happiness from within. Despite my confidence in this new perspective on marriage, I knew I was risking being a three-time loser. George Harrison upped the risk to being a *dead* one.

It was my call to him, just two days before Juanita's report that prompted the threat. I hadn't spoken to her father since our only meeting in January, earlier that year. The conversation didn't go as I had hoped.

"Mr. Harrison, this is John Maberry."

"Who?" His deep voice boomed back.

"John Maberry. The one with the green telephone van." I instantly regretted my words.

"Oh yeah, I remember you! Why are you calling here? I got nothing to talk about with you." He spat out, sounding ready to hang up.

"Well, I know we met under awkward circumstances, but I want to put that behind us. I was calling to let you know that your daughter Juanita and I are planning to get married next year." The silence was deafening for a few moments, before the explosion came.

"Married? You say you gonna marry *my* daughter! Don't you think I got something to say about that?"

"Well…sure, that's why I was calling you. But she is 30 years old. I was calling as a courtesy, out of respect to you as her father."

"Respect! You don't respect me. You don't know nothing about respect!" He snorted.

"I'm sorry you feel that way." I stammered, unsure how to respond.

"You're sorry all right! You stay away from my daughter and don't you be calling back here again," he said, hanging up the phone. At the time, I was surprised by his anger but unconcerned. An unpleasant conversation to be sure, I thought, but of no lasting consequence. I was mistaken, of course. By the time he threatened to kill us, he had undoubtedly given this call much thought.

What could Juanita and I do? Should we just forget about our marriage plans, give up our relationship and start over with somebody else? Maybe we could run away to a proverbial Timbuktu where her father couldn't find us. Could I get him before he got us? I had nothing against him, even if he did want to kill me. But if it were he or I to live or die, then I either would have to strike first or be prepared to fight back. Not a pleasant thought to contemplate. Or should we try to change his mind? A very difficult undertaking and potentially fatal if we failed to convince him.

Why was this happening to me? Of all the women in the world I could get involved with, why did I choose one whose father wanted to kill me? I had no strong feelings one way or the other toward George Harrison, having met him only once. Yet he felt strongly enough about me to contemplate my death. When Juanita and I got to the point of discussing marriage, I considered that George Harrison might not warmly welcome me into the family. Some opposition I could understand, but killing us both seemed a little excessive. I knew he had a couple reasons to be upset, the first of which was my skin color.

Her father didn't care much for white folks. He had endured plenty as a black man in a white world. Juanita told me of his military experience during WW II, in a segregated unit, and what happened after his discharge. He had fought in the South Pacific, becoming a platoon sergeant. Although they all fought as Americans on foreign soil, U.S. military policy prohibited black soldiers from fighting alongside the whites. As a returning Army sergeant, the local bus company was more than happy to offer him a driver's job sight unseen. Upon showing up in person however, they said he must have misunderstood. The only openings were for janitors. I couldn't blame him for how he felt about white people. Why should he view me as being any different from the rest?

My complexion wasn't the only problem. There was that unexpected encounter, our only face-to-face meeting, the previous winter. I had gone to pick her up for a party later that night. We were having a little pre-party party at her place beforehand. Juanita lived in a house only a few blocks from her father in northeast Washington, DC. He had encouraged her to buy it, cosigning the mortgage and putting his name on the deed as a co-owner. Driving by her house that night, he was suspicious of the old telephone van with Virginia tags parked along the curb. After a knock on the door failed to produce an immediate response, he let himself in. The sweet smell of marijuana hung heavy in the air as he ascended the stairs to her bedroom, yelling, "Juanita, what the hell's going on here? Who you got in there?"

"Nobody, Daddy," she lied, as I ducked into the closet—where I was quickly discovered.

"Get your clothes on and get the hell outta here," he said to me. I scrambled into my clothes and quickly departed.

So I was white *and* I smoked dope. Although reason enough for some people to kill, there was more to his threat than that. The fundamental reason for Mr. Harrison's threat wouldn't become clear for more than 20 years. I had asked for this to happen, although I could have no conscious memory of that. I needed this threat to happen, in order to transform my life. It's really all in how you view things. It's a choice of waiting for Westmoreland or going ahead without him. It's a choice of viewing negative karma as an opportunity or as an ugly destiny. The long chain of cause and effect I had created to reach this point wound far back in time from my experiences with George Harrison, through Vietnam and all the way back to my childhood dream of being a writer. So I better start where the dream began, in Minneapolis.

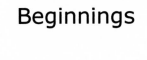

Beginnings

Chapter 1 — Lessons Learned Early

I SPENT MY FIRST 11 years living in a small stucco house in Minneapolis, the second one in from Humboldt Avenue, where the first block of Victory Memorial Drive began. The mile-long boulevard commemorated America's successful end to the First World War. How odd it seems to me now, growing up on a street by that name. My war, Vietnam, had a somewhat different conclusion. It would leave me not a sense of victory but one of loss, both for my country and for myself. My parents bought the house new, in 1929, 18 years before I was born.

No longer new by my time, the blackened walls of the former coal bin were now just a reminder of an old furnace that once warmed the dwelling. The detached garage at the end of our small back yard had a current-leaking rotary light switch that would give a mild shock on rainy days. A dirt alley next to the garage separated us from an out lot next to the Soo Line tracks. Further back was a switchyard, with engines shuttling boxcars back and forth most days of the week. Through trains rumbled by during the night, with steel wheels clicking and clacking on the rails and whistles sounding in advance of the grade crossing at Humboldt Avenue. I slept through the sound, growing accustomed to it much as I later would the sounds of distant artillery and helicopter gunship fire during Vietnam nights, waking only when the battle grew too near.

Except for the trains, it was a quiet enough neighborhood. At least I thought so. I was eight or nine years old when my mother read me a newspaper report about a gruesome murder. The killers had dragged the cook out of the Bandbox, a burger joint in Camden, a tiny business district in north Minneapolis about a mile from our house.

"They banged his head on the curb until he was dead—because he was Chinese," she cried, tears welling up in her eyes. "It's just like the Ku Klux Klan, dragging black people from their homes—whipping, beating or killing them because of their skin color."

I said nothing, unsure how to reply either to her sorrow or to her disgust, but the image of people being dragged out and beaten remained seared in my mind. Her reading was an instructional moment about racism to which she returned on other occasions. I never thought to ask her why or how she came to hold so strongly these views opposing racism. Perhaps her own Norwegian parents, both immigrants to America in their youth, had instilled this virtue. It was enough for me to know that her kind heart's embrace extended beyond the walls of the home.

Minnesota didn't have then, and still doesn't have, a large African-American population. Most of this minority population is concentrated within the Twin Cities of Minneapolis and St. Paul. Although not quite next-door, there were minority households not far from my own, literally on the other side of the tracks just a few blocks away. My class of 25 students at nearby Hamilton Elementary School, where I attended kindergarten through the first half of sixth grade, had a couple of Asians and two or three African-Americans. I don't recall the teachers or my fellow students treating them any differently than the white majority, but perhaps my mother's viewpoint clouds my memory.

Hamilton was a very old school. It had been old when my mother went there 30 years before me. It's long gone now, replaced by an assisted living facility. While I attended, it already smelled like a nursing home with aged architectural details all around. The school had tall window sashes and transoms over classroom doors opened by those long-handled poles with a black metal stub on the end. Cracking-black-painted telephones hung on the classroom walls. The old phones had rayon-covered cords running from clarinet-bell-shaped earpieces and short-funnel mouthpieces centered on the face of the phone. Like most libraries, courthouses and other government buildings, the school also had the requisite black and yellow fallout shelter signs above the basement stairs.

Like everyone else in 1950s American elementary schools, I learned to duck and cover under my desk—in case of a nuclear attack by the Soviet Union. A fat lot of good hiding under our desks would have done in a real attack, but such were the illusions of safety from fallout at that point in nuclear warfare knowledge. No one told us in grade school about Mutually Assured Destruction—the facile concept that a massive nuclear arms race between the U.S. and the Soviet Union (and later China) would prevent either side from nuking the other, in the certain knowledge that retaliation would wreak destruction of both. No, just duck under the desk, we were told. Then we could live on to fight the Communist menace.

Over time, I came to accept the notion that communism was a bad thing and democracy a good thing. Was it the teachers at Hamilton, what little television news I saw back then, or was it my much older brother Doug, born 19 years before me that supplied my perspectives? Probably it was a combination of all three. "We will bury you," said Nikita Khrushchev (then Soviet Premier) in 1956, commenting on the political fortune of communism versus democracy. To my impressionable mind, communism seemed an oppressive political regime imposed on unwilling people. The people in Communist-led countries were not bad, just those evil leaders who ran the countries were bad. The leaders personified and maintained the wicked system. Democracy, on the other hand, was that most wonderful thing which had arisen from the Declaration of Independence, the Constitution and the Bill of Rights. Somehow, this amalgam of ingredients produced a higher-principled political system, precluding the evils and oppression that communism allowed. If only the people could be liberated from that oppressive Communist system, they could be happy and free like Americans. Ah, the bliss of simple belief!

While the Cold War was a fact of fifties life, we were not obsessing about it in school each day. Like most children, I suppose, I went through most school days unconcerned about larger world events. In fact, my dream of writing sprung to life during second grade at Hamilton School. Mrs. Libby thought so well of my short story with the surprise ending that she submitted it to a children's literary magazine. Alas, it turned out to be my first rejection letter, but the idea that I could be a writer seized me. It puzzles me now, how I was able to develop that dream given my father's illness.

Cancer was already ravaging my father's body while I was in kindergarten. I have only a few memories of him either well or sick. I recall riding with him in small boat on Cross Lake, trolling for pike. Sunlight sparkled off the shallow waves tossed up by the wind. That peculiarly distinctive smell of an outboard motor's exhaust fumes bubbled through the lake water. I must have been three or four, because he wasn't sick then. He wasn't sick, or at least not very sick, when he and my mother came home later than expected one night, to find me in tears worried about where they were as darkness fell. My most vivid memory of him came when I must have been six or nearly seven years old. I opened a door to the front bedroom and saw my father lying grimacing on a day bed, while the family doctor inserted a catheter into his urethra. I watched as bloody urine streamed into a bag below the bed. My father turned and saw me then. He motioned to my brother Doug to get me out of the room. Once outside the room, Doug said, with tears in his eyes, "You weren't supposed to see that."

"Why did the doctor do that?" I asked, bewildered by the torturous treatment.

"He can't pee anymore, because of the cancer. He has to have that tube in his peepee to get the pee out," Doug struggled to explain, seeming to feel our father's pain almost as much as he did himself. Dad returned to Asbury Methodist hospital soon after. The pain he felt was more than he could bear to show his wife and sons, Doug told me later.

During the summer of 1954, between my first and second grades of school, Mom came home from Asbury crying, "Your father's gone to heaven," she said. I cried too, because she was crying, not really understanding why. Sunday school had taught me that heaven was a good place.

He was just 48 when he died, and I was seven. I saw him for the final time, a few days later, a waxy-faced facsimile of a father I barely knew, lying in his satin-shrouded coffin. What I said, what I felt, I do not know. I do know that once school began in the fall, a school psychologist pulled me out of class at times, for one-on-one sessions. My mother told me it was because my teacher thought I didn't interact well with other kids. I think now perhaps my behavior problems came from being undisciplined at home. Whenever my brother Doug, 19 years older than me, attempted to curb my behavior, I would yell at him, "You're not my father. You can't tell me what to do!" From the hurt look it gave him, I could tell it stung him, reminding him of our father's death. I know now that I was hurting too, but I didn't know it then.

My mother blamed Dad's cancer for my behavior. When she got exasperated with me, she would always say, "Your father was in such pain, that he always said, 'Oh, just leave him alone' whenever I told you to stop doing something." As bratty and spoiled as I was, I still wanted to be a good kid and do the right thing. Wanting to be good and doing good, unfortunately, is not the same thing. From the things she said and did, it was clear that my mother felt it important always to do the right thing. So did Doug.

I went to Sunday school at North Methodist Church every week back then, while Mom attended services. There I learned to sing, "Jesus loves me, this I know, for the Bible tells me so." If he did, I had no other way of knowing. All the pictures I ever saw of him showed him looking up and away, not at me. Later on, I went to some neighbor lady's house after school from time to time for something she called the "Good News Club." I guess it was a home version of Sunday school, complete with a board on which she stuck felt letters and religious figures to illustrate Bible passages. I invited my friend Nick, who lived next door to us, to come with me but he told me his father wouldn't let him because they were Catholic. It was probably my first inkling that not everybody looked at religion or God in the same way. From having dinner with Nick one night, I learned that every meal at the Polivka house began with saying grace. Meals at my house never did. It didn't seem to make Nick much different from me. Church and religion seemed just as much a separate part of his life as it was of mine. Something we did mostly on Sundays and forgot about the rest of the week. While church and the "Good News Club" provided some glimpses about morality, I think my mother's influence was more important.

Before Dad died, my mother had worked for a time at the Kenwood School lunchroom, a long bus ride away in the more affluent area of St. Louis Park. Crippling rheumatoid arthritis that contorted her fingers like twigs on a branch forced Mom to quit the cafeteria. With Dad gone, her sole income became Social Security, including a widow's survivor benefits for herself and dependent benefits for me. With an eighth grade education and no experience managing the family's finances, she was ill equipped to deal with a mortgage and other financial obligations on her own. This left 26-year-old Doug responsible for seeing that the bills got paid. My other brother Bill, two years younger than Doug, could provide no help. Bill had moved out the house a few years before when he got married. Now he was going to college.

Doug couldn't handle the pressure. He had enlisted in the Marines right after graduating from high school in 1946. He had completed two years of college after his service but the Marines called him back to active duty in 1950 for the Korean War. There he faced combat in the Chosin Reservoir. He returned early from Korea, with an accidentally inflicted gunshot wound to his ankle. He went back to Hamline University to finish his education. I remember that he wanted to be an English teacher or a speech therapist, but I'm not sure which one it was. I do recall that he helped me with some pronunciation problems.

"It's all in where you place the tongue. You have to touch the gums with the end of your tongue, at the bottom edge of the hard palate, right behind your front teeth to make the gl sound for glass," Doug demonstrated. "Otherwise it will sound like grass." I still looked up to Doug then, before my father died and before Doug's dreams died as well.

Instead of teaching, he took a job at a loan company in Sioux City, Iowa early in 1953. When my father's cancer progressed, Doug returned home. First, the Korean War experience, then my father's lingering illness and finally the financial responsibility at home must have become too much for him. Alcohol became his refuge and his curse. Perhaps he should have been better than my mom was at managing money, having earned a college degree and having worked first at a small loan company and then a debt counseling service. Apparently, the booze reduced his capacity for handling money at home.

First, my father's two-year-old car was repossessed due to missing payments. Within a couple more years, the bank foreclosed on the home mortgage for the same reason. By age 11, I had only contempt for Doug. My mother blamed his drinking for our losing the house. She blamed Bill as well. "He could have helped out," she complained, "instead of just thinking about himself and his wife." I was in no position to know who was at fault. All I knew was that my mother was crying a lot again, as she did for several months after Dad died, and everything in my house was being divided up among relatives and friends. With the little equity remaining in the house, Bill did arrange for my mother to buy a house trailer (now known as "manufactured housing") in Phoenix.

Shortly before leaving for Arizona, I took the opportunity to antagonize Doug while we said our goodbyes to other family members gathered at Bill's house in Wayzata for the occasion. Sitting around a card table, I swung my feet wildly under the table, kicking Doug in the shins.

"Stop kicking me!" Doug scolded me.

"I didn't do anything," I lied.

"You were kicking me," he said again.

"Was not! You're always picking on me," I whined.

"Stop picking on him, we'll be gone to Arizona soon enough," my mother said, totally snowed by my award-winning performance.

Despite my antipathy to his drinking and my spoiled nature, I somehow acquired values and ideals from Doug. Compassion and sympathy for his weakness would come only much later, as I looked more closely at my own means of escape. He had found alcohol in Korea. I would find marijuana in Vietnam. Doug clearly wanted to do good deeds, to serve others. He sometimes replayed the 78-rpm recording he had made in a coin-operated recording booth (much like the once common photo booths used by teenagers all across America) memorializing his spoken commentary on the perils of the atom bomb. Aided by the liberating effects of alcohol on the store of fond memories, Doug often spoke with pride of his protecting a polio-stricken classmate at the expense of his own knees. He had taken a misstep off the grandstand at the football field while carrying the young man to his wheelchair. Falling to his knees, he had managed not to drop him. Doug's self-medication generated frequent melodrama and emotional undercurrents. It annoyed me, yet at the same time, I somehow internalized the underlying values he expressed during those episodes. Finding a purpose in life and creating value in the world were the goals I should pursue. While I continued going to church and the "Good News Club" for some time, neither of them seemed to offer a purpose or direction in life.

So we went on to Arizona, driven there by Bill while he was on winter break from his fifth and final year at the University of Minnesota. The trip was unremarkable except for the raging snowstorm we drove through in the Salt River Canyon. After a brief stop for food at a diner, we came out to find an inch of snow covering the car. While he brushed snow from the windshield, I heard him arguing with a local man on the wisdom of continuing onward from Show Low to Globe, about 90 miles east of Phoenix. As the man had warned us, the snow did pick up once we were in the canyon. A solid wall of white reflected back the headlights' beams. We drove slowly and close to another fool out on the highway that night, able to see only the taillights ahead and not where we were going. Fortunately, that car we followed must have known all the curves by heart or we surely would have not survived. To me it was a thrilling escapade. For my mother, I later learned, the trip had been a terror.

Bill set Mom up in the trailer park before returning to Minnesota. It felt strange, but like an adventure, moving into an 8-foot wide by 32-foot long trailer after living in the house in Minneapolis. There was no mantle displaying Dad's many trophies from table tennis and ski jumping. Nor was there a dank basement, a well-worn player piano or an attic to which I could escape. The trailer was just a metal-clad shell broken into compartments. Mom had a bedroom at the back, spanning the width of the trailer. Mine was along the side, a little larger than a sleeping car train berth, but not by much. In the dry Phoenix heat, an evaporative cooler on the roof was sufficient to keep us cool, with a fan drawing the hot air across a wet bale of straw.

The park was on Maryland Avenue, in what was then the Northern outskirts of Phoenix. There were no shops, restaurants or gas stations in either direction for close to a mile, except a few widely spaced homes on large lots. Maria and Ivan Krutosf, some relatives of one of her long-time friends from Minneapolis had moved out there a year or so before to run the park. The Krutosfs had a house, rather than a trailer, in which to live. Alongside the house, they had a large chicken coop, with a flock of 20-30 hens. Living in the city, the only chickens I had ever seen before were the featherless dead ones my mother cooked in the kitchen. Watching them one day, not long after our arrival, I saw one of the hens being pecked at by several others, each taking turns pursuing and drawing blood from the struggling bird.

"What are they doing? Why don't you stop them?" I asked Maria Krutosf.

"That's what they do with sick birds," she replied with a laugh in her voice, "they kill them."

I was shocked and disturbed at the sight, but I was more disturbed by the amusement of Maria at my question and her matter of fact disinterest in what was happening. Without saying it in so many words, Maria was telling me that this was just the way life is. It is OK for the strong to kill the weak or disabled. Did everyone feel this way? Perhaps she only felt that way about chickens, perhaps not.

Ours was the last trailer in the row, seven in from the chicken coop. A dusty field lay beyond the narrow strip of grass next to the cement patio alongside our trailer, the turf surviving only by regular watering. Next door lived a much older lady who soon earned my contempt. She didn't particularly like kids, it seemed. She too had arthritis, like my mom, but not nearly so crippling. She got around in an electric golf cart, which she used for going shopping at a store a mile or so down the road. She would take my mom with her on shopping trips, but not me.

"Mom, can I go along with?"

"Is that OK, Evelyn; can John come with us?"

"No, I'm sorry, the extra weight of one more person means I have to charge the batteries much more often. I can't afford to keep charging the batteries just to keep Johnny occupied. Besides, we need the space in back for groceries."

I did wear husky clothes, but I wasn't that big or heavy. To my young mind, this seemed like an implausible excuse. But in thinking back, perhaps she did believe it. She did incessantly warn my mother about the dangers of the Melmac cups Mom used for tea and coffee.

"You shouldn't use those; they're dangerous. They're made with formaldehyde. Hot liquids will release the chemical and poison you. It will also counteract the benefit of the copper bracelets I gave you for your arthritis."

"Hmm, I'll have to look into that, Evelyn." That's what Mom always said in response, after my brother Bill, assuaged her concerns. In his last year of studying chemical engineering, he should know.

"Take it from me, Mother, the formaldehyde and all the other chemicals that go into making Melmac are bonded into the material. Boiling water isn't hot enough to release anything from the cups or saucers," he had told her. As I would come to learn later on, Bill was always right—and most annoyingly, knew that he was. He also told her the copper bracelets wouldn't help in any case. He was right about that too.

School was a couple miles away in the opposite direction from the store Evelyn carted my mom to now and then. It required a bus ride, a new and sometimes ugly experience for me. Back then, Phoenix still included 7th and 8th grades with elementary school. This meant we had one teacher for the entire day, for all subjects. It also meant that kids further along in physical development were lumped in with smaller and more immature kids on the playgrounds and the buses. Despite my mother's occasional lessons about racism, I was unaccustomed to seeing racial or ethnic conflict around me. So I was surprised at the problems I saw between Anglos and Mexicans in Phoenix. The school bus on which I rode from the trailer park sometimes became a battleground. On one trip to school, a Mexican kid grabbed an Anglo around the neck from behind while another undid the kid's jeans and exposed his genitals.

"Hey Rosa, take a look at the chilito [little penis] on the gringo," the kid said to a nearby girl.

I froze in fear, looking quickly away lest I become the next victim. Maria Krutosf had warned us of this, laughingly telling us about the nature of things at the school, "The Mexican kids don't care too much for fancy dressed Anglos. They think a kid's pants are too fancy, they'll just pull them off him." She thought it hilarious. I thought she was pulling my leg until I saw it for myself.

When my mom, over my objections, bought dressy flannel pants for me to wear to school, I was more than a little concerned. On the playground at recess, I managed to rip a good-sized hole in the knee of the pants soon after the bus incident. It traumatized Mom, my ripping the costly pants. She could ill afford my tearing up expensive school clothes on her Social Security income, but I didn't really understand that then. She acceded to my wearing nondescript jeans after that. Meanwhile, the school remained an ugly, unhappy and dangerous place with frequent fights on and off the playground between browns and whites or bullies and victims. So stomachaches, buses intentionally missed and other means of avoiding school became routine for me and a continuing challenge for my mom.

A year after we arrived, the Krutosfs sold the land to a developer and moved back to Minneapolis. We had to move again. Trailer and all, we moved to another park on the Western end of Phoenix, 3211 West Van Buren. The park was much larger, with a bigger pool. Municipal buses ran into the city from in front of the park, although my mother much preferred the expensive comfort of taxicabs. Missing the bus to avoid school was not an option here. The newly built school I transferred to was within walking distance at a rear corner of the park, 150 yards away.

The school was relatively new, in a better part of town than the one I had attended the year before. But this was not an affluent suburb, this was still a school populated with low to middle-income students at best. The same problems with browns and whites continued. While the school building was new, the educational fashion was old. In Phoenix, corporal punishment was not only permitted in public schools but also encouraged. The preferred paddle among teachers and principals had a wide blade and narrow handle, with air-resistance-foiling holes drilled in the business end. Perhaps fear of the pain it would bring kept the timid like me in check. It didn't keep the tough kids in check, who boasted of swats as a badge of honor. That was not the worst of it.

My 8th grade classroom had one student with a disability. I don't know whether it was muscular dystrophy or something else, in those less enlightened days both the condition and the person were simply identified by the term "spastic." He walked with the use of crutches in a stumbling gait, had some speech problems as well as an occasional problem with drool. Being "mainstreamed" (in current parlance) was not easy for either him or the teacher. His slow walking impeded others. His slow talking delayed and frustrated discussion. Other students laughed and teased him, making him angry at times. On one occasion, I vividly remember the teacher choosing to punish him, rather than his provocateur. While the boy's eyes teared at the paddle's sting, the teacher's blazed with an adrenaline-fueled rush at the illicit thrill of paddling this cripple, this unwelcome and repulsive addition to his class. The man's tomato-red face shouted words unspoken, *See, I've done it! You all wanted to do it, didn't you? Having to put up with this drooling, disgusting thing. But I did it. And you'll all back me up, won't you, if it comes to that? I had good reasons to do this. For all of you.*

I did feel annoyed by the kid, unsettled and squeamish in dealing with him. But even then, I knew what the teacher did was wrong. The kid had been mercilessly provoked. His physical disability had been prodded and poked into an emotional outburst. More wrong was the spirit in which the teacher punished the boy and the rush he so obviously received from it.

Meanwhile, on weekends and during the summer, Mom compensated for her suffering and mine by taking me to movies and restaurants. I don't recall its name or its location, but I can still taste the Swiss steak, Thousand Island dressing and soft rolls of a favorite restaurant we frequented. It was nice while it lasted that second year in Arizona, but the cost of movies, meals and the taxis that got us there quickly depleted the funds remaining from the sale of the house in Minneapolis. That became clear to me when Mom asked Doug to rejoin us, in hopes that he would add some cash to the household. The income from Social Security couldn't sustain the lifestyle to which Mom had become accustomed. I really don't know why she thought Doug could help after the way things went in Minneapolis before we left. She really had little other choice, I suppose, in looking back on it now. Doug got a bill collection job at a sewing machine company. It didn't last long, when they found out that he had credit problems of his own. I think he found a job as a skip tracer at another company after that. That is what he usually did those days, always something to do with debts. It seems ironic now, given our family finances.

Shortly thereafter, my uncle John (my mother's brother) and his wife Margaret moved to Arizona as well. They hoped that the dry desert air would be good for her allergies, but it wasn't. Too many Northerners had already planted and irrigated grass in the area, generating plenty of pollen to irritate allergic sinuses. Phoenix also turned out to be too hot for Margaret, in more ways than one. During the brief time, they were there, Margaret stopped by on occasion to help my mother. One day, in my typically spoiled state of mind, I didn't take kindly to Margaret telling me to put away my socks, or her intrusion into how I preferred to while away the time on my back if I wasn't down at the pool.

"Come on Johnny, get up and put your socks away," said Margaret.

"No, I don't want to," I yelled.

"John, do what Margaret tells you," added my mother.

Angrily grabbing my socks, I said, "Damn you, Margaret!"

"Why you little brat! Here I am coming to help your poor crippled mother with her housekeeping and you're lying around on your backside doing nothing! And for you to talk like that to me!"

"I'm sorry Margaret," my shocked mother said through tears, "you know Dick always spoiled him while he was sick."

"I know, Emma," she said, shaking. "I think I better just leave." She did leave—both our trailer and soon thereafter Arizona. The state wasn't doing for her health what she expected. It wasn't doing much better for my mother's health either.

The doctors at Maricopa County General Hospital were dangerously incompetent. For some unknown reason, they abruptly stopped her prednisone. With Mom suffering greatly from steroid withdrawal the summer of 1960, Doug convinced her we had to head back to Minneapolis for the known evil of Hennepin County General Hospital. So we sold the trailer and headed back to Minnesota in the old four-door Chevy Doug had arrived in several months before. With the trailer now sold, what few belongings we still had all fit in the car. Mom was not doing well during the long drive, so he put her on a plane before we got through New Mexico. Unfortunately, we arrived in Minneapolis first, because the flight attendants thought she was too ill to stay on the plane and put her off in Kansas City. I don't remember now, how we were reunited, but I do remember seeing her in Hennepin County General Hospital, a place I came to know very well.

As a teaching hospital, Hennepin County General attracted bright young interns and residents eager to learn the newest and most innovative techniques. It was also the place where people like my mom, without insurance and living on Social Security, went for treatment. That meant long waits on hard benches in crowded corridors. As sick as she was when she came back from Arizona, I doubt she waited long this time. I only recall the parting visit by the resident treating her on this occasion.

For years, Mom had been taking prodigious quantities of aspirin, sixteen tablets a day, to deal with the pain of arthritis. She had increased the dose even more, to compensate for the Arizona doctors taking her off prednisone. The results were two-fold: a bleeding duodenal ulcer from aspirin and an ulcerated cornea from unleashed Sjogren's syndrome, which she first learned about when she went to Hennepin County General Hospital immediately upon her arrival back in Minneapolis.

"Sjogren's syndrome is an autoimmune disorder in which white cells attack tear and salivary gland production," the resident told her at the hospital. "There is no cure but corticosteroids suppress the symptoms," he added. "You have an ulcer on your cornea. You will have to use eye drops several times a day to keep it from getting worse. If you don't, any little piece of dust or debris that gets in your eye could scratch it further. Oh, and you will want to keep a pitcher or glass of water handy too, to keep your mouth from getting too dry."

"Oh no," she said. "So that's why my eye was hurting so much."

"Yes. I am going to put you back on prednisone. That will keep the Sjogren's system in check, get rid of the fatigue and the extra joint pain you have been having since they took you off the drug in Phoenix."

"Thank you, doctor. I don't know why they refused to give me any more prednisone in Phoenix."

"I can't understand it, either. It is a big mistake suddenly to stop administering a corticosteroid like prednisone. I am going to give you some medicine for the duodenal ulcer, too. But you are going to have to try and cut back on all that aspirin you are taking or it won't get any better."

"OK, doctor, I'll try," she said, "but my hands and feet really hurt, especially when I am trying to do stuff around the house like cooking or washing dishes."

"Well you have a healthy boy here who should be able to help you."

"Oh I know, but he doesn't like to do stuff in the kitchen." That certainly was true enough. At age 13, in 1960, most boys I knew didn't want to do "women's work." Most boys didn't have mothers who had spilled a couple quarts of boiling water on a terry-cloth covered foot, as had mine, when her arthritic hands failed in an effort to drain the pot of potatoes she had cooked. Despite her difficulties in the kitchen, I offered little help. It's a truth that pains my heart and soul today as much, I imagine, as the arthritis pained her contorted joints then.

"Hmm, I see. Well here is your prescription for the pharmacy, downstairs. I must get on to the next patient now. Good luck."

We moved into a two-bedroom furnished apartment at 44th and Logan Avenues North. The apartment was in the rear of a two-story building owned by an insurance agent. His office fronted on 44th Avenue, with the apartment in the rear, under the agency. The place had only two bedrooms, forcing me to share a bed with my brother Doug, which pleased neither of us. The apartment was the most we could afford, I guess, back in our old neighborhood and only a few blocks from the home my parents once owned. Mom never said so, but I imagine she hoped to find comfort for us in the familiar surroundings.

Mom happily returned, at least at first, to the Sunday services she had left behind when we went to Arizona. There were no Methodist churches accessible to her in Phoenix. She encouraged me to go to Methodist Youth Fellowship (MYF) activities at North Methodist Church, just six blocks away. I recognized the need to reinforce the moral principles Mom imparted. So, for a time I did go, as she asked. We got together in the basement of the church on Friday or Saturday nights. I suppose it kept teenagers away from more risky or decadent behaviors. It must have worked for me, because I had no interest in smoking, drinking or drugs. Then again, I don't recall that these problems were widespread among 12 or 13 year-olds in Minneapolis in 1960.

Going to MYF meant walking past homes whose doors I had once knocked on years before back in third grade, selling Christmas cards to earn spending money. That reminded me of what I had lost in the five years past. Walking past Jan Cucvara's corner grocery store, where Mom had sent me to buy bread, milk and other small items a young boy could be trusted to bring home, illuminated the different path the Maberry family's lives had taken once Dad died. So I had mixed feelings about going there.

Mom must have thought moving back could give us all a fresh start. Despite all that had happened, she still had hope then. People did welcome us back, surprised to see her again after we moved away. But seeing the look of pity on so many faces must have made it painful, reminding her too of the life she once, but no longer had. Her home had been sold at foreclosure. With the money left after the sale, she bought a trailer to live in and set aside a small reserve for other expenses, which she burned through quickly. Now the trailer too was gone. The proceeds from selling the trailer offered only enough money for the trip back to Minneapolis, with a few months surplus above the cost of renting an apartment. Of course, at age 13, I didn't know all these details of our downward financial spiral. I couldn't fail to see, however, that we were becoming poorer and poorer.

At least the apartment we moved into put me within walking distance of a school, Patrick Henry. My brothers Doug and Bill had both attended there, while the school was still fairly new. Patrick Henry was both a junior and senior high school, covering grades 7-8 and 9-12. In Arizona, students still had one teacher for all subjects through 8th grade. So the first few days were very confusing to me in the abrupt transition to six different teachers for various subjects. Since Minneapolis Public School students had already made that transition in 7th grade, the 8th grade teachers assumed all the pupils were accustomed to this routine.

The teachers were a mix of the new and the old-fashioned. My history teacher, appropriately enough, was something of an artifact himself. He had attained the age at which men's ears and nose sprout prolific hair and their gray brows become bushier than a squirrel's tail, or at least his did. His mode of instruction was the rote learning of historical sentence outlines. I found little redeeming educational value in his simplistic and unreasoned routine.

"Alright, class, this week's outline is up on the blackboard. I expect you to be able to reproduce this exactly as you see it here, on the unit test next week."

"No, put your hand down, you don't need to ask any question about this; it's all here on the blackboard. This is history. It doesn't change." Perhaps he was correct, at least in terms of the dates that battles were fought, treaties signed, laws passed or presidents elected. But what scholars make of historical events changes. Opinions, interpretations and analyses of history change. Why did this event happen? Was the outcome good, bad, or indifferent? Did it achieve an intended purpose? Answers to such questions change and provide a reason to acquire historical knowledge beyond trivial pursuit of fact.

Meanwhile, he walked around the classroom passing out square sheets of minimally processed paper, some of which seemed to have visible signs of knots, and short-stub pencils like those handed out at miniature golf courses.

"Put away your pens and notebooks, the outlines will fit perfectly well on these squares. Use the pencil, in case you make a mistake copying them down." Mr. Palm was an odd anachronism at a time when the Cold War had become nearly hot. A more meaningful study of history might have had value as the threat of World War III or at least war between the U.S. and the Soviet Union got more real in the minds of many.

In the early 1960s, newly formed companies began mass marketing home fallout shelters to be buried in back yards. Shelters ranged from cheap prefabricated units to models custom built on site and offering a quiet retreat for harried homeowners. My family did not have one, of course. The Cuban missile crisis in October of 1962, stimulated sales like no advertising could. Aerial reconnaissance confirmed that the Soviet Union had placed offensive missiles on Cuba. President John F. Kennedy ordered a naval blockade, closing the port of Havana and threatening World War III. The first leader to blink was Soviet Premier Khrushchev, who had the missiles removed. Many people said then, and still say now, that it was a close call from an all-out nuclear war. I watched it all on our rabbit-eared black and white Philco. I didn't fully comprehend then how close we came to war or how serious it would have been. I was simply proud that our president had made the evil Communist premier back down.

There wasn't a lot to watch on television back then, but there was enough selection to fight with Doug about what we watched. He had been on the debate team at Patrick Henry. He and his partner, Cal Peterson had won the Region 5 debate competition in April 1946 and went on to the State contest. I sharpened my verbal skills in argument with him about such mundane matters as which TV show to watch. Having the advantage of sobriety somewhat leveled the field between us. Doug generally didn't drink during working hours, but he usually drank himself into oblivion every evening after dinner. Of course, he often started earlier on the weekend. "Let me see the TV guide," he might ask.

"I'm looking at it."

"Well you weren't a minute ago," he would say in frustration.

"Well I wasn't then. I am now."

"You're just stalling. You read faster than that," his anger rising.

"All right, all right—take the damn thing," I would yell, tossing it at him.

Only once did we actually come to blows. It wasn't over a petty argument; it was in the bed we shared. Tired of his rolling over into me, I punched him in the face, breaking his glasses. He refrained from retaliation, perhaps from the surprise and from my age. The commotion woke Mom.

"What's going on?" Mom said, appearing in the doorway.

"He broke my glasses! He hit me in the face and broke my glasses!" Doug said, still stunned.

"Why did you hit him?" Mom asked, patient in exasperation.

"He kept rolling over on my side of the bed. He does it all the time," I whined.

"Well you know, Doug, you shouldn't have been wearing your glasses in bed." Mom ended the discussion.

In the meantime, high school continued to be alternately boring, irrelevant or frustrating. It could be dangerous too, contending with kids in gangs and isolated bullies. The Baldies predominated at Patrick Henry, where I had gone to school. They favored the unlikely combination of close-cropped hair, hangar-loop Gant shirts, cuffed pants pulled up high above the waist and wing-tipped Florsheims that served well the purpose of a quick introductory kick to the groin before a fist to the face. A rival gang, called the Animals were found at Edison, a school in northeast Minneapolis. The Animals allegedly filed their teeth to sharp points, the better to bite people with. I never actually saw any myself, but I heard it from kids who didn't make up stuff like that. Fortunately for me, I acquired a friend/bodyguard, the knowledge of which kept bullies and gangs away from me for fear of retaliation from him.

Gary was a tough kid living in foster care. We would go to the Patrick Henry hockey games together during the winter, play baseball in the summer and listen to music year round. Mom got mad when I sold him a present she had given me but I had since grown tired of, one of those electric football games—the ones where the players have flexible nylon strips on their base and move as the game table vibrates. She didn't think he was good company but I continued to hang out with him. I didn't want to explain how staying in good graces with him was essential for my own protection. I can't really say he was a role model, but I suspect I learned something from him about being your own person, how he was able to transcend the circumstances in which he found himself. Besides, for a kid like me who didn't really fit in, he was my only friend.

Not long after the eyeglasses incident, the insurance agent said his business was picking up and he needed the space in which we were living. So we moved again, this time to an old house we rented at the corner of 36th Avenue North and 3rd Street. As a result, I had to ride a city bus to get to school, but I didn't have to share a bed with Doug anymore. Doug had his own room at the rear of the house, down a long hallway. He could keep his boozy self in there for all I cared. Perhaps it was the space that now separated us that allowed an occasional truce to go bowling, an interest we had in common. Despite our limited resources, on Saturdays, I bowled in a junior league. It didn't cost too much, $.35 a line or something like that. Doug used to bowl in a league too, but not anymore. We also had in common a taste for Hormel chili. Once, with Mom on one of her many extended stays in the hospital, he bought a whole case of it just for the two us. It was cheap and simple to make. Despite not wanting to do work in the kitchen, it was now mostly up to Doug or I to get meals together. Mom's hands and fingers just were not up to it. Still, we needed cheap even more than we needed simple.

Mom was horrified on the occasion I came back home with my hands dripping blood, explaining I had tripped on a buckled sidewalk while running downhill to cash in some empty Mason root beer bottles I had scavenged around the neighborhood. I still have the scars from the unstitched cuts. It was there, at the house on 3rd Street, that I tried to wrest control of the finances from Doug. I hated math in school, but figured all we were dealing with was simple arithmetic. I thought I could do better than she and Doug at managing the family's money. The issue was to make sure Doug was putting more in than he was taking out for whisky and cigarettes. A fifth a day and 1-2 packs of Pall Malls cost plenty, even back then before the big run-up in cigarette taxes.

"Mom, why don't you let me take care of the money after we cash the [Social Security] checks? I can buy stuff from the store and give you and Doug enough money for stuff. I'll make sure we have enough for the rent and food, so you don't have to worry." That is what I told her one day, when she was counting out the money in her purse to see if she had enough for bread and milk.

"I appreciate it John, but I think you're too young for that."

Doug was relieved when she wouldn't go along with it.

I may have been young, just turning 15, but circumstances had already forced me to become more independent. Like my friend Gary, there were places I wanted to go and things I wanted to do. It was easy to get around anywhere, living in a medium-sized city with a good bus system. Gary and I, like other non-driving students, went to high school hockey games at Dupont Arena that way. I would have liked to have been on Patrick Henry's team myself, but I wasn't that good a skater. Before we went to Arizona, I often played goalie in the pickup games at the outdoor rink at Camden. By the time we got back, it was too late for me to catch up on essential skills others had already acquired. So riding the bus to root for the team was the best I could do.

I rode the bus to Junior Achievement as well, in my sophomore year. There I received an introduction to, or perhaps indoctrination in, the capitalist system. My fellow students and I learned the structural components of a business by doing: incorporation, selling shares of stock, electing directors and the various company officials, and last but not least, selling an actual product door-to-door or to friends or family. In our case, the product we made and sold was a window cleaner, no better or worse than regular retail brands sold in the stores. I don't recall now how or why I got involved in Junior Achievement. Perhaps it came at the suggestion of my civics teacher. In any case, it was an interestingly quaint activity, showing me a facet of American life I had never seen. However, I didn't see Junior Achievement leading to a future day job for an aspiring writer, the importance of which I learned during career exploration in that civics class.

I called Clifford Simak, a science fiction writer whose books I enjoyed. His day job was city editor at the Minneapolis Star and Tribune, the main newspaper in town.

"So you're interested in writing science fiction?"

"Yes, I want to be a writer and I've always liked reading science fiction, so I thought that's what I might write. I really enjoyed reading Ring Around the Sun, Empire and City." It was exciting, talking to a real writer!

"Well, thank you, I enjoyed writing them. You know science fiction is popular with some people, but it's considered genre fiction—like mysteries or westerns. That means a smaller pool of book and magazine readers than for mainstream fiction. It's very difficult for most people to make a living writing fiction full time, let alone niche fiction like science fiction or fantasy. Since I began writing science fiction in 1931, I have had 5 novels and over 20 short stories published, but I am still working at a newspaper. So if you really want to be a writer, what you need to do is go to college, learn as much as you can about the English language and then get a regular job you can depend on for income."

Given my family's financial history, it made eminently good sense to me. I had always planned on going to college, like both my brothers. After my father died, Doug had often said, "Don't worry about money, Bill and I will pay for your college." It was his way of encouraging me to go, I suppose. It was one of the few suggestions I didn't have a problem accepting from Doug. The value of college became more apparent to me the further along in high school I went. I needed courses in English to be a writer. I needed that day job. College would be my ticket out of poverty and into a writing career. The purposeful pursuit of doing good, which I had felt strongly about in elementary school, had receded into the background somewhat during high school. Never gone entirely, it would return much stronger, after the real life experiences of war provided an education that school did not offer.

Before I could get to college, I needed to make it through high school. That was not a sure thing, given the C's and D's I had received. I didn't like most of the teachers I had the misfortune to have had in Phoenix or in Minneapolis. Ever since grade school, I had missed an average of 30 days of school a year for some real and many more feigned illnesses. Now there were my mother's health problems to contend with. Since returning from Arizona, one or another of Mom's various ailments would flare up and it would be back to General Hospital. By our third year back in Minneapolis, my sophomore year, her trips to the hospital had become more frequent and the stays longer.

As a teaching hospital, Hennepin County General wanted to be innovative. As a poorly educated woman on Social Security, she was a fitting guinea pig for trying out new treatments for arthritis. They tried digitalis, a heart drug, perhaps hoping to reduce fluid buildup and thereby relieve the arthritis but it didn't work. Instead, after the treatment, she developed a heart murmur, a problem that wasn't there before. Next came the painfully unsuccessful hand-surgery. After cutting the tendons in all the fingers of both her hands, the doctors then attached rubber-band powered splints to the outside of each digit in hopes that the joints could be straightened out by stretching the tendons. This didn't work either. However, while under anesthesia for the hand-surgery, she did suffer a collapsed lung. And so it went.

The staff must have gotten tired of seeing her after awhile. What appeared to be a flare up of her asthma, wheezing and shortness of breath, came on suddenly in March, 1963. She first called the hospital emergency room but the intake person said this wasn't really an emergency and they couldn't send an ambulance to get her. "You can take a bus or taxi if you think you need to be seen today. We will get to you when we can, but you may have to wait awhile," the person told her, matter-of-factly. Then she called a doctor who used to treat her for asthma back when we had health insurance, many years before. Given her lack of insurance and inability to pay, he refused to see her. With her lips turning cyanotic blue, she was getting desperate. She called the fire department and the dispatcher did agree to send an ambulance.

The crew took it's time getting there, running with no siren. A cop arrived as well, a common procedure on ambulance runs. One of the medics casually exposed one of her withered breasts as he applied a stethoscope to her chest, while the bored cop stood by callously observing. I was angry at his indifference to her embarrassment. Confirming that her breathing wasn't up to par, the medics took her on to the hospital. She had pneumonia, it turned out, and so the hospital was forced to admit her once again.

I visited her every day, riding a Minneapolis Transit bus to the hospital after school. She was in an oxygen tent, in an open ward with many beds. On Saturdays, I went directly from the bowling alley to the hospital. One Saturday, April 4th, I bounded up the stairs to her floor, just missing my uncle John coming down to wait for me in the lobby and Doug going back up in the elevator. Finding the curtain drawn around Mom's bed, I figured she was on the bedpan or getting washed up. The patient in the next bed motioned, telling me to go check with the nurse.

"I'm here to visit Mrs. Maberry," I told the first nurse I saw.

"Oh didn't you know? She passed away this morning," the nurse casually blurted out.

With my chest constricted and my stomach knotting, I could say nothing more. In a daze, I turned and made it back down to the lobby before the sobs broke free. Doug and John found me sitting on a bench, with my hands vainly trying to hold back the tide of tears. It was two weeks before my 16th birthday in April 1963.

Perhaps her death should not have been so unexpected to me, given all her ailments. But none of them were typically or obviously fatal. They were just painful and numerous. Despite her being in and out of the hospital and sick in so many ways, no thought of her death had ever occurred to me. She was only 54, six years older than my father was when he died of cancer.

Chapter 2 — A Small Town Expands My World

WELL BEFORE SHE DIED, MOM had run out of hope. Her physical ailments kept worsening while new ones kept attacking. Her drunken oldest son and her unruly youngest son were of little aid or comfort, while her other son was hundreds of miles away, living a detached and comfortable life of his own. I had begun to think in the previous couple years, what a wonderfully different life I could lead if I were living the life Bill had. He didn't have fights with Doug every day. He didn't eat TV dinners or meals from a can, his wife Lorraine made sure of that. He didn't haul clothes to the laundromat and hunt for change to feed the washer and dryer. His home would be a refuge of peace and hope from the battleground at school rather than another place of merciless combat. But I never wanted, I never hoped for and I never expected this new life to come at the expense of Mom's death. Still, it was a relief and a bittersweet dream fulfilled when Bill and Lorraine offered to take me in after her death.

Just two weeks after the funeral, Bill provided my first plane ride, in a two-seater V-tailed Bonanza. As a teenager, Bill had wanted to own a cabin cruiser. By the time he got out of college, his interest had moved from aquatic to aerial. So he took flying lessons and bought his own plane, a little Piper Tri-Pacer. Before getting an instrument rating, he cracked the plane up in a thunderstorm a few years later. Since then, he had joined a flying club from which he could borrow the speedy Bonanza. Flying the 400 direct air miles from Minneapolis to Midland, Michigan took just two hours, offering little time to ponder the very different world I was entering.

Lorraine met us at the airport, in the Volkswagen Bus. She introduced me to Spook, the excitable Dalmatian, who came along for the ride. With their equally excitable two-year-old daughter Chris, we drove the short distance to their home in a well-manicured subdivision. They gave me a tour of the house and showed me to my room. I had my own room! The room had a built-in desktop next to a sliding-door closet. It was a modest-sized home by current standards, but still much newer and larger than any I had ever lived in and most I had even visited. I looked around outside for Wally and the Beaver, but they were nowhere to be seen. Still, I felt sure the Cleavers lived somewhere nearby.

In the space of a few hours, I had gone from a big city to a small town. A town so small that Bill could come home for lunch, unless traveling to one of the pulp mills to whom he sold "slimicide" chemicals for processing paper. The home of Dow Chemical, where Bill worked, had less than a tenth the population of Minneapolis. The town, the people, the house and now living with Bill and Lorraine—this was all so different!

There was no stench of cigarette smoke (Doug had smoked a pack and a half a day). There were no empty bottles of booze because neither Bill nor his wife drank any alcohol—period! There were regular meals at regular times. I had breakfast, lunch and dinner all cooked and served from scratch by stay-at-home Mom, Lorraine. The only exception was Saturday night, when Bill gave Lorraine a break from cooking. That was McDonald's night, or now and then, the Dog-'N'-Suds for root beer and a hot dog. Lorraine had been an executive secretary to one of the bigwigs at General Mills. Like dutiful wives across America, she had encouraged Bill to go to college, which he began a full six-years out of high school, leaving a warehouseman job for the University of Minnesota. Now he was a five-year employee at Dow, with a master's degree in chemical engineering, earned with Tau Beta Pi honors.

Neither Bill nor Lorraine attended church services. They didn't talk about religion at all, except, when I first arrived, to offer to take me to services if I so desired. I declined the offer. In the midst of what initially appeared to be paradise, church seemed an unnecessary exercise. I figured that I knew right from wrong as well as I needed to and no longer needed moral instruction. Nor did my life really need the Sunday only purification anymore, as far as I was concerned. Besides, by this time, I had become something of an agnostic. As my mother's pain and suffering progressed, my faith declined in direct proportion. It seemed that the hope for a better life promised in church could only be realized in the after-life. God could not be counted on to answer prayers for help in the here and now. We were all on our own in this life. What had my mother to show for her faith? Not much, to my mind. What had Bill and Lorraine to show for their apparent lack of it or at least of outward display or devotion? Nothing unpleasant, that I could see. That would change however, upon my arrival.

It had to have been a major adjustment for them, having a lazy teenager in the house. In fact, they so informed me of this point later on. They had hoped I would be cutting the grass, but I (honestly) told them it aggravated my allergies to pollen, etc. and avoided it. At least, after awhile, I occasionally deigned to watch my two-year-old niece Chris or to walk the dog. Indeed, after struggling through the remaining six weeks of 10th grade, I spent my first summer in Midland lying on the living room sofa while reading 75 science fiction books checked out of the local library.

Looking back on it now, it couldn't have been only typical teen laziness. The books allowed escape from guilt and dulled the pain of my mother's death. While she lived, I had begrudged the time I spent cooking, cleaning and washing—despite her obvious pain and incapacity. Alien cultures amid far-flung galaxies engaged my mind, enabling escape from regrets that I hadn't been more help than hindrance in her difficult life. Space operas and time traveling heroes kept me from dwelling on her death. Remorse postponed is remorse compounded, of course. Thankfully, when it visits me now, the effective prayers of Buddhist faith transmute the suffering into Nirvana.

Midland's one high school was way ahead of those in Minneapolis; the college-educated crowd at Dow demanded it. There were no gangs, like the Animals or the Baldies from my Minneapolis schools. In Midland, instead there were learning tracks, separating the academically talented and inclined from those not so interested or capable. Entering Midland H.S. with the educational baggage I had, I couldn't get into the best tracks at school. I hadn't put forth any substantial efforts studying since grade school. School had held no interest or challenge. To me it was just a legal obligation. Still, the Midland classes at least offered a new perspective on the academic compartment of my life, just as the life with Bill and Lorraine gave a new perspective on home. During my junior year, my history teacher showed us graphic films from Nazi Germany.

He began with footage of a Hitler speech predating the invasion of Czechoslovakia, his initial offensive in World War II. As Hitler spoke, his henchmen dragged a few men onto the stage in a large auditorium, for the offense of disagreeing with his words. Like the scene I witnessed on an Arizona school bus, one goon held the men around the neck while another pulled down the men's trousers, exposing their genitals to the audience. But this was no childhood bullying, it was a more sinister humiliation intended to out circumcised men as Jews or if not, at least show the consequences of daring to dispute the Fuehrer.

He went on to show us footage of starving people with flesh barely covering their bones, scraping food from garbage cans or entering trailers set up as portable suicide facilities for those whose Hitler's policies had driven to such despair. I watched the wide-striped prison uniforms billowing around living skeletons that were dumping bodies from the gas chambers into flaming pits. From all of this, I concluded that there must be such a thing as a just war and that armed intervention could be the morally correct thing to do. Unfortunately, for millions of Jews in Europe, I learned that it took an attack on Pearl Harbor to get America directly involved in World War II.

While learning about WW II in school, current television news reports were covering events in Vietnam. Communists from the North Vietnam, it was said, were trying to subvert and take over by force, if necessary, the democratic government of South Vietnam. It was the height of the Cold War and American political leaders feared a "domino effect" in Southeast Asia. If Vietnam fell, next would fall Laos, Cambodia, and so on. President Kennedy, who had thwarted Communist threats to America by challenging Khrushchev's placement of missiles in Cuba, said it was essential for the U.S. to help the South Vietnamese repel the Communists in South Vietnam. Backing up his words with action, he sent U.S. military advisers and military equipment there to aid in the effort. It seemed reasonable and the right thing to do, given what I knew then, but I was troubled by news about the Vietnamese leaders we were supporting.

Newspapers and network TV showed graphic pictures of Buddhist monks engulfed in gasoline-fueled flames in Saigon's public squares, their self-ignition a suicidal protest of South Vietnam's President Diem. The news reports indicated that Diem was repressing religious and political groups that didn't support his policies. More disturbing were the comments of Madame Nhu, Diem's sister-in-law, who laughingly called these incidents "monk barbecues."

Before 1963, I had not understood or experienced much of death. My father's death was an abstraction to me, a remote event I had pushed to the back of my mind. Following my mother's death in the spring and the initial glimpses of Vietnam horrors, the fall of 1963 brought to me an unwelcome knowledge of murder. The killing began November 2, 1963, with the assassination of South Vietnam's President Diem. Only much later did I learn that the U.S., if not actively involved, tacitly accepted this outcome to rid itself of a troublesome ally that had become an embarrassing political liability. Twenty days later, while sitting in chemistry class, the news of John F Kennedy's assassination came over the PA system, shocking students and teachers alike. Only two days after that, while watching live TV coverage of Kennedy's alleged assassin Lee Harvey Oswald being led through the Dallas Courthouse, I heard the shots and saw Oswald doubling over, grimacing in pain, as Jack Ruby's handgun ended his life.

As the world's violence impinged on my self-absorption, I struggled to grow and to go in directions more typical of a sixteen-year-old, like out with friends to the movies or on dates with girls. At the time, I was inexperienced at dating. Although I could have gone somewhere on the bus with girls in Minneapolis before my mother died, that had not happened. Now that I lived in the small town of Midland, I suffered from limited mobility. There was no public transportation and Bill would not allow me to drive their Volkswagen bus, the one vehicle he and Lorraine owned at the time. The cost of his car insurance would have more than doubled had he allowed me to do so, he pointed out. Nonetheless, I asked out this girl in my chemistry class. She had blazing red hair surrounding a freckled face, with green eyes and an intriguing gap between two front teeth, like Brigitte Bardot. Much to my surprise, she agreed to meet me at the movies. Bill would drive me there and give her a ride home. Alas, she didn't show up. When I saw her in my next chemistry class, she made some excuse about her Irish father. After that, she simply turned a cold shoulder to me. I was too embarrassed to pursue it further.

I made a couple male friends, both of whom lived nearby. With one, I played chess, expanding my mind a bit. With the other friend, I expanded my knowledge and appreciation of the opposite sex. He shared his *Playboy* magazine collection with me, explaining that once he got a subscription, there wasn't much his mom or dad could do about it. So what the hell, I thought, why not me? Lorraine was flabbergasted when the first copy showed up in the mailbox, but I think she was also amused at my chutzpah in daring to have it delivered there. If I couldn't have them in the flesh, I could at least have playmates in print.

Lorraine was not so amused at my more public outreach to the local newspaper. Midland, like many small towns in Minnesota, differed from Minneapolis in having very few minorities. At the time, Dow Chemical apparently made little effort to seek out minorities. Affirmative action would not become a concern for major companies for several more years. Not long after my arrival, the local newspaper published a letter to the editor that crudely characterized African-Americans as inferior to Caucasians. The letter writer, passing through town, expressed satisfaction that Midland had so few members of the inferior race visible. Although signed William Campbell, the letter bore remarkable similarities to an editorial I had recently been surprised to read in *Analog Science Fact and Fiction* magazine. Written by John W. Campbell, Jr., a major figure in the science fiction world, the editorial expressed praise and agreement with the views of William Shockley, a physicist who led the development of the transistor at Bell Labs. Shockley had put forth some poorly reasoned theories outside his scope of knowledge or experience, asserting that African-Americans were genetically inferior intellectually to Caucasians. I wrote a letter to the Midland paper's editor myself, disputing the opinions expressed by Campbell. A few days after my letter's publication, Lorraine answered the phone one evening. An obviously puzzled Lorraine asked the caller, "Join the NAACP? Why would we want to do that?" She paused to hear the caller's reply, then continued the conversation.

"You say the letter was signed by John Maberry? That's my brother-in-law, not my husband. He's only sixteen. No, we don't care to join NAACP, thank you," she said as she hung up the phone.

"Who was that on the phone?" Bill asked.

"A local NAACP official, asking if we wanted to join. He said he saw this letter in the newspaper about racism in Midland. It was signed by John," she replied, clearly annoyed.

"What do you mean sending in a letter to the newspaper about racism in Midland?" He asked, indignation in his voice.

"Bill has a reputation in the community and his career at Dow to think of!" Lorraine added in a rising voice.

"It wasn't about racism in Midland, at least not for the most part. It was a response to a racist letter the newspaper published from someone else," I quickly blurted out, before Bill and Lorraine could continue. "I wasn't talking about Midland, other than complaining that I was shocked and surprised that the newspaper would print such a crudely racist letter. Mom always taught me that racism was wrong and that man wrote a hateful, disgusting letter."

"Well, all right. It's fine to have your own opinions, but you should consider the effects on us when you put them in the local paper," Bill said. "This is a small town and we are the only Maberrys living here."

"OK, fine," I replied, suppressing my own indignation and replacing it with amusement. I had succeeded in disturbing the equilibrium of Bill and Lorraine's carefully cultivated and detached world. From this promising beginning, I began augmenting my lazy and spoiled traits with the attitude and behavior of a smart-ass. I didn't know then how much this development would cost me later on in life. In the meantime, only a year later, Bill and Lorraine succeeded in disturbing my equilibrium.

The shakeup came in the spring of 1964, only a year after my arrival and subsequent adjustment to the Cleaver life of Midland. I came home from school to find the ambitious Bill and pregnant Lorraine considering an opportunity he had for advancement. It meant a move to Dow's corporate sales office in Manhattan. I listened in stunned silence at the thought of being uprooted yet again while they discussed the pros and cons of the transfer. How promising did future promotions in the field look versus headquarters proximity to bigwigs? What about Midland's qualities of life for their growing family versus the quality and affordability of unknown neighborhoods from which Bill could commute to Manhattan? Finally, I spoke up, initiating the only big blowup we had, exposing a culmination of mutual frustrations that had been left unstated to this point.

"Well I don't think it's a good idea. I don't want to go to another new school for my senior year. I finally got used to Midland; I don't want to move again."

"What do you mean YOU don't want to move? You don't have a say in the matter!" Lorraine snapped. "It's Bill's career. It's OUR family's future."

She was right, of course. I didn't have a say in the matter, at least not like hers. But I certainly had an opinion, an opinion colored by my sense of entitlement that they owed me something.

"She's right John. It's our decision. I'm sorry if it inconveniences you, but you know you didn't have to be here in the first place—and you don't have to go with us! I don't see that you're contributing a lot to this household.

Whenever we ask you to do something, you always have some excuse. Like you can't cut the grass because of your hayfever." Bill said with irritation.

"All you do is lie on your backside on the sofa every day after school. It's what you did all summer last year. I could barely get you to take care of your own dishes or watch Chris for a few minutes when I had to do something!" Lorraine added.

"I do have hayfever and if it gets out of hand, my asthma kicks in. I take Allerest and my nose dries up but I feel like a zombie. Bill and Doug didn't inherit it from Mom, just me. I don't know anything about little kids; I've never been around little kids. I did push her on the swing some times." I protested.

"Yeah, and you pushed her down one time while she bothered you when you lying on the sofa reading!" Lorraine replied.

"That was an accident! She startled me and I just bumped her!"

"So what else have you done?" asked Bill.

"I take Spook for walks sometimes."

"Oh, like the time you walked her near the end of the runway, off her leash? She could have been killed!" Lorraine said.

"Lorraine and I talked it over after Mom died. We thought it would be the right thing to do, bringing you into our home. We thought it would be interesting and fun, having a teenager around. We didn't expect it would be so difficult." Bill added.

My experience, my skill at verbal combat, honed over the years in daily quarrels with Doug, had atrophied over the year of peace with Bill. Emotion overtook what little I then had left.

"Interesting! Fun! You care more about a damn dog than me! You didn't have any worries about me getting killed at the end of a runway!" I replied, tears welling up. "You could have helped out Mom while she was still alive, helped her out so she didn't lose the house. She often said all you cared about was yourself and your family; that you didn't care about her. It was the least you could do, to give your own brother a place to stay after she's dead! You expect me to be grateful and do chores when you get a check for me from Social Security every month?"

"I, I never heard that from Mother," Bill replied, off balance at the accusation and the tears.

"Bill was in the Marines when your father got sick and starting in college when your father died. We didn't have any extra money to help you or your mother."

"I drove you and Mom down to Arizona while I was on winter break from college. I got her set up in the trailer and suggested a budget and spending plan. That was all I could do. She just wasn't good with money. And then she had Doug come back down there to help spend it."

"We do care about you, or we wouldn't have invited you to live here. It's been a difficult adjustment for all of us," Lorraine said.

"Whatever we decide about Manhattan, you're welcome to come along with us," Bill added.

What else could I have done?

So in the summer of 1964 we all moved to Kendall Park, New Jersey, a bedroom community between U.S. 1 and N.J. Route 27 about 50 miles from New York City. It was another difficult adjustment for me, augmented by appendicitis striking me a few weeks before school started. The surgeon said it was a good thing I came in when I did because the appendix was ready to rupture. If it had, that could have been fatal. Spending several days in a Princeton, New Jersey hospital was not fun. Bill was commuting by bus and rail to Manhattan, getting home to Kendall Park at 7 p.m. Lorraine was taking care of 3-year-old Chris and now 3-month old Dave. So I was on my own for most of the week I spent in the hospital, alone with the candy stripers and the Demerol. The Demerol was my first experience with serious drugs. It colored my world in a rosy glow of exhilaration. But I soon found the mood elevator was short-lived. Each time the drug's effects began to wear off, I rode an emotional roller coaster down to subterranean depths. If this is what narcotics were like, I wanted none of them. The hospital stay did provide a good diet plan, however, taking off ten of the pounds that had accumulated on my body from Lorraine's good cooking and my own indolence. The loneliness I felt in the hospital served as a reminder that I would soon enough be on my own altogether. I needed to begin making exit plans from Bill and Lorraine's for after high school.

Around the same time, President Lyndon Baines Johnson (LBJ), who had assumed the office from the Vice-Presidency upon Kennedy's death, got a blank check from Congress for waging an undeclared war in Vietnam. Johnson claimed that North Vietnamese boats attacked a U.S. vessel off the coast of North Vietnam. Congress adopted a resolution at Johnson's request, giving him the right to send troops and material there as necessary to defend U.S. interests without any further authorization. The Gulf of Tonkin Resolution would come back to haunt LBJ and Congress alike.

After Labor Day, I began my senior year in another new school, South Brunswick High School, in nearby Monmouth Junction, New Jersey. The school itself was very small and very new. It's first graduating class of students that began there as freshmen, graduated in 1964. A year later, the senior class I joined in its final year totaled only 126 students or a third the size of Midland's class. The students were very different as well. Midland had a narrow demographic of middle-class, mostly white kids. South Brunswick's mix of rural and suburban kids ranged from poor to upper middle class, with an equally wide distribution of racial and ethnic minorities.

Despite its size, like most high schools, there was a variety of cliques: jocks, thugs or hoods and the popular crowd (including cheerleaders and class office holders). I continued my role as an outside observer, never wanting to join or feeling I ever could belong to any of them. Without any obvious difficulty, it seemed that membership in the cliques transcended race and ethnicity. I found it interesting how South Brunswick students shattered popular stereotypes, demonstrating that not all Jews are rich or smart and not all African-Americans have rhythm or athletic prowess.

Meanwhile, with the time for college drawing near, I had to make the best of my final year of high school. Getting good grades in school hadn't been either easy or a priority to me since early on in elementary school. Even then, my fifth grade teacher had me pegged when she once told me, "John, you're a bright boy but you really need to buckle down." As smart as *I* thought I was, it finally dawned on me that the college admissions officers might not agree. Now, many years later, I was finally ready to take that fifth grade teacher's advice. My determination didn't start out well. Although I had received a number of D grades, especially at Minneapolis' Patrick Henry from 8th through most of 10th grades, I had never failed a class. That changed the first quarter at South Brunswick, when I flunked physics. I had never liked or done well at math, a key component of physics. The fact that I was working part-time as a supermarket carryout boy, reducing my available study time, didn't help either.

I needed to turn this around quickly, so I quit the supermarket job. As much as I despised Doug for his weakness for alcohol, I had somehow acquired an appreciation for the common sense of doing what works, something that he preached from his book of William James' *Essays in Pragmatism*. The lab component of the physics class was supposed to demonstrate the empirical validation of theories we studied. Unfortunately, experiments did not always turn out quite right. Even when they did, the documentation of my observations was lacking in sufficient detail. James would say, among other things, that truth lies in the value created, not simply in empirical fact. That the sun is shining may be a fact, the value lies in the truth of knowing its effects on growing crops. Studying a bit harder in the second quarter, I realized how to adjust and fully explain my lab results to validate the theories. For example, I could not always succeed in getting a steel ball to roll down a track in the precise manner to leave a track replicating a physicist's proof of particle theory. But while my experiments were not empirically valid, I learned the outcome that should have occurred and satisfactorily explained what I should have observed. It shocked both the teacher and me when my second quarter grade became an A. I learned an important lesson both for school and later for work. Give people what they expect from you in the manner they prescribe, and you will be appropriately rewarded. Many people probably learned this well before their senior year in high school; others never do.

Meanwhile, I found my first hip teacher in Jeanette Ritzenthaler. She opened and stimulated the closed minds of know it all seniors in her English class. She was the one who revealed that, contrary to conventional wisdom, it is men who are romantics and women realists. Don Quixote might be fiction, but not so far from reality. It all made sense, once I thought about it. This was the whole point—to think and observe, to analyze and synthesize.

In light of my advice from Clifford Simak, the science fiction writer and city desk editor, that an author needed a day job, I felt compelled at least to explore the newspaper business. Fortunately for me, South Brunswick not only had a journalism class but a free daily subscription to the New York Times for class members. Ms Lehet, my journalism teacher, could perhaps have been the inspiration for the 1984 David Lee Roth song, "Hot for Teacher." She drove a Thunderbird convertible to and from school. She had a singular talent at emphasizing a point of instruction: While sitting atop her desk at the front of the classroom, she would rapidly cross her legs, which were only partially covered by a tweed skirt that stopped well above the knee. Although there were no Sharon Stone *Basic Instinct* moments, it certainly grabbed my attention. Despite the distraction, I did learn something about the "five Ws and how," which are essential elements in any news article. I also learned the technical aspects of layout, including editing content to fit the space available while retaining consistency with the import of the story. That was important not just from a journalistic perspective but also in living up to our high school paper's motto. In a play on the New York Times, our masthead said, "We print all the news that fits." All in all, however, the pressure of meeting deadlines didn't seem a good fit for a procrastinator like me. Halfway through the year, I concluded this wouldn't be the right day job for me.

During my year in New Jersey, I made another lame attempt at dating. How ignominious, having your much older brother as a chauffeur! This time I made certain we actually picked up the girl at her home. A disaster ensued nonetheless. The downward spiral began with my comment on her clothes.

She came to the door in a sweater and a plaid wool skirt, with a wide belt. The belt had a large square buckle, repeated in miniature on her black flats. Having recently finished a unit on colonial America in history class, I innocently but thoughtlessly observed,

"Hey, that reminds me of the Pilgrims."

"Are you saying my clothes are old-fashioned!" she hissed, with eyes blazing in fury beneath furrowed brows.

"NO, no!" I stammered. Digging the hole deeper, "I just meant the buckles looked like what the Pilgrims wore—you know, like what we saw in class last week."

"These are not at all like the Pilgrims wore. These are gold buckles; they wore plain and simple stuff."

"Sorry, I didn't mean to offend you."

"OK, let's get going."

The tension subsided but the mood never lightened. Bill dropped us at a nearby strip mall, promising to return in 2 hours. Sitting stonily side-by-side in the theater, we watched a now forgotten movie. Midway through the show, she rebuffed an abortive attempt at an arm around her shoulder. Oh well. Bill was there at the curb as we exited the theater.

"Did you have a good time?"

"Oh sure, fine," I said.

"It was a good movie," she added.

We dropped her back home. Before she could reach the door, a light came on and the face of her father appeared. He waved a quick goodbye to us on her behalf as he closed the door.

"Didn't go too well, huh?" Bill asked, as we pulled away.

"No, not really. That'll be my last date with her I'm sure."

That turned out true enough and the last one in high school. Dating hardly seemed worth the aggravation at this point.

Meanwhile, Bill made adjustments of his own to the new job and its very different commute. There were no more lunches at home for him, but he soon found ways to shorten the time away from home, despite his 50-mile commute each way to work. In his methodical and self-disciplined way, he managed to organize his client calls and other business so he could be out of his office earlier and earlier. Eventually he wound up arriving home each day before 6 p.m. instead of after seven. He was caring, sympathetic and playful within his own nuclear family but almost completely detached from the world outside. Bill was so unlike Doug, whose romantic idealism and bleeding heart sentimentality colored his world. Yet Doug could manage or accomplish little, devoid of self-discipline as he was.

After Chris and Dave were in bed, somewhere around 9 p.m., Bill and Lorraine would have coffee and some goodie (like apple crumb cake) Lorraine had whipped up. Along with other high school seniors in my class, I had finally acquired a taste for coffee. So I often shared the snack with Bill and Lorraine. It wasn't perhaps the best time for it, but it also afforded me the opportunity to challenge Bill's positions on issues. He had the most annoying attribute of not only being correct about virtually any factual matter but also knowing that he was. Why couldn't he be wrong once in awhile? He simply wasn't. But when it came to value judgments, his opinions were fair game. So one evening at snack time, I asked him an open-ended question, sure to lead into a hot discussion.

"Bill, what do you think about the death penalty? We were discussing it in government class today."

"I'm for it. Why not? If someone kills somebody, don't they deserve the punishment of death?"

"But that's just revenge isn't it? Why is it wrong for one person to kill another but OK for the government to kill somebody? Two wrongs don't make a right."

"Yes, but if people know that they will be executed for committing murder, don't you think that keeps some people from killing?"

"I doubt it. It doesn't really make sense. If somebody kills out of anger, in the spur of the moment, they aren't thinking about the punishment—they aren't really thinking at all. People who plan it all out, they don't figure they're going to get caught. If they did, why would they do it? Besides, studies show that deterrence doesn't work. So it all comes back to revenge."

"I don't see anything wrong in retribution—paying for your crime. What value has the continued life of a killer? Why should I, as a taxpayer, pay to feed and house him in prison for the rest of his life."

"Ah, but that's another fallacy—thinking that the government saves money by executing people. Because the stakes are so high, the verdict keeps getting appeal after appeal. By the time you add in the time and expense of the trials and appeals, it actually costs more to sentence a person to death than to simply give him life at the outset."

"I find that hard to believe. Even if it is true, then they're getting too many appeals and too many delays. Things need to be streamlined so they can be executed more quickly."

"But what if somebody is wrongly convicted? Once they've been executed you can't bring them back and say 'oops, we had the wrong man, sorry.' That's why the trials and appeals take so long."

"Well, you haven't convinced me. I still think the life of a killer has no value; they should die."

"You don't think crazy people should be executed do you?"

"Maybe not, if they really are crazy."

"You know Doug always said that he thought that people who commit murder must be crazy. I know what he means, that society and religion say killing is wrong so if somebody does it anyway, it's a kind of insanity. But I'm not sure if I agree with that. Anyway, I think human life is valuable, even the life of a killer. Who knows, if given the opportunity in prison, they may sometime change and become a better person. That's not possible if they're dead." It was a humanistic notion, not fully formed or believed by me at that time, that even the life of an evil man or a killer might have potential value. Later on, I understood how integral such a perspective is to the Buddhist faith.

I felt good, getting at least a draw with Bill, but disappointed I couldn't move him to value more highly all human life. Later, I remembered how he had laughed along with Madame Nhu, describing as "monk barbecues," the self-immolation of several Buddhist priests protesting her husband's policies in running the government of South Vietnam. While he and I were in essential agreement that the monks had been desperately foolish in their martyrdom, we had disagreed on Madam Nhu's way of expressing her view. By 1965, that issue had become old news, as President Johnson began making effective use of the Tonkin Gulf Resolution.

In February 1965, B-52s began bombing targets in North Vietnam. Known as Operation Rolling Thunder, the bombing continued nonstop for three years. From a handful of military advisers a few years before, the spring of 1965 found 200,000 U.S. ground troops in South Vietnam. To fill the ranks, the Selective Service System cranked up the draft system, inducting double the 112,000 young men who were drafted in 1964. Upon my 18th birthday, I dutifully registered in New Brunswick, with Local Board Number 31 for New Jersey. I was classified 1-A, qualified and ripe for induction as soon as high school ended. It was not a happy thought. It was a scary thought. I had other things on my mind, to keep thoughts of the draft away.

After nearly two years living with Bill, my idealized expectation of family paradise had been only partially disproved. Most things really were better or at least more stable, calm and rational. Bill and Lorraine proved a good model for a happy home life and a good relationship. They hardly had disagreements, let alone arguments between each other. They lavished attention on each other and their children. Still, I wasn't comfortable with his cold detachment to those outside his family. Bill showed little empathy for those outside his nuclear family. He took care of his own, but seemed to feel no imperative to reach out a hand to others. That is not to say he did anything unscrupulous or dishonest to get ahead. He was meticulous in observing the laws and norms of society. In fact, I found his dismissal of all vices somewhat annoying. My brief stint as a carryout boy at the supermarket had introduced me to cigarettes. Bill and Lorraine told me it was a stupid and unhealthy choice but didn't try stopping me from smoking. They did, of course insist that I not smoke inside their house. Despite my observation of alcohol's effects on Doug, I also couldn't simply accept Bill's belief that drinking any alcohol at all was a stupid waste of brain cells. Stubbornly, I had to find out for myself.

The legal drinking age in New Jersey as well as Connecticut was 21, but only 18 in New York. So, shortly after my 18th birthday, I took the bus into Manhattan, where I bought six bottles of Thunderbird and a bottle of rot-gut high-proof gin from a liquor store on 42nd Street, right off Times Square. It wasn't all for me, I was making a run for younger friends as well. In a field somewhere in Kendall Park, several friends and I polished off the fifth of gin and one of the bottles of wine. Not surprisingly, we got wretchedly ill. I blacked out for a time. When I woke up, I had to knock on someone's door for directions home. I still recall how puzzled they were when looking past me and seeing no car, they realized that I was on foot. At least after this episode, becoming a heavy drinker seemed very unappealing. Nor would I ever again drink anything that tasted like juniper.

Bill and Lorraine were not amused by my indiscretion. With high school ending in six weeks, I couldn't blame them if they felt it was time for me to move on. For some students at South Brunswick, the prom seemed an important thing. It held no interest for me. For other students and their families, graduation seemed like an important ritual. For some it was a relief that they had made it. For others, it was an opportunity to relive and revel in their accomplishments during the preceding four years. There were few golden memories and little in the way of achievements for me at any of the three high schools I had attended. The end of high school seemed like nothing other than a transition point for me. Graduation came and went. So did I.

I had no reason to remain in New Jersey or even on the East Coast to go to college. Now that the time for college neared, Doug's promise from ten years before that he and Bill would pay for my college education held no hope of fulfillment. Doug could barely support himself. As for Bill, who had obviously never been consulted about the glib promise, he needed to be saving money for his own family's education—not for mine. College would be on me, assuming I could get in with my less than wonderful GPA. Although it seemed like a very long time, it had only been a little over two years that I lived with Bill and Lorraine. I still considered Minneapolis home, so it was there that I headed after classes ended at South Brunswick High School, intending to attend the University of Minnesota as had Bill.

Chapter 3 — On My Own; Caught in a Draft

AS A VERY LARGE STATE school, the University of Minnesota was relatively liberal in admitting residents. I did well on the SAT and ACT tests so, despite my mediocre grades through the 11th grade, I hoped to be accepted. Unfortunately, since I had been away living with Bill for two-years, college officials told me I no longer qualified as a resident. I would have to live and work for a year in Minnesota before applying, unless I were able to pay non-resident tuition. With only a little cash in my pocket, I needed to work for a while anyway. I would be at risk of the military draft, but that was a risk I would have to take.

Upon my arrival, I took up residence at the YMCA, downtown. I had a single room with no cooking facilities and a communal shower down the hall. It was a big step back from suburban Cleaverdom, but at the right price. It was Doug's suggestion, from his own personal experience. Doug had been a member of the Y for some time. He used to take me swimming there now and then, before we went to Arizona. He thought it was a safe and wholesome place for a young man. Well, sort of. Years later, when the Village People came out with their disco song about the YMCA I knew exactly what they were talking about. One older guy was always checking me out in the showers. As a trim 18-year-old, I suppose I was prime meat. I wondered about those pool visits earlier, when we had to observe the requirement that no trunks be worn while swimming, allegedly for health reasons. All the guys had to swim nude. Hmmm.

After settling in at the Y, I looked for work. According to aptitude tests during high school, I had strong persuasive abilities. I took this to mean I would do well in sales. Hah! Knowing no better, I first hooked up with some outfit selling crummy console stereos out of a basement. We were the clowns with clipboards that still stop people today, in the malls of America, claiming to be taking a survey. In our case, it was a music survey. We targeted young working girls. If they bit at listening to our music, we showed the merchandise, promising a choice of a Lane hope chest or a synthetic, cheap-looking wig as an added inducement. The stereos were crap and I hadn't been popular with girls during high school, so I was not successful. The next month I briefly tried telemarketing, cold calling people to subscribe to *Reader's Digest*. It was an unglamorous but reputable job at which others were successful enough to make ends meet but not one at which I could meet minimum quotas. After two weeks, they let me go. So much for my persuasive aptitudes.

I gave up looking for work on my own and went to an employment agency. What a mistake! To think I actually paid someone a percentage of the piddly little wages I received for working at Westling Manufacturing, the auto parts rebuilding company where they sent me. Tearing down power brake units from large trucks was a horrible, smelly and somewhat hazardous job. Many of the units were recovered from salvage yards. They were nasty. They were rusty. Bolts were stripped. Nuts were frozen. Seals were torn, letting brake fluid, rusty water and dirty oil mix together in a foul-smelling brew. One large unit was particularly dangerous to disassemble. A tiny pin, about the length and diameter of the needle used to inflate soccer balls or basketballs, was all that kept a huge coiled steel spring from flying out of the unit. The quarter-inch thick spring was compressed down from six feet to about two feet under the hydraulic piston. Tear down required carefully removing the pin running through the piston shaft with one hand, while further compressing the spring with the other hand atop the piston. One slip and the spring would shoot out faster than a jack-in-the-box but with much more serious results. At least there was a guaranteed paycheck, even if I did have to pay part of it to the agency that referred me there.

In the meantime, with the assistance of a loan from my uncle Ed, my mother's younger brother, I bought a cheap used car. While living with Bill, I had taken driver's education at school, but Bill wouldn't let me drive his car. Now it was a bit of a challenge getting my driving skills back up. I felt especially challenged driving a standard transmission, since I had learned to drive on an automatic. Having the car and a little bit of money from my crummy jobs enabled me to move to a seedy old apartment building on West 15th Street. I saw an ad posted on the bulletin board at the Y, "Looking for a male roommate." The apartment was just south of Loring Park.

Shortly after moving in, I came home surprised to find the two-bedroom apartment filled with drunken revelers, a previously scheduled party ongoing that my roommate Rick had forgotten to tell me about. By then, I had sufficiently recovered from the gin and Thunderbird incident in New Jersey to feel comfortable knocking back a few beers myself. I was more surprised to find a female friend of Rick's in my bed at the end of the night. She quickly disabused me of any notions I might have. "I'm just here for sleep, not for sex," she informed me. "There's nobody here sober enough to drive me back home."

"Where's home?" I asked.

"Gibbon, where Rick's from."

"Oh, wow. Ok."

Gibbon is a small town, about 80 miles west-southwest of the Twin Cities. Rick was still out of it early Sunday morning, so it fell to me to drive her back home, so she could teach Sunday school. How odd, I thought. It was the closest I had come to a church since my mother's funeral. But I didn't stay for services.

For reasons unknown, Rick had some attitudes about race I didn't care for, which came up most often after a few beers. And Rick often had a few beers.

"You gotta watch out for the 3 "M"s—the Muslims, the Mau Maus and the Motherfuckers," he would often say.

"Rick, you shouldn't talk that way," I'd tell him.

"What—are you some kind of nigger lover or something?"

"I don't **love** black people, I just don't hate them. They're just people, like you and me."

"Oh no, not like me! Not like me."

This roommate thing wasn't working out well. A month later, the FBI came to the building. Two men outside in front, two in back, one outside the window and two on the door, just down the hall. The guy they were after couldn't have been one of the "M"s, since he was white—but he must have been a bad MF anyway, given all the agents there to arrest him. *I don't need this*, I thought to myself. With the regular check coming in from Westling Auto Parts, I got a small apartment of my own in northeast Minneapolis, not far from Edison High School. Fortunately, I didn't see any Animals in the neighborhood—perhaps the Baldies had overwhelmed them. Moving there made sense anyway, since the auto parts place was northeast. While the small, but regular paycheck was nice, I didn't much care for the constant badgering by a roving supervisor.

"You're behind. You've got to work faster. We need to get five of these units torn down each hour and you're only getting three or four."

"I'm working as fast as I can Mr. Spencer. The rust is really thick on some of these bolts. It takes a lot of penetrating oil and time to break them loose."

"They're always like that. You need to spend less time talking to Tommy [a coworker] and work faster—otherwise I'll have to let you go."

As it turned out, he didn't have to fire me. I quit. After several months of enduring the nasty smells and the aggravating supervisor, I had had it. From this frying pan, I leapt to the fire. I began selling encyclopedias door-to-door. I learned the fine art of deception from a man who took pride in his ascension from a dirt-under-the-nails farm boy to a blustering bully. He thoroughly enjoyed conning people in the small Midwestern towns we pillaged. We shouldn't have had to be so sleazy to sell something edited and published by a reputable national company, but we were. Although I made a few sales, my sales aptitude had not improved markedly during the time spent tearing down power brake units. A couple months passed before three events compelled me to quit this job.

The first was when I was accused by the former farmer and now encyclopedia office manager of "fronting" (putting in the down payment myself) an order. The second event was when a man whose door I knocked on invited me in not to see the encyclopedias, but to detail his prior experience with my employer. He had contracted a serious illness, leaving him unable to work. All his creditors were sympathetic and understood that he would need more time to pay—all except for the encyclopedia company. Fearful of not getting the rest of their money and despite his being ahead several months on the payments, they demanded he pay the balance at once. They were not nice people. The final straw came in April, was when I got busted in Huron, South Dakota.

The company had a set policy of never complying with local ordinances requiring permits to sell door-to-door. The wonderful man I worked for claimed it was unconstitutional and besides, too costly. So if stopped by a cop, we would play dumb and innocent. After waiting an appropriate time, we would turn the corner and knock on another door. I didn't wait long enough that particular night. The local police hauled me in, fingerprinted and booked me. Before putting me in a holding cell, they took away my tie, shoelaces and belt so I couldn't hang myself. *Did traveling salesmen often hang themselves over this?* The crew boss managed to get a magistrate out to hear the case at 10 p.m. I got a fine of $50, half of which was suspended. Thankfully, a sentence of thirty days in jail was also suspended. The company paid the fine. But ever since then, I have had to recite this silly episode when answering the question on various forms "have you ever been convicted of a crime."

With no other job lined up, I quit a couple days after returning from South Dakota. With a decent income no longer certain, it seemed like a good time to head back to the inexpensive YMCA. In May of 1966, almost a year after leaving Bill and Lorraine's house in New Jersey, I was back where I started on my arrival back in Minneapolis. I needed a decent job if I had any hope of paying for college. While still working for the book peddlers, I had applied for fall admission to the University of Minnesota. I got my letter of acceptance just after I quit. Now I needed to find a way to pay for it, assuming that they also would now agree I was a state resident. Doug suggested I take the Postal exam, since it paid well for a job not requiring a college degree. But like most government jobs, getting hired took time. You couldn't just walk in, apply, and get a job in a few days or even a few weeks. I took the exam the next month. In the meantime, I took a dependable job as a stock boy at a department store, one of the anchor stores in Southdale, a mall in the affluent Minneapolis suburb of Edina. This was a very different environment than the ones I had been frequenting. The middle-aged moms who frequented the mall tried to disguise the aging process by dressing like their teenaged daughters.

What the moms didn't know (or maybe didn't care about anyway) was that they weren't getting as good a deal at the frequently advertised sales as they thought. Before bringing the newly arrived merchandise from the loading dock to the sales floor, I had to make a stop at the back room where others put the price tags on the clothes. The tags had a printed "regular" price, which the markdown ladies had first lined through, and a "markdown" sale price they had then wrote in. Coming straight from the warehouse, none of the items was ever offered for sale at the "regular" price. It was useful, if disturbing, information to learn. At age 19, I had not realized how cavalier at deception were America's retail stores. I had a lot to learn about business ethics. Less disturbing and at least as valuable an educational experience were my trips through gift-wrap. The nice ladies working there taught me how to wrap packages. That would be a useful talent if and when I had an opportunity to give someone a present. The opportunity came sooner than I expected because of my living at the Y. Despite its well-earned reputation heralded by the Village People, the YMCA did encourage interaction with the opposite sex.

"John, you should go to the dance tonight," said Bill Casbohm, a fellow Y dweller I had recently met.

"I don't know. I'm not much for dances," I replied truthfully, having had little experience with them. Even when I had tried to make a connection, in Midland and Kendall Park, it hadn't gone well.

"That doesn't matter; most of the guys that live here can't dance either, if that's what you're worried about." He was reading my mind. "It's your chance to meet some girls."

"Oh sure, meet girls at the YMCA? Are you for real?"

"Hey, the girls that come here aren't looking for a wild time or a great dancer. Their moms figure the guys that go to dances at the Y must be safer than the ones at the clubs and the parties."

"Yeah, I suppose you're right." What did I have to lose? After my limited and ill-fated efforts at dating while living with Bill, I needed to do something. Of course, there was that missed opportunity, if it could be called that, when a woman wearing only a negligee answered my knock on her door. She had invited me in to tell her all about the encyclopedias I was peddling. I declined the offer, insisting (honestly) that the company required me to talk with both a husband and wife. I left her standing puzzled in her doorway, that a young man could be more interested in making money than her.

So I went to the dance that night. Bill was the first one to spot Gloria, a trim dark-haired brunette in a snug-fitting shift. Like most American females aged 15-30 in 1965-66, her hair was teased up in a pile resembling a hair dryer hood and held in place with high viscosity hair spray. Not my idea of beauty but that's what they all did. Then again, who was I to be fussy given my nerdy look and lack of dating success or even experience? After taking her for a few spins around the floor, Bill brought her back to meet me,

"John, this is Gloria."

"Hello, Gloria."

"Hi."

"Why don't you ask her to dance," Bill whispered generously in my ear, as Gloria's head turned toward the music.

"So, you want to dance?" I inquired, as manfully as I could.

"OK," she replied with a disarming but unreadable smile.

I did my earnest best in faking an ability to dance. Thanks to occasionally watching Dick Clark and Lloyd Thaxton, I wasn't totally clueless, just not adept.

"You're a good dancer," she said, over the unintelligible lyrics of "Louie, Louie," playing loudly in the ballroom. *Hah, what a come on,* I thought to myself.

"Oh, thanks; so are you." *No, not really,* I lied.

A few songs later, adorned by the sheen of perspiration, we took a break. Sitting down next to Bill Casbohm, I asked both of them,

"You want a pop?"

"Sure," replied Gloria.

"Sure you can carry three of them?" Bill, partner-less, asked.

"Yeah, what do you want?"

"I'd like a cherry Coke, please," Gloria said.

"Root beer for me," Bill replied.

"OK, I'll be back in a couple minutes."

It took a little longer than I thought. A long line at the pop stand held me back. By the time I got there, Bill and Gloria were back out on the floor. They came back soon, as a slow dance started up.

"Hey, John, you were taking so long, I didn't want Gloria getting cold sitting here," Bill said with a laugh, his short blonde hair still dry along the edges in the chill air of the well air-conditioned room. He hadn't been dancing as much as I had.

"Will you watch my drink, please? I need to go to the ladies room."

"You bet," I said.

As she walked away, Bill wasted no time pumping me up.

"I think she likes you."

"Oh yeah, sure."

"No, really. Next time there's a slow dance, just get her on the floor and you'll see."

"You saw her first. I thought you were interested in her?"

"Well I was, but I don't think she's interested in me. So go for it!"

"Oh, all right."

We sat in silence through the Beatles, Stones and Chuck Berry, before the return of Gloria. With face back in place and hair restored and re-glued, she sat down beside me, in the only open chair, with another inscrutable smile.

"Thanks for the Coke. I needed that."

"You're welcome. Do you come here often for the dances?"

"Well, I've been here a few times. I haven't seen you here before."

"This is my first time here. I just moved back in."

"You live here?"

"Yeah, I need to save up money for college."

"You're going to college?" Gloria's eyes opened a little wider. The corners of her mouth rose and her breath quickened.

"Well, not yet. I just got accepted at the U for the fall. I would have started last year but I graduated from a high school in New Jersey. Even though I lived here most of my life, I couldn't qualify for resident tuition because of living out of state with my brother for two years. So I had to live and work here for a year to get in-state tuition. I needed the money anyway."

"What are you going to study?"

"Well I really want to be a writer, but people have told me not to count on writing to make a living. So maybe I'll do technical writing or go into advertising. I guess I'll be taking a lot of English classes."

"Wow, that's neat."

Right about then, the DJ started playing the new chart-topping single, "Gloria," by the Shadows of Knight.

"Hey it's a song about you! You want to dance?"

"Sure!"

More enthusiastic faking later, Gloria the song concluded and Gloria the girl grabbed hold for the slow dance. Step, step, turn—clinching all the while, tentatively at first but then more firmly. Feeling no psychic resistance and recalling the moves I saw my more confident friend Gary put on the girls back at Henry High School, I boldly pressed a knee between her legs and lifted up. Alas, there was physical resistance, in the form, apparently, of a girdle. But not too much. She reciprocated my advance, rather than rejecting it, limited by the girdle's constraint and the contours of the shift she wore. The slow dance and the grind ended in a comfortable but silent embrace. Bill had been right all night. It had been a good idea to go to the dance. Gloria liked me. *So now what?* I wondered.

"I need to be going home now. I told my mom I'd be home by midnight. I need to catch the 11:30 bus." Gloria said, as the music stopped.

"You don't have to take the bus. I can give you a ride home. Where do you live?"

"I live with my parents, on Harriet Avenue, south of Franklin. It's not far but you don't have to give me a ride."

"It's no problem, if it's OK with you."

"OK."

Fifteen minutes later, we pulled up in front of the apartment building where she lived.

"Thanks for the ride. I had fun dancing with you tonight."

"Yeah, me too. Maybe we could get together again. Why don't you give me your number so I can call you?"

"Here, I'll just write it down for you," she said, pulling a pen and small notepad out of her purse.

Back at the Y the next day, I caught up with Bill Casbohm.

"Hey Bill, thanks for encouraging me to go to the dance. It all worked out really well."

"You're welcome. Did you get her phone number? Are you going to see her again?"

"Yes and yes."

"Great! It must be the answer to a young man's prayers."

"Uh, well I'm not much into praying. It's more like the answer to a young man's fancy."

"Yeah, I guess so. Still, I'd like to think God fits in there somewhere."

"Why?"

"I don't really know. My parents never had much belief, but I feel like there has to be a reason I am here. There has to be purpose in life. I want to have faith but I just haven't found it yet."

"Well I had it once. I used to go to Sunday school when I was a little kid. Later on, I went to MYF, Methodist Youth Fellowship. I can't see how it gave me any answers. It just gave me more questions. Like how come my father died so young? Like how come my mother suffered so much?"

"Yeah, those are hard questions."

"Well, if you find out the answers, let me know. It really makes me wonder whether there is a God or not. I mean, if there is, why would he let things go on like that, letting people suffer? Am I supposed to be grateful and thank him for it not being any worse?"

"I don't know for sure, but I think it has something to do with love. When I find out, I will let you know."

"Like in 'God so loved the world he gave his only begotten son to die for your sins'?"

"And 'love your fellow man'."

"You bet. That's where we came in, with the young man's fancy turning to love. I could go for some of that."

True enough, it was spring and the sap was rising. Now, for the first time, I began exploring a close relationship with someone. Over the course of the next month, Gloria and I saw each other often. By the end of the month, if not physically together, we were on the phone. It was a new experience for Gloria as well, despite her being two years older than I was, a month past her 21st birthday. Gloria, however, had the advantage of a mentoring mother. Alice Nelson clearly was impressed. Her daughter's fortune might be assured after all, now that she was dating someone college-bound. Gloria's father was a shipping clerk with only a high school education (like my own deceased father). Upon hearing my potential career goals of being in advertising, Gloria's mother promptly bought and presented me with a book on the industry. She didn't want this fish getting away. Happily enough for her, because I lived at the Y, I couldn't spirit Gloria away to my own room. But Alice Nelson wasn't dumb; she knew we needed privacy. She was considerate enough to go in another room of the two-bedroom apartment so Gloria and I could make out on the sofa in the living room.

Of course, we couldn't actually "do it," as Gloria referred to sex, there or anywhere else. She was saving herself for marriage. That didn't keep her from getting "hot," as she put it, while engaging in some serious fondling. It was my first inkling of the advantage that women have over men, the ability to have an orgasm while fully clothed. Despite feeling a little frustrated, I accepted her restraint without complaint—after all, nobody else had ever offered me anything more in the way of sex play.

The play would not last for long. While working that first year after high school, the draft remained a dark threat, a boogeyman kept at bay by more pressing matters like finding and keeping a paying job. Early the next month, the New Brunswick boogeyman sprung. Local Board No. 31 in New Brunswick, New Jersey sent unwelcome "Greetings ..." informing me that my number had been drawn in the draft lottery. This was not a lottery I wanted to win. The letter was an icy blast colder than an Alberta Clipper ordering me to report to Fort Snelling, for a pre-induction physical on June 24. Unless found deficient in some way, I would soon find myself in the armed forces. What about my acceptance at the University of Minnesota? Didn't that get me off the draft's hook? Tough luck, I learned. Student deferments didn't apply until you enrolled and were attending classes. Simply being accepted into college was not enough to avoid the draft. At the physical, the doctors found me sufficiently fit. The armed forces personnel assured me my little legal problem in South Dakota wouldn't keep me out either. Oh well, getting drafted would get me the GI bill to help finance college. That had worked for both my brothers, Doug and Bill. I didn't know it then, but the military experience that awaited me, ugly as it would be, also would be crucial in putting me on the path to my own enlightenment.

Gloria was sympathetic and concerned at the news of my impending induction, which perhaps played a part in us becoming more and more seriously involved. The family was very religious, attending a Lutheran church every Sunday. While my friend Bill Casbohm continued exploring the world of faith in hopes of finding answers, the spiritually uplifting effects of romance were providing me a more subtle epiphany, leading me back into the fold. Perhaps the feelings of what I took to be love, what little I knew of it, were evidence enough of the existence of God. So I began attending church with the Nelsons, at first to humor them, but soon enough more seriously.

During a summer, especially a summer of youthful romance, a dilation of time occurs. Minutes spent lolling on a blanket spread atop a sunny knoll, exploring the contour of your lover's cheek, seem like a lifetime. A series of those minutes can be an eternity. So it's not surprising that we, Gloria and I, should have begun thinking about marriage before summer's end. Having passed its physical, the military ordered me to report for induction into the Army on October 6. I reasoned that if I was old enough to go off and fight in a war, I must be old enough to get married. My brother Bill had already married by the time he was my age and it had worked out well for him. I didn't dwell on how unalike we were. If I had given it much thought, it would no doubt have made little difference in my decision in any case.

If we were to be married, it should be in the Lutheran Church. If it was in the Lutheran Church, I should be a Lutheran—or so Gloria and her mother told me. It was now August, giving me just enough time to complete the process of becoming a Lutheran before becoming a soldier. It meant repeating confirmation, which I had completed in the Methodist Church not long after returning from Arizona. The Lutheran Church had a bit more ritual, and the observance of its tenets was a bit more formal, than were those of the Methodist Church in which I had grown up. So I began learning all about the Nicene Creed, the Apostle's Creed (its shorter alternate) and other elements of Lutheran catechism. I listened and accepted uncritically the admonishments of religious dogma. Jesus Christ was the Son of God. He rose from the dead after being crucified. And so on. It required a lot of faith, but I had already decided to get married.

Perhaps I accepted the dogma a little too uncritically. The fact that Mr. Palm was an usher at the Nelson's church should have been a clue that I did. He was my 8th grade history teacher, the one who passed out those square sheets of paper on which to regurgitate an outline of American history. Now he was passing out offering envelopes and the program for the day's services. At the time, I failed to see the irony through love's rosy tint coloring my glasses.

Meanwhile, the Post Office had called to let me know I could report for work the beginning of September. *What wonderful timing*, I thought. The Post Office job would have paid enough to fund college, but I wouldn't be going to college this fall. The Post Office said I should start the job anyway. Federal law required them to rehire me when I got out of the Army and with all the pay increases I would otherwise have received. That would definitely be a better job to come back to than being a stock boy at Southdale! In the meantime, all I had to do was make sure I came back alive. As the number of U.S. troops on the ground grew, news reports about Vietnam put the numbers of dead and wounded well into five figures. While still thinking that fighting in this war was the right thing for America to do, I didn't care to be a casualty.

The draft required you to serve two years. The Army could train and assign you to do anything anywhere during those two years. Rather than take the chance of the Army sending me to Vietnam as an infantryman, I enlisted for an extra year on the promise they would train me in a safer MOS (Military Occupational Specialty). According to the tests they gave me, I qualified for 31B20, radio mechanic training. I took it, figuring that fixing radios would likely keep me out of combat. But first, I would have to go through Basic Training, eight weeks of Hell at Fort Bliss, Texas. I can't say I experienced any bliss while there, but then the Army hadn't named the post for an emotional state but for a deceased colonel by that name.

Chapter 4 — You're in the Army Now

MY EXPERIENCES DURING BASIC TRAINING were much like those of the characters depicted in any of countless movies. Some were serious and some were hilarious. Then again, since many of the NCOs had seen those same movies, as well as the TV shows, this shouldn't be surprising. Looking back on it now, it had its very funny moments, like the occasion when the drill instructor (DI) said, "That Marine sergeant has it good. He only has one Gomer Pyle. I have 55 of them. Right, Mundhenke?"

"Right, Sarge," replied the hapless trainee. Only with great difficulty did the platoon of trainees stifle the laughter rising from their bellies.

More often, the eight weeks were intense, beginning with my arrival at the induction center. They shaved my head nearly bald there. Then I proceeded along a line of windows, holding my fresh green duffel bag open like a trick-or-treater for the supply personnel to toss in Army-issued clothes from socks and underwear through belts, pants, shirts and boots, etc. From there it was on to the training company, where the Smokey Bear-hatted DIs barked a bulldog's welcome to the fresh meat of new recruits and provided initiation into the pecking order of rank and proper syntax when speaking to them.

"When I give you an order, you say 'Yes, sergeant!' Is that clear?"

And for those slow on the uptake, "Don't call me sir! I work for a living!" Only commissioned officers were called sir, never NCOs.

Calling us out by name, the DI's told us our platoon assignments and pointed us to our barracks, where we would spend our sleeping hours for the next several weeks. Metal bunks with thin mattresses, spaced at a prescribed distance from one another, were assigned to each trainee. The DIs told us how to make up the bunks, with the foot and the head alternating from top to bottom and from adjacent bunks, to avoid transmission of communicable disease. They assigned each of us a footlocker and an upright locker. The footlockers were in pairs, at the aisle end of the bunk; the standing lockers were against the wall, at the other end of the bunks.

We learned how to fit the Army issued sheets and blankets so tightly that a quarter would bounce off the surface. They instructed us in the precise manner of folding, rolling, hanging and otherwise storing or displaying all of our military belongings. We didn't need and were not supposed to have much of any civilian clothes during Basic. Those who somehow managed to bring too much with them were instructed in how to ship it back home. Outer shirts, pants and coats, had to be hung in a specific order and direction within the upright locker adjacent to our cots. All other articles had to be placed at specific points within the footlockers. The DIs conducted frequent, unscheduled inspections to reinforce the prescribed displays. An improperly set up footlocker tray would be dumped on the floor.

Basic Trainees had to absorb a great deal of knowledge that is foreign and peculiar to normal civilian life. Important things like military nomenclature and vocabulary were drilled into our brains. Pointing alternately to the bullet clip-equipped weapon in our hand and then to the bulge in our pants, we learned to say, "This is my rifle and this is my gun, this is for fighting and this is for fun." We also had to acquire such important military skills as marching. While on duty, two or more soldiers could not simply walk. Walking would be too disorderly, too undisciplined. Soldiers must march in formation. We learned to fire and maintain a rifle, surmount physical obstacles or crawl under barbed wire. We also had the fun of becoming more physically fit through calisthenics, pushups, and other ordeals intended to make us capable of carrying a load of military gear on long marches.

Aside from instilling knowledge and skills, basic training's major function was making human beings into interchangeable parts in the military machine. To do so required replacing the unique individual behaviors of a diverse group of young men (and later women) with consistent and collective responses to military order and discipline. If the selective service system failed to weed out some of those who were physically or emotionally unsuitable for military service, then Basic Training would complete the task. One superficially cruel, but probably life-saving, example of this that I recall involved the first sergeant of my training company. The first sergeant continued berating one somewhat unstable trainee until succeeding in provoking the individual to attack him with the working end of a broom. The first sergeant was unharmed, but as he intended, the assault was sufficient to get the trainee tossed out of the Army. Had he remained in the service, the trainee posed a risk to both himself and others should they wind up in combat. If the kid couldn't handle the stress of the NCO's duress, how could he have stood the stress of being under fire?

The same DI who made the Gomer Pyle joke frequently offered chilling codas to the combat classes, transcending the otherwise chicken-shit appearance of military dictates. For example, each boot must first have a white paint strip marked inside, then the trainee's name and serial number written in black ink. The same went for all other articles of clothing. Beyond the practical utility of identifying your own stuff should items get intermingled somehow, the critical point he made was, "If you step on a land mine or get hit with an RPG [rocket propelled grenade] or a mortar, you may wind up with your body parts spread all over the place. You got your name and serial number on all your gear, what pieces of you they find will be in the body bag shipped home to your mama." I didn't find it very reassuring, but it was one of the few sensible explanations I ever heard for some of the rules in the military.

The military, beginning in Basic, is a very profane place. It was in Basic, I believe, that I first became accustomed to the use of "fucking" as a universal emphatic modifier. "Fucking" could be inserted before, after or between any two syllables of another word—as in "outfuckingstanding!" Other examples include such gems as, "AfuckingOK" and "allfuckingright." Or for even more emphasis, adding "mother"—as in "Hell, motherfuckingyes!" To be fair, the language among young college students, I later learned, was not that much different. The juxtaposition of Army chaplains attempting to interpose some decency was very different, however.

The schedule of Basic did not permit attending services each week, but on one of those Sundays when I was able to attend services, I recall the chaplain assuring us that, "I take seriously the concerns of your mothers who write to me complaining about the language used by our drill sergeants. I am admonishing the company commander to do something about this."

It was welcome comic relief. While marching, the trainees would work on their esprit de corps by stentorian renditions of cadence call and response. It was not quite like the call and response that one might hear in a church.

"I know a girl, her name is Lil. She won't do it but her sister will!"

Or, from our rhythm-challenged first sergeant, "Lulu's got a boyfriend; he drives a truck. Lulu's got a boyfriend; he likes to fuck."

From the beginning, I found it odd to be attending religious services conducted by ministers in military officer's uniforms. What would prompt a man of the cloth to become a chaplain? Undoubtedly, it was for some of the reasons above, to attempt (unsuccessfully for the most part) to keep their flock pure following their transition from civilians to soldiers. Yet here we soldiers were learning how to kill people. That was not what I thought religion was supposed to be about. Of course, it's good, many people think, to have God on your side when fighting a war. It seems that many people are convinced that God, in fact, *is* on their side *and* that those on the other side are very mistaken if they think God is on their side. This, I am sure, is why the military at least tolerates, if not enthusiastically embraces, chaplains. At least they do so long as the chaplains know their place. They should support morale but keep their opinions to themselves about the military mission, unless those opinions are militarily correct. To cite one example, the famous quote attributed to a Navy chaplain at Pearl Harbor who reportedly said, "Praise the Lord, and pass the ammunition."

I didn't want any ammunition. I didn't want to kill people. Yet I did learn to shoot a rifle. I was not a good shot, qualifying at the most minimal passing level. It was a good thing for me that I was headed for training on fixing radios rather than being an infantryman. Following the excursion known as "bivouac," when we camped out in the deserts of New Mexico at the Northern end of Ft. Bliss, Basic Training concluded with a graduation ceremony. I could find humor in this pageant only much later. It was remarkably similar in import, if not style, to the show put on by Bill Murray, Harold Ramis, et al in the movie, "Stripes." All of the training companies marched in review before a high-ranking but forgettable and faceless functionary, the commanding officer of the training brigade. If they chose to do so, family members were welcome to be present at this momentous occasion. None of mine were there, nor was Gloria. She would see me soon enough, coming home the next day, on the brief break between Basic and Advanced Individual Training (AIT).

Arriving home, Gloria and her mother wasted no time in reorienting my faith from the odd religious experiences during Basic Training. We needed to complete pastoral counseling to assure our readiness to be married. Hah! In my state of relieved confusion having survived Basic, the visit to the minister reinforced my grasp of rapture. No, not the rapture of Judgment Day—the rapture of love and the ecstasy to follow. More importantly, it reaffirmed the promise of a secure and stable sanctuary, an emotional refuge. I would leave the wedding planning to mother and daughter, the result mattered more to me than the process of getting there. Besides, I had only a few days leave before reporting to Ft. Benning for AIT, where I would learn how to be a "radio mechanic."

It seemed odd to me then and still does now, to call someone a "mechanic" who fixes radios. But perhaps its oddity shouldn't be surprising. Radio school was my first introduction to the wasteful mismanagement of human resources in the military. My course was a basic one, limited to lower power radios. After the training, we would only be able to do simple tasks like exchanging plug-in components, replacing fuses or repairing connectors. Among my fellow students at this lowest level course was a design engineer from RCA. Meanwhile, at the same Ft. Benning site, a man who had been a professional musician in civilian life was attending a six-month course in fixed-station transmitter repair. The guy from RCA could have taught that course. Another classmate of mine became an Army cook, wasting his radio repair training. Oh well.

The radio mechanic classroom was in a brand new building, part of the Army's Infantry School complex at Ft. Benning (near Columbus, Georgia). Class was a long ways from our old barracks. We marched there every day in the cold freezing rain of a Georgia winter, Army field jackets doing little to keep the damp cold from penetrating our bones. Nonetheless, it was a welcome relief from the rigors of Basic Training. Military discipline had been successfully instilled in Basic. There was no more shouting and no more intimidation for us. We weren't being trained in a combat specialty, unlike the macho masochists who volunteered for Airborne Ranger training or Officer Candidate School (OCS). The Army used OCS for quickly producing commissioned officers from among draftees and volunteers. The output of officers from ROTC and the military academy was not enough to cover the quantity needed during the Vietnam War. Many infantry officers had the misfortune of a short lifespan while in combat there.

My fellow comfort and safety-seeking classmates laughed every day, passing by the Airborne Rangers in training. We watched them double-timing everywhere, jumping off high platforms in their jump gear to toughen up and get the landing roll down or pulled up and then dropped from tall towers with their chutes open. We thought they were chumps, fully sucked in to the alternating facets of domination and submission common to military life— except taken to a much higher level, approaching sexual craving, by these commando types. The guys in OCS had it tougher still. But they did have a nice new building, with good equipment.

The OCS played a part in my introduction to "Midnight Requisitions." At our old dumpy barracks, we didn't have the best supplies or even decent access to them. Our Supply sergeant instructed us in a simple solution. We would simply steal what we needed from OCS. A late night raid on the OCS mess hall netted half a dozen brand new mops, hanging on the wall outside the back door. It was easy pickings for us and tough luck for some poor sods at the OCS unit!

Meanwhile, Gloria and her mother kept working on the wedding plans. Without knowing whether we could be together after radio school, it seemed like a good idea to schedule the wedding before AIT ended. Unfortunately, as the time for the wedding approached, the duty roster for March came out showing me performing KP the weekend of the ceremony. The church was reserved, caterer scheduled and invitations sent. So I went home anyway, confident that another trainee would perform the KP for me in exchange for my doing it for him the following weekend. He "forgot" to show up for my shift as we had agreed. As soon as I got back, the training company's first sergeant called me into his office. He asked me,

"Did you go AWOL this past weekend?"

"Yes, sergeant," I said.

"Did you get married?"

"Yes, I did."

"All right. Don't go AWOL again! Dismissed."

Perhaps he thought she must have been pregnant for me to go AWOL to get married. She wasn't pregnant of course, since we had yet to have sex. I just couldn't be bothered with explaining to my superiors that I needed that particular weekend off. Based on what I had seen of military flexibility so far, it seemed unlikely I could have had a leave request approved, so I didn't ask for it. I figured it was none of the Army's business anyway.

I was less willing to cave in to authority than most guys were. That attitude would cause me serious problems in Vietnam. Soon after I returned from the wedding weekend, the first sergeant tried to sign me up for a savings bond allotment. I told him I didn't need or want one. So he sent me to see the training company commander for some arm-twisting. It was a big deal in the Army, peddling savings bonds. The Army sold bonds on the installment plan, deducted from pay. Given the piddly amount of money that privates got paid ($89 a month at the time, if I remember correctly), I didn't think I should have to buy one.

"So, Maberry, the first sergeant says you haven't signed up for a savings bond. What's the problem? Don't you want to save some of your pay for your future?"

"Well sir, I would like to, but I don't really think I can afford to on a private's pay."

"Well you know that most people buy them on the installment plan, a small deduction each month. He also told me you got married recently. Don't you want to save money for your wife, and eventually a family?"

"Yes sir, but I don't think that savings bonds are the best way to do that. They don't really earn a lot of interest. I don't really want to get one and I don't think you can order me to."

"I hate to admit it, but you're right. I can't make you take one. You can go. Dismissed."

I went on to learn what I needed to know about fixing radios, doing very well in the class. Within two weeks of returning from my brief weekend wedding trip, I graduated from the radio school as the top student. Shortly before classes ended, I got my orders: Report immediately to the 6th Armored Cavalry at Ft. Meade, Maryland. I was gratified not to have orders for Vietnam, at least not yet. When I arrived, I learned that the unit had been reactivated a few months before and was being restocked with personnel for eventual shipment to Vietnam. While that process went on, Gloria and I could have an initial foray into married life. It wouldn't be easy. Ft. Meade was midway between Washington, DC and Baltimore. The nearest town, Odenton (AKA "Boomtown" on post) had apartments for low-ranking enlisted men like me. I had disposed of my cheap used car in Minneapolis when I went in the Army and couldn't afford another now. Gloria had never owned a car since neither she nor her parents drove and it wasn't entirely necessary living in a moderate-sized city like Minneapolis that had good public transit. Living near an Army post would be a different story. Most of them are miles from civilization. Although that was not the case for Ft. Meade, there were no good public transit options. I needed to be on a main travel route into Ft. Meade, so I could get a ride onto post with some other soldier or civilian. I found a small furnished apartment, one bedroom atop a storefront, where Gloria and I could live.

I met Gloria at BWI airport a few weeks later. I can't say it was the heart that had grown fonder in the six weeks apart since our wedding day. Physical obstacles had prevented consummating the marriage before now. We barely managed to restrain ourselves on the bus from Baltimore, sitting in a back corner away from other passengers. Once in the apartment we quickly made up for lost time, with zest and passion. The zest and passion was short-lived. I had to be up so early to get into post on time that I found myself falling asleep shortly after dinner most nights.

Dinner was a bit of a problem anyway. Gloria's cooking skills were less than stellar. Large servings of Hamburger Helper, Rice-a-Roni and other simple dishes were the staple of our diet. To an already sleepy person, the high-carb/high glycemic dinners had a sedative effect. When Mrs. Nelson came to visit six weeks later, she couldn't understand why I didn't want to stay up and talk. With a belly full of food after being up for 16 hours, I wasn't being rude, I just couldn't do it. Beyond that sour note, my choice of reading material dismayed Gloria's mom.

I had casually left on the dresser a paperback I picked up during overnight duties at Ft. Meade. I hadn't bought the book or even read much of it. The book was just something someone else had found to pass the time when he had to stay on post overnight. When I left post, I grabbed it by mistake along with my own stuff. The book had some explicit sex scenes describing a variety of practices other than the acceptable missionary position. My mother-in-law found it luridly disgusting. The resulting discussion she had with Gloria, put such "dirty" practices as oral sex off limits. Sex could be fun, but it shouldn't be too much fun or indulged in too often to her way of thinking. So after mother Nelson's visit, sex was a lot tamer. I felt like I had taken a few bites of a steak dinner only to have it yanked away and replaced by a peanut butter and jelly sandwich. What a bummer!

In the meantime, while reporting to my unit every day at Fort Meade, I had no radio repair duties to perform. The 6th Armored Cav had little or no equipment, especially radios. Instead, we drilled daily on the parade field, a grassy square a football field length in either direction. Practicing interminably, we marched to and fro for hours on end because only in precision could we properly honor and impress retiring fat cats. As First Army Headquarters, Ft. Meade always had one general or another entitled to a parting parade. We looked so spiffy in our pretty yellow scarves, covering the t-shirt space from the open neck to the first button of our khakis. Oh, and the thrill of standing at attention in the summer sun with fixed bayonets on our rifles (the heavier old M-14s, not the newer and less esthetically appealing M-16s). I often wondered, would anybody pass out today, slashing or impaling themselves or the guy next to them?

When we weren't playing at pomp, we were practicing riot control. A straight-line formation used for blocking and pushing back, an oblique line used for turning the rioters at a corner and a v-wedge for splitting them. Keep moving, in a stagger-step while thrusting a bayonet-tipped rifle or a shield (assuming we were issued them for an actual deployment). Close as we were to Washington, D.C., we might be used to protect federal property if large-scale riots spread there.

Race riots were widespread in major cities throughout the U.S. in the mid to late sixties. Los Angeles (Watts), Newark, Detroit, Cleveland, Atlanta and Chicago all erupted in violence even before the 1968 assassination of Martin Luther King. Ironic would be too weak a word to describe this prospect for African-American soldiers. Much the same, I suppose, for many of the white soldiers in the South. Like the Arkansas National Guard members who were ordered by President Eisenhower to escort African-American students through the doors of Central High School in Little Rock Arkansas (in 1957) past the resistance of then Governor, Orval Faubus.

I learned long after leaving the service that President Truman had desegregated the military by executive order in 1948, with the first integrated units fighting together during the Korean War. By the time I entered in

October 1966, there were many African-American NCOs and officers. Nonetheless, military discipline didn't alter the underlying attitudes that individuals brought to the service. If anything, the discipline made things worse. When the draft was reinstituted to fill the ranks for Vietnam, a whole lot of America's racial problems were inducted along with the recruits. Many white soldiers didn't care for taking orders from African-Americans. At the same time, it was a real struggle for the brothers from the big cities of the North and from California to deal with white NCOs from the deep South.

Many African-American soldiers thought that the Army wasn't that far removed from the antebellum plantation. Not everyone shared Martin Luther King's dream, expressed only three years before, for an American society where all races could coexist peacefully and amicably. Sam Jackson, a brother from Pittsburg, California (a neighborhood in Oakland) was illustrative. I can't say he was quoting Huey Newton or Bobby Seale, but he had the West Coast strut and a surly look that said, "If you feel froggy, jump." He barely controlled his contempt for white superiors and some fellow blacks (mostly career soldiers) whom he considered Uncle Toms or Oreos. His favorite expression, which I never really understood, was "Coo cluck [Ku Kluk?] the duck. Doesn't matter anyhow. He's a web-footed mother-fuck." But Jackson and I got along. He and I had already spent 12 weeks together at the Radio Mechanic School at Ft. Benning before spending four months at Ft. Meade. I was jealous, though, that he got into the radio school as a draftee, without having to take an extra year of military service as I did.

By the fourth month at Ft. Meade, we still didn't have radios or much in the way of equipment. All we had was one or two tanks and a couple of trucks. In the meantime, they trained us on M-16s, the rifles used in Vietnam. A lieutenant who had already been there ran us through an escape and evasion course, designed to help you avoid capture or if caught, how to get away. Despite the Army's stated goal of sending the 6th Armored Cav overseas as a unit, they kept siphoning off individuals to fill immediate needs in Vietnam. It seemed only a matter of time before it happened to me. And so it did. I had a few weeks leave and travel time before reporting to the Replacement Station at Oakland Army Base. En route, I dropped Gloria off at her parent's apartment, where she would remain while I spent the next year in Vietnam.

At Oakland, masses of soldiers destined for Vietnam were processed quickly through the replacement system. We got a variety of shots to protect us from tropical diseases that the United States didn't have. We got a bunch of jungle fatigues, lighter in weight than the standard working uniform for stateside. We got two pairs of jungle boots with canvas sides (no Gore-Tex back then). We got travel documents for the commercial flight we all would board for travel to Vietnam. All during the process, we heard the routine harangues from the local NCOs, "Get in line. Stay in line. Close it up." In one ear and out the other, the simple commands did little to keep my mind from wondering how bad it would be in the combat zone. *Would the Lutheran faith I had acquired little more than a year before keep me safe?* Now I would have killer Communists to contend with. At the same time, I had to deal with fellow soldiers, especially the people giving the orders, who seemed downright crazy, incompetent or both.

Vietnam

Chapter 5 — Arrival in-Country; Hello Dali

ON THE GROUND AT LAST, after the long flight from Guam, the plane taxied past sandbag-clad heavy steel revetments surrounding bombers and fighters on three sides. As we rolled to a stop, the flight attendant popped the door, allowing the cool cabin air to escape. Tropical heat—asphalt-softening, frying eggs on a sidewalk heat—washed in like a sunny surf, carrying unfamiliar smells. It was Saigon in late September 1967. A throng of cheering khaki-clad soldiers in loose formation waved and beckoned to us from the tarmac at Tan Son Nhut. They laughed and shouted as kids on a playground, all the while looking about as secret service agents do during a presidential walk on a crowded street. A year later, I would better understand their uneasy excitement. Barring a last-minute attack, they had survived their year in Vietnam. They would fly back to "the world" in the plane we exited.

Wasting no time assembling here, we went straight from the ramp onto a prison bus. At least it looked like one. The kind of bus that hauls convict work gangs around some places in America, guarded by shotgun-shouldered Bubbas in Smokey hats. Only we weren't the criminals. The bars and mesh covering the windows were there to protect us. *How odd,* I thought, *we were here to protect the Vietnamese but we must be protected from them.* Yet, on the busy streets we traveled, other military personnel walked freely about or rode in jeeps while Vietnamese civilians sped about on mopeds and bicycles. Other locals fearlessly shopped at the colorful stalls crowding sidewalks along the narrow streets. It was the first of many incongruities, in a year filled with them.

Wealth and poverty, filth and beauty fought for my attention along the 16-mile route to Long Binh for in-country processing. Shacks of wooden ammo crates topped by rusty tin roofs stood next to trash-strewn alleys plied by scavenging birds and occasional cats. Nearby, women emerged from stone buildings of faded grandeur, wearing brightly hued pastel ao dais, snug from neck to waist but billowing in the breeze over their black silk pants. People of all ages carried huge loads on bent backs—bags from the market, bundles of straw or wood. Nearing a river away from the city, workers with conical straw hats strapped under their chins and pants rolled to their knees waded in muddy rice paddies. Further on, we passed the lush green of a rubber plantation, its opulent mansion only slightly tarnished by this or previous wars.

I don't remember at all, the afternoon arrival at Long Binh. So much of military existence is filled with an unremitting and unremarkable sameness. Hurry up and wait. "Assemble in a column of twos. Close it up 'til your buddy smiles!" I do remember that first night in-country bunked under the cover of a circus-sized tent. Intermittently throughout the night, bright flares fell from the sky on parachutes, illuminating the nearby countryside as they swung to and fro. Muffled sounds of rifle fire, far away artillery and other ordnance unfamiliar to my ears rumbled through my head. Adrenaline-fueled wariness overcame weariness, shorting my sleep. Later, I would learn there was no fighting nearby and the flares were just routine. On the first night, however, fear filled me with dread.

It could have been worse, I suppose. I was not among those selected for KP, awakened at 4 a.m. to set up the trays, utensils, garbage cans and washing barrels. Nor was I among the still more unlucky ones selected for shit-burning detail. For toilet facilities in non-permanent bases like these, three or four-seater wooden outhouses were built. Under the holes were the bottom third of 55-gallon drums, cut off and half-filled with diesel fuel. When 2/3 full, the drums were removed through a door at the back of the outhouse and the material burned. It is hard to say which smelled worse—the unburned fecal-fuel blend or the thick black smoke of the burning mix.

Fortunately, for all us new arrivals, the mess hall was upwind from the stench. I had a couple hours' wait after an unappetizing breakfast, before getting a ride to my unit, the 7th Battalion, 9th Artillery, 54th Artillery Group. The E-5 sergeant in charge of the radio repair shack met me in Long Binh. From there, another private, like me, drove us to Bearcat, a base camp our battalion shared with the much larger 9th Infantry Division. Upon our arrival, much to my surprise, I immediately spotted Sam Jackson, my former radio school classmate and fellow Ft. Meade parade participant. I knew that he too was heading to Vietnam when he left Ft. Meade, but I hadn't expected to see him again here. Jackson's orders had come two days before mine and he had arrived in the unit two days ahead of me. He knew I was coming from his first day there. From that knowledge, despite the friendship I thought we had, my problems in Vietnam began. The E-5 introduced me to Master Sergeant Seagram, Chief of the Communication Section. Seagram greeted me with what I would soon recognize as his trademark, bushy-mustachioed grin.

"Jackson here says you were one of the best students in radio mechanic school."

"Well, I did OK," I said, unprepared to provide a more sensible answer. As it turned out, no answer would likely have sufficed to avoid the fallout from this.

"No Sarge, he was really tops," Jackson helpfully added, in a respectful tone very different from the one I was accustomed to hearing from him when addressing white NCOs. Whether sincere or calculated as a setup, I soon learned it would be difficult to live up to Jackson's buildup.

Since we had no radios to work on at Ft. Meade, I hadn't seen the inside of one in six months. Not only that, but the radios here were newer models on which we had received very little repair training. Seagram had a good laugh at my expense, asking me to look over one of the radios before letting me out of his sight. I didn't have a clue about the radio. I doubt that Jackson did either, but he had one big advantage over me, he had arrived two days before I did. As I learned more than ten years later from my study of Buddhism, there is no such thing as chance or coincidence when it comes to the timing of human events. When I arrived in Bearcat, I knew none of this. I had no clear idea then what the significance was of the sequence of events or my first exchange with Sgt. Seagram, but I had a bad feeling about it nonetheless. I didn't have time for idle speculation then, so I pushed the feeling out of my mind. I needed to find my bunk and unpack my stuff. I needed to find out about Bearcat, the place I would be spending the next year of life.

Someone told me that Bearcat was about 22 miles due east of Saigon, five miles from the village of Long Thanh. Over the course of the year, the assurance that this was a relatively safe location to be in Vietnam, turned out to be true. Because of its location on the eastern side of the country, north of the Mekong Delta, Bearcat was free from heavy Viet Cong activity, supply or transportation routes. Still, no place in a country at war could be completely safe. That is why a few feet out from the walls of our hooches lay a stack of sandbags, offering some protection from mortar or rocket attacks and a convenient place for hiding a dope stash, I would later learn.

Having been in the army for a year already, I was used to sleeping in barracks. In lieu of barracks, troops at Bearcat (and at similar base camps) slept in "hooches." They were wood frame buildings walled by screens. They were a step up from the large tents some units had and definitely better than a foxhole in the field. For the first four feet up from the ground, wooden slats sloped down at a 45-degree angle, covering the screen much like permanently open jalousie windows. More secure bunkers were available should we ever be under serious attack. My bed for most of the next 12 months would be an olive-drab canvas-covered cot, topped by an air mattress. Like a mini four-poster bed in jungle chic, a framework of dowels held up mosquito netting surrounding the cot. Soon after arriving, I sent Gloria a letter, covering only the bare details of my Bearcat existence, that I slept indoors and wasn't out in combat.

When I arrived, the hooches were still relatively new. Without electricity, flashlights provided the only light at night. A couple weeks later, our platoon sergeant led a "midnight requisition" on a supply depot a couple miles away. We liberated enough solid core copper wire to brighten our nights. We powered up the hooches per the staff sergeant's directions by running the wire between simple porcelain sockets nailed to the trusses under the tin roofs, and on out to a utility pole connected to a nearby generator.

Once the lights were available, evenings became a strange odyssey. For some it was rereading letters from their wife, girl friend or mother back home and then crafting a message to send back—thanking them for "CARE packages" of cookies or other edibles and asking for more. For others, it was listening to tapes from home and recording their own to send back. Playing cards, usually Hearts or Spades, sometimes Gin, but rarely Poker, took care of most evenings for myself and three or four other guys.

We had a regular mess hall, constructed of the same wood frame and screen material. There was no plumbing however. The mess hall relied on the 400-gallon potable water trailers that could be towed behind trucks or brought in by chopper. Dishwashing was field style, using galvanized steel garbage cans filled with water heated by immersion heaters. They were dangerous devices, tricky to light and adjust, with burning gasoline dripping down a stovepipe into a larger base submerged in the water. The very hot exhaust stack may have been marginally cooler than an idling automobile's tailpipe but it certainly was able to char skin. With an actual mess hall, we had some of the regular army fare we were accustomed to, including creamed chipped beef on biscuits (AKA "shit-on-a-shingle") for breakfast. But we still had to put up with powdered eggs and reconstituted milk. The latter was drinkable only if it was chocolate flavored.

Like the Replacement Battalion processing center in Long Binh, we had a diesel-fuel drum outhouse (a three-seater). We didn't have to burn the stuff here, though; they paid Vietnamese civilians to do that. Nearby was a single stall shower with an overhead tank of unheated water. Given the tropical heat, this wasn't usually a problem. It was sometimes better just soaping up outside during an afternoon thunderstorm, although a premature end to the rain left me soapy on a couple occasions, requiring a dash to the shower stall. Although it was nearing the end of the summer rainy season, it was still hot— so hot that shortly after sunup sweat would soak through my light jungle fatigues while sitting perfectly still in the shade. The least exertion resulted in a salt-water drizzle from my wide-open pores. Soon enough, I would become intimately familiar with the jungle GI's constant companion, crotch-rot.

Like most military posts, we also had a laundry/tailor. Military units must always have someone available to sew on nametags, unit insignia and the lasting mementos of service, such as the silky jackets with messages embroidered on the back. Messages like, "Yea though I walk through the Valley of Death I shall fear no evil, for I am the evilest son of a bitch in the valley!" or "When I die I know I'm going to heaven cause I spent my year in Hell (Bearcat, Vietnam--or fill in the blank of the applicable base camp or village).

A Vietnamese civilian took our dusty/sweaty fatigues off-site somewhere for washing. His English was good, better actually than some of the ARVN (Army of the Republic of Vietnam) interpreters. He seemed too smart to be simply running a laundry. He always would ask about and discuss troop operations.

"You going out in field, soldier?"

"Where you go?"

"When you come back?"

The questions seemed somewhat logical, coming from someone responsible for getting your clothes back to you, but I wondered why none of the officers or NCOs ever cautioned anybody about providing too much information to the guy. He asked for more details than I thought necessary. Perhaps he was a plant for the VC to get information on troop movements. In ironic contrast were the precautions Sergeant Seagram took concerning me. On the single occasion I went into the commo trailer to repair the long-range transmitter, he took care to drape a cover over the crypto equipment attached to the radio and specifically cautioned me against raising the cover. I didn't have the requisite security clearance allowing me even to see the gear. Typical of my military experience, Seagram exalted form (security clearance regulations) over substance (apparent risk).

More sensibly, officers cautioned us about the barbers. It was suggested that we not go along with the neck-pops they offered (twisting the head rapidly to either side to pop the cervical vertebrae) because the result could be hazardous to one's spinal health. We were also cautioned about the nose-hair trimming, given the barbers' tool sanitizing practices (or lack thereof).

Only a Salvador Dali painting could do justice to life at Bearcat. It was that surreal. Eating, sleeping, showering were all so different even from the austerities of military bases in America. Jungle foliage surrounded the hard-packed mud/dirt of the base camp, kept at bay only by tractor blades and defoliant. Much more peculiar was the human environment. These were people whose language and culture I did not understand—not the Vietnamese as much as my fellow soldiers. We were in a hostile, very foreign place, most of us for the first time in our young lives. Partially freed from the constraints of military discipline applicable on American soil and with drugs and alcohol readily available to assist, suppressed quirks and previously hidden subcultures came out in the open. Vietnam was a crucible, heating and compressing psyches. Necks got redder. Drawls got longer/slower. Moonshine making/drinking possum hunter/eaters were a puzzle to Down East lobstermen or Windy City slickers, and vice versa. Open discussions were mumbled in my midst about Toms, Jemimas and Oreos. My friend Jackson's name never came up among the accused, despite his transformation.

Since I had seen him at Ft. Meade, barely a month before, Jackson had shed the guise of Huey Newton. Now he played the role of Rochester, Jack Benny's man. Instead of the "Yass, boss," that Rochester always said to Benny, it was "Yass, sergeant" from Jackson. It was accompanied with a happy hop-to-it attitude, instead of the sneer common to earlier times. *What the hell had happened to Jackson?* Later on, I would see the wisdom of his change in behavior. This was a cloak of compliance, shielding him from harm in a place where opportunities abounded to deal with "uppity niggers." Clearly, some other brothers had quickly clued him in. Why risk a "friendly fire" accident for the sake of ego or pride while here in Nam? The score against whitey could always be settled later on "back in the world."

In retrospect, I am sure Jackson's change in attitude played a part in who continued to work on radios and who wound up doing detail work for 11 months. *Why had the Army sent me to this battalion, which already had an E-5 and Jackson to repair radios? More of the typical mismanagement of resources or carelessness,* I supposed. The unit didn't need two radio mechanics plus the E-5 working on radios. When the E-5 who ran the radio repair shack mistakenly sent a radio to C Battery that actually belonged to A Battery, he blamed the error on me. Before the end of my first month in Vietnam, Sergeant Seagram used this as an excuse to remove me from repair duties. I was neither as sensibly adaptable nor as disposed to yield to authority as was Jackson. Serene in the knowledge that I had been able to go AWOL to get married and to resist buying a U.S. Savings Bond while at Ft. Benning, I felt confident my rights would be vindicated when I spoke up. Well no, it didn't quite work out that way. When I protested to the company commander, he backed up the NCOs. This initial challenge and loss was only the opening round. Seagram would turn out to be the bane of my Vietnam existence. I said nothing about it in my next letter to Gloria. She wouldn't understand anyway. Of course, I didn't understand either, not then at least. I had been cheated out of the job the Army trained me to do. I had taken an extra year to get that training. I had been the top student in my class. Now Jackson had that comfortable job to himself and a red-necked asshole lifer named Seagram was going to make my life miserable. *How could this happen to me? Why was it happening to me?* Many years would elapse before Buddhism supplied an answer to the questions running through my mind.

Chapter 6 — Getting to Know Stubby

SEAGRAM WAS ABOUT 5'5" AND built like a burly fireplug. From his stature, another guy in the unit aptly nicknamed him "Stubby." Of course, we didn't call him that to his face, a face with more craters and gullies than that of Keith Richards. Stubby often said, to anybody in earshot of his frequent rants, "I've been in this Army 26 years; I was here before you were and I'll be here after you're gone. You don't have to accept me, I have to accept you!" Or he might add, whenever he had the least suspicion that someone doubted the wisdom of his orders, "and I outrank anybody in this unit except the CO (Commanding Officer)!" Which wasn't literally true. Stubby was a master sergeant. Although they were at the same pay grade, the E-8 first sergeant outranked him, but then he didn't appear to respect the first sergeant anyway. He certainly didn't appear chummy with him or the other NCOs. He seemed to be on the best terms with an officer, the major who was Battalion S-3.

Stubby drank hard and heavy. Everyone learned to stay away from him the morning after, as well as in the evening after he got his load on. But stone cold sober, he was still a mean son-of-a-bitch. Spanish is the native language of most Puerto Ricans, but that didn't exclude them from the draft. On one occasion, Stubby started baiting a Puerto Rican kid he overheard conversing with a friend in Spanish.

"You're in the American army, speak English!" Seagram said.

"Que?" ["what" in Spanish] The kid reflexively responded.

"What's the matter, puta [Spanish for whore; equivalent to calling a guy a bitch today], you got trouble with English?"

At this, the kid glowered, appearing roused to fight. Stubby egged him on.

"Come on, puta, want to fight me? I'll take my stripes off, and then I'll kick your fuckin' ass!"

"Go on, you can take him!" The kid's idiot friend urged him on. Reluctantly but wisely, the kid backed off. Stubby may have been 25 years older than the kid, but he was still a muscular guy, undoubtedly with many of those 25 years offering abundant bar-brawling experience and who knows what other opportunities for hand-to-hand combat. While he was less than half Stubby's age, the kid was obviously no match for him.

Stubby never challenged anybody else to a fight, directly. I think he always held out hope that by jerking guys around enough, one would challenge him. Nobody ever did. In my case, he and I developed a burning antagonism, flaming brightly for a month and then smoldering the remainder of my tour in Vietnam, flaring up as events unfolded. The accelerants to our blazing hatred occurred out in the field, within a week or two of my wrongful exile from the radio shack.

In November of 1967, a major operation was underway to clear Viet Cong from the periphery of Highway 1. The ARVNs, soldiers in the Army of the Republic of Vietnam, were supposedly doing the front-line work with air and artillery support from U.S. forces. The 7th of the 9th Artillery, my battalion, was among those forces providing support. Like other soldiers in Headquarters and Service Batteries who had no specific job keeping them at Bearcat, I was detailed out to back up the firing batteries.

A short bumpy ride on a banana-shaped CH-47 transport chopper brought us to a clearing in the jungle. Wet heat soaked through our jungle fatigues in the noonday sun as we unloaded the galvanized steel culvert halves we would use to make sandbagged bunkers. As artillery, especially the Headquarters Battery, we were several clicks (kilometers) from where things were really hot, although not entirely without risk of harm. Rome plows, giant tracked vehicles with plow blades as big as the side of a barn, had knocked down most of the foliage in what may once have been a rubber plantation. But like anything else that didn't get doused with Agent Orange, it was growing back. Leafy ground cover underfoot encroached on fast growing bamboo shoots and a few resilient rubber plants, forcing us to scatter our tents shouting distance apart. We were 2 men to a tent, 20 tents in all. Stubby's tent was nearest to mine but shielded from view by some remaining foliage.

Whether it was one of the ARVNs or one of our guys (not likely), somebody stole Stubby's 35-mm camera from his tent the first day out and he was really pissed. On the way to breakfast the next morning, I reminded the guy sharing my tent: "Take your camera; you don't want to get it stolen like Seagram." Unfortunately, with my back turned away from his tent, I failed to notice Stubby coming into earshot.

"There's something that goes before my name—sergeant!" He yelled. "When we get back to Bearcat maybe your signature on an Article 15 will help you remember!"

Arrogantly amused at his petty rage I said nothing to him. It was obvious to me that he was mad, not so much that I, a mere PFC, should be disrespecting his rank, but because I had noticed and commented on his careless loss. Failing to add his rank before his name, when not even addressing him, was far from an actionable infraction. An Article 15 is non-judicial punishment under the Uniform Code of Military Justice (UCMJ; applicable to all branches of the military service) for a minor offense, such as a disciplinary infraction. Typical punishment is loss of a few days' pay or a restriction on leave, but can include reduction in one grade for lower ranking personnel. Only commanding officers can impose the punishment, not NCOs—although the offense could involve insubordination to an NCO. I had not been insubordinate; I had been careless in making a comment he overheard. So I wasn't worried about an Article 15. I remained, however, careless in keeping track of Stubby's whereabouts.

Later the same morning, we were clearing brush around our tent site. As soldiers often do, we were talking about life in the Army and the NCOs and officers that make it harder. "Hey, I must be a celebrity," I casually joked to the guy sharing my tent, "Seagram wants my autograph," referring to the paper agreeing to accept an Article 15 in lieu of a court martial. Damned if he wasn't in earshot again!

"Autograph these," Stubby said, tossing me a bundle of sandbags. "I want these 40 sandbags filled before noon!"

"Yes, sergeant," I quietly replied. It was not the time for any equivocal or smartass response.

So I began filling the bags, holding a sandbag in one hand and the shovel in another. It was an awkward task. With Stubby gone, my tent mate laughed at my predicament, but after awhile, seeing how hard it was, he offered to help. But then Stubby came back.

"That's Maberry's job! Let him finish it unless you want to be doing the same thing by **yourself**!"

With difficulty, I kept at it until done while an odd brew of emotions swirled through me. Both angry and amused by Stubby's rising bile, I was annoyed with myself for not looking before speaking. My escapades with Stubby continued a few days later, when a general visited our camp. It was a perfunctory inspection, I supposed. The width of a football field away, Stubby escorted him past my line of sight. I ignored the procession. Stubby caught up with me later.

"Maberry, you didn't salute the general! What do you mean embarrassing me like that, having the general thinking my men don't know enough to salute!"

"I've heard you're not supposed to salute officers out in the field," I paused, "in case there are VC out in the woods. They could target the officer." I said in honest confusion.

"That's bullshit! We're not out in the jungle. This is a camp. There's no VC here," he said.

"You were too far away. You don't salute an officer when he's that far away." I quickly saw where this was heading.

"You do in my army," Stubby said. "You seem to have trouble with authority, Maberry. Since you're so full of shit, I have just the job for a shithead like you. You get to dig a pit to bury the shit in. Then you can cover it when it's full."

Another unfortunate fuckup like myself was detailed along with me to dig a four-foot deep pit, three feet wide by six feet long. We then emptied the contents of three cut-off 55-gallon drums, a stinking mix of diesel fuel and human waste, into the pit. Although the stuff had already been burned, the smell wafting from the pit as we tossed dirt on top the waste made me gag. Bent over in a stomach wrench after one shovel full, I missed seeing the swing of my partner. He caught me above the eyebrow with his shovel blade. Our unit's doctor took this opportunity to give one of the medics some practice in sewing up a cut with a few stitches. The doctor also put me on light duty for a couple of days, greatly pissing off Stubby since I would miss a turn refilling the pit.

Chapter 7 — Far from Stubby; Far from Home

I NEVER DID GET ANOTHER turn. A few days later, we headed back to Bearcat. No more C-rations, the successor to K-rations and the predecessor of MREs (meals ready to eat), with their chewy-dry cheese chunks and gritty stale peanut butter packed with crackers. No more cans of Spam-rejects to open with our P-38s, the thumb sized rotary can opener usable only by the strong and nimble fingers of youth. Relief from the strange Hershey bars with their sometimes ashy pallor and sometimes gasoline-on-water iridescent shine that came from a special coating to keep chocolate hard in the tropical heat that should have liquefied it. We would step up to the not quite fine, but better than the field, cuisine of the mess hall.

Getting an early start in breaking camp, we were unstacking sandbags around the field mess area under the light of a full moon. Enough to see what we were doing but not enough to see a black scorpion between two bags. It struck Andre Labeau, a brother from New Orleans, in the palm of his hand. Over the course of several days, the wound festered and grew, eventually leaving a scar where dead tissue had sloughed off. From then on, we were all very careful when moving sandbags. I remember Andre more for his profound lucidity in relating to his fellow soldiers.

"First sergeant, I done found you out. You ain't shit!" Andre once remarked in jest.

"And you eat shit and bark at the moon," the first sergeant replied.

It was an exchange two black soldiers of very unequal rank could share, but not one that two whites would dare—not to mention a white and a black unless looking for a fight. The first sergeant was very easygoing with low ranking enlisted men, too easy going perhaps. I would rather he not have shared with me the details of his diarrhea on exiting the outhouse one day. "You ever have it so loose it starts runnin' down your leg before you can get to the shitter?" he asked me one day.

"Uh, no," I said, quickly continuing past him. Fortunately for me, the daily anti-malaria pills didn't have that effect on me. They did on some guys.

The first sergeant was a wheeler-dealer. He took care of the men under him as well as himself. Coming back from the field operation, one of my early detail jobs was helping stake out the boards for a basketball court—not the boards to play on, boards to contain cement. In exchange for a fifth of whiskey, he got some guys from a construction unit to drop several yards of cement in an open area, giving our unit a place to shoot hoops. On other occasions, I saw him drive off with the unit's ARVN interpreter in a ¾-ton truck fully loaded with equipment or supplies. The truck always came back empty. I heard he went to Bien Hoa. The trips were profitable, evidently, since guys who worked the bar at the NCO club said drinks were always on him after these trips.

Another first sergeant I encountered was equally well connected. He was able to get good food and booze, but I don't know if he was into the black market at all. He, a first lieutenant and another ARVN interpreter were responsible for liaison with the ARVN units and Regional Forces/Popular Forces (generally called "Ruff-Puffs) continuing the operation for clearing the Route 1 area. Although all of Headquarters Battery had returned to Bearcat, the operation was ongoing. Artillery units with long range, 175 mm guns were now supporting the operation. They needed to be sure that the areas receiving artillery fire were clear of friendly forces. The lieutenant checked the map personally. The first sergeant talked to the Ruff-Puff advisers/coordinators, who apparently were contract workers (mercenaries) with the CIA. The small liaison unit needed a Radio Telephone Operator (RTO) to communicate directly with the artillery. A couple weeks after I first returned from the field, volunteers were requested for this job.

I jumped at the opportunity to escape from Stubby. Since returning, in addition to helping with the basketball court, I had been stuck with a variety of hot, hard and dirty details. One of the most tedious tasks was filling replacement sandbags, for the ones the jungle damp had rotted away. It meant swinging a pick at the rock hard ground to get a few shovelfuls of dirt. At least this time I had help with the job. We took turns hold the bag and filling the bag. Still, it was hard work. The sandbags came in two varieties, a muslin-like cloth or woven polystyrene. The former rotted faster but could more easily be handled wet or dry and when rotted simply torn off hardened dirt. The green polystyrene bags were slippery and even when torn were harder to deal with. Even if it meant sleeping back out in the field again to escape these details, I was ready to go.

How ironic, after taking an extra year in the Army in hopes of staying out of harm's way in Vietnam, I was now volunteering to go out in the field. It wouldn't be the last time I did so either. Since the VC hadn't shot at us while the large detail was out there, this couldn't be too dangerous, I thought, especially since this location was further away from the action. I was partially right. While the VC posed no major risk at the time, I later learned that the roads did.

It was late November, but in tropical Vietnam that didn't mean a chilly winter but a respite from the heat and humidity. It was less than 90 degrees during the day and nighttime temperatures went down to 70. Six months of the year, it was very hot and wet. The other six were just hot and dry. It was easy duty working with the lieutenant and the first sergeant. The lieutenant was young, maybe 25, and seriously earnest about his job. He was ROTC, with a couple years in the Army already so he wasn't a greenhorn OCS type, nor was he into chicken shit games. He had a job to do and expected me to do mine. He was a welcome relief, a rarity among the many officers I had seen so far who were incompetent, were assholes or were both. The first sergeant probably had as many years in the Army as Stubby but was nothing like him. Like the first sergeant at my HQ Battery, this one knew how to get what he needed to get the job done and still enjoy doing it. He had connections with MACV (Military Assistance Command Vietnam) in Ham Tan, a village on the coast. Perfectly capable of driving himself the several miles to MACV, he chose to have me drive him there. He did so not from the privilege of rank, but out of consideration for me and another guy from the Commo Section also detailed to the small camp. He gave us the opportunity to go swimming in the South China Sea while he conducted his business at MACV.

A clean sandy beach merged slowly with the calm water while gentle waves rolled in from far away. With the shallows extending out far from shore in a protected cove, we swam and splashed for half an hour in our Army-issued underwear. Arriving back at the camp, the first sergeant revealed the supplies he'd rounded up at MACV. Following his instructions, we scavenged wood from the surrounding jungle and dug a small but deep fire pit. Once we had a good hot set of coals burning in the pit, it was "surf and turf." The first sergeant expertly grilled sirloin steak and baked lobster over the pit. Washed down with champagne, the meal was a uniquely satisfying alternative to the missing turkey on Thanksgiving Day. I wondered, not that I cared, if some general's cook or valet would be catching hell for a table less well set than expected. While the Generals might eat like this on a regular basis, I was back on field rations the next day and soon enough back to the fine cuisine of our unit's mess hall. The Liaison RTO duty was too good to be exclusive. I had to share it with Cooper, the guy who went swimming with me at Ham Tan. I had two weeks out there and then had to go back to Bearcat while Cooper enjoyed his two weeks in the field.

When I returned to base camp, I got a pass to go to Bien Hoa (before it became off limits to GIs). I intended just to do some shopping and sightseeing. But Jerry Roberts, another guy from the Commo Section, was after sex. I was reluctant, still clinging to my sense of morality that a husband should be faithful to his wife. But with a little convincing, Roberts persuaded me it didn't count. After all, we were in a war zone, thousands of miles from our spouses. Besides, since he was driving the jeep, I needed to stick close to him. So like another more famous man who lived at 1600 Pennsylvania Avenue many years later, I rationalized that if I only got a blowjob I wouldn't really be cheating. Hah. Long before I learned about the karmic laws of cause and effect, I received a quick response to my bad behavior. While Roberts and I walked back to the jeep, a young boy stole my watch right off my wrist. The watch was a gift from Gloria. I chased the boy past a few shacks but he was too fast for me. Besides, Roberts convinced me, I might lose more than my watch if I kept pursuing the kid further into the neighborhood away from the main road.

Despite the loss of the watch, I didn't immediately associate this with my infidelity. Of course, I realized that but for the trip to Bien Hoa, I would still have the watch and wouldn't be wondering how to explain its loss to my wife. I just didn't recognize it as a negative effect of my action. Not quite blissful, but certainly ignorant, at the next opportunity for sex I was somewhat less reluctant. Still, like Bill, I limited it to oral gratification. Sex was readily available. Women on the street would ask, "You want short-time GI—three dollar?"

Blowjobs were $5. Actually, we didn't give them dollars because we didn't have any. In Vietnam, on payday we received scrip, military payment certificates in denominations identical to American currency. The Vietnamese used piasters, a relic of French colonial rule. One dollar equaled 100 piasters (Pees). We were supposed to get MPC converted to Pees before buying stuff from the Vietnamese. MPC could be converted to U.S. dollars, which was a black market problem and why we got MPC in the first place.

Wherever we went, outside Bearcat, most of my fellow soldiers assumed that any Vietnamese woman was fuckable for a fee. It didn't matter whether they were young or old, exhibiting any overtly sexual behavior or not. Many GIs would simply ask for sex from any woman they saw on the street. Embarrassed looks or angry frowns from those who declined were little deterrent. It embarrassed me too, eventually. *How it had come to this,* I wondered only later, back in the States. *Would they ask just any woman they saw on a street back home, "Hey baby, you wanna fuck?" Or "How much for a blowjob?"*

As we were corrupted, so too were the Vietnamese. War-induced poverty had made sex a valuable commodity. When we needed sandbags filled but didn't need holes dug in our area of Bearcat, a laterite pit just outside the base camp had plenty of dirt we could dig up. It also had a flow of Vietnamese women, many of them middle aged or older, willing to provide sex. In the ladder of prostitution, this was the bottom rung for both the soldier and the provider—but it was convenient for that time of desperation when better wasn't available.

Meanwhile, my letters to Gloria became less frequent, a little more awkward and even less revealing of the goings on at Bearcat and elsewhere. What could I tell her? What we wrote, mostly, each of us in our own way, was "I miss you. I love you. It will be over in 9 more months." Then "8 more months," then 7 more and so on.

Chapter 8 — Waiting for Westmoreland

DESPITE MY INDISCRETIONS, OR PERHAPS because of them, going to church seemed like a good idea since Christmas was coming up soon. I held only a smidgen of hope that the chaplain would provide any profound message of inspiration. It was more the ritual that I sought. A way to make a connection with something more pure than the immoral morass in which we lived as soldiers in Vietnam. Given the number of Protestant denominations, chaplains for each and every one of them were not available at every base. Oftentimes, a somewhat generic Protestant service was all there was. This was the case at Bearcat.

So I went to the Protestant chapel where I waited and waited. Chaplain Vladimir kept conferring with his enlisted aide, spec-4 Estragon (the names have been changed to protect the guilty and gratify those who enjoy literary allusions). They were stalling—5, 10, 15 minutes after Sunday services were supposed to have started in the chapel at Bearcat. The civilian church services I had attended typically followed a tight schedule. If anything, unlike other military activities, the timing of religious services conducted by chaplains was even tighter. Finally, as the chaplain's face brightened, the reason for the delay became clear. Preceded by his junior officer flunky, General Westmoreland strode sharply into the back of the room, taking a seat in the last pew. After the services, the general shook hands with each of the departing soldiers, greeting them somewhat like a parent in the receiving line at a wedding, but even more like a politician at a campaign stop. As I approached and shook his hand, an aura of power seemed to emanate from him, as much as two or three inches from his crisply starched uniform. Startling as this was, it certainly was understandable. He was so important that God had to wait for him! After all, he was a man in charge of 500,000 American soldiers.

As soldiers, we were not paid to think. All we had to do was follow orders of our NCOs, who followed the orders of the officers, who followed the orders of their superior officers and all the way on up to General Westmoreland himself. The general, in turn, was following the directions of the Commander in Chief, AKA President LBJ. We of course, as American citizens and soldiers, naturally wanted to believe in and follow our president and Commander in Chief. Only later would I learn the annoying fact that I couldn't trust what the president tells the American public, then or now. Waiting for Westmoreland was no different from waiting for Godot or for Lefty to tell us what to do. Or for the chaplain, pastor or priest to tell us what was on God's mind. In this best of all possible wars, as Voltaire might say if he were alive today, there could be no doubt that Westmoreland was doing God's business, killing Commies. After all, that's what some of the bumper stickers of the time said: "Kill a Commie for Christ." In fact, the official position was that the more we killed the better.

That was so because, unlike in previous conventional wars, there were no land-related strategic objectives. During the time I was there, the primary goal was to eliminate Communist political power. As a war of attrition, the measure of progress toward this objective was the body count of killed enemy (both NVA and VC) relative to their perceived ability to put additional men in the field. Unfortunately, the CIA and the Defense Department apparently didn't agree on the replacement numbers available to the Communists. That was a major reason the Vietnam War became subject to such conflicting opinions on its winnability. There were also questions about the actual number killed, so much so that Westmoreland eventually sued Mike Wallace of *60 Minutes* for allegedly libeling him, by saying the general was overestimating the number of enemy killed.

I didn't know all of this then. I wasn't even too suspicious yet, about why we were there or what we were doing. I felt fortunate, yet a little guilty, that my existence was relatively safe. Unlike those going on search and destroy missions in the jungle or fighting the VC in rice paddies, I was in base camp or in the rear. I had noticed the difference in how we enlisted peons lived and how the generals lived, at least the ones at Long Binh. They lived in air-conditioned Quonset huts that were spic and span, with manicured lawns and shiny jeeps (polished by their drivers at least daily) parked in front of them. How fortunate for them. For those of us at Bearcat living in hooches, we still had it better than the poor grunts in the field living in tents or bunkers with scorpions and snakes—or with even more unwelcome visitors like Charlie, the Viet Cong.

We were trying to help the "good guys," i.e., the local non-Communist Vietnamese. Unfortunately, since few of the VC wore distinctive headgear, had tattoos or carried ID cards advertising their membership in the Communist bad guy group, it was difficult to tell them apart from the good guys. Still, we tried to help the locals through programs like MEDCAP (Medical Civic Action Program). MEDCAP provided outpatient treatment to villages, using an Army doctor, medic and an ARVN interpreter. MEDCAP also gave me another opportunity to escape the tedium of details and the scrutiny of Stubby. I volunteered to ride shotgun, serving as a bodyguard to the medical personnel, on MEDCAP trips to Long Thanh and other local villages. The VC apparently viewed the humanitarian gesture with annoyance because it would engender good feelings toward Americans and the South Vietnamese government. If we were to be successful helping a very foreign nation fight what appeared to be a civil war, it would seem valuable—if not essential—to win the trust of the people. Or their "hearts and minds," as the Washington policy makers would say about the process. Despite apparent good intentions, that was never too damn likely.

As we all waited for Westmoreland to tell *us* what to think, I later learned what *he* himself was thinking. During a segment in the Peter Davis documentary *Hearts and Minds,* [1] (Academy Award for Best Documentary, 1974) Westmoreland says on camera, "Well, the Oriental doesn't put the same high price on life as does a Westerner. Life is plentiful, life is cheap in the Orient, and as the philosophy of the Orient expresses it, life is, uh, is not important." Perhaps the general was mistaken. Juxtaposed with his comments was footage of a Vietnamese boy crying while holding a picture of his dead father, a South Vietnamese soldier. Fellow mourners repeatedly pulled the boy's mother from the man's grave as workers filled it in. She kept jumping in to be with her dead husband.

The fact is that while we were supposed to be here helping these people, most GIs treated them with contempt, thereby demeaning the Vietnamese and corrupting themselves in the process. To most NCOs and officers, all Vietnamese were "Gooks," "Slope-heads" or "Slant-Eyes." That didn't stop any of us from getting "short-times," of course. During my entire year in Vietnam, I recall only one occasion on which an officer or NCO made any effort to educate us about Vietnamese customs and encourage us to treat the people with respect. He was a first lieutenant. I don't remember his name or his position. He told us not to cross our leg and point our foot toward anyone, that this was the local equivalent of the American insult of giving someone "the finger." He explained that seeing two men holding hands doesn't mean they are gay, it's just a local custom. He also informed us that "gook" really means foreigner, so we are the gooks, not them. Everyone waited until we were dismissed and out of the lieutenant's earshot before laughing. Although I joined in the laughter, I had never called the Vietnamese names and continued to resist doing so. My mother's lesson about the Bandbox murder remained with me. I always remembered her disgust at someone brutally killing a man because he was Chinese.

It surprised me hearing even African-Americans referring to Vietnamese as gooks. Color was a major issue in Vietnam. Anger could redden any complexion as hostility and mistrust swirled among black, white and yellow human beings. While I sat in another hooch, a brother played back a portion of a tape he was sending home. The part I remember was his lament to his woman that " 'Here we are fighting two Charlies—whitey and the Cong.' "

"Why're you playin' this for me?" I asked, puzzled and embarrassed.

He laughed and said, "Yeah, you all right, man. I didn't mean nuthin' by it about you. But you know there's plenty a rednecks and crackers here that are askin' for trouble."

"You got that right," I agreed.

Not all the brothers did call the locals names or have problems with whitey. A guy named Alford actually chastised fellow African-Americans about this. He and I had some good discussions about race before he got infused to some unit up near the DMZ.

Relations between blacks and whites could be explosive. Although we were in a combat zone, subject to attack, our rifles were kept locked up in a bunker, kept there because we were more in danger from each other than from the Viet Cong. Personal weapons were prohibited altogether. Locker inspections were relatively infrequent in my unit but I think it was no coincidence that one came soon after a new guy transferred in. Unlike other brothers who kept outward shows of aggression in check, he seemed to hold little back. It wasn't that he seemed particularly angry with whites, he seemed angry with everyone. He wasn't interested in getting friendly with the other brothers or anybody else. I wasn't real comfortable having him in the next bunk to me. He was about six-feet tall and a muscular 200 pounds. I didn't have long to worry about him. During the surprise inspection they found a loaded 45-caliber, non-standard issue, pistol in his locker. That offense earned him a quick ticket to LBJ (Long Binh Jail, not the U.S. president). I never saw him again.

---

[1] *Hearts and Minds.* Directed by Peter Davis. 112 minutes. BBS Productions, Rainbow Releasing, Touchstone Pictures, 1974. Criterion Collection, 2002. DVD

Chapter 9 — I Almost Lose My Head, Then I Become One

IN LATE DECEMBER, I WENT back out in the field as a liaison RTO. I didn't mind that at all, because I was escaping Stubby. Cooper was ready to rotate back to Bearcat but before he left, we got another chance to go to Ham Tan. It was Christmas day, 1967, a little after nine in the morning. This time Cooper was the driver, with the lieutenant in the front seat and me in the back of the M-151 jeep. Unlike the very wide Humvees used by today's Army, the M-151 had a narrow axle and a suspension designed so that the wheels tipped a little inward at the bottom. This made the jeeps prone to oversteer-induced rollovers. Why the Army used a vehicle made this way was a mystery to me. The road to Ham Tan, like most in this area of Vietnam, was dirt. Large potholes were widespread; maybe they came from mortar-rounds or bombs, or maybe just from the effects of rain and heavy vehicles. Trucks, buses, and other large vehicles including tanks used the road.

A Vietnamese bus, going the other direction, threw up a cloud of dust as it passed by, hiding a large pothole from Cooper's view. He hit it at about 35 mph, causing the rear-end to swing to the right. Trying to correct the skid, he oversteered. The jeep first swung the other way, then back again. The fishtailing grew worse as Cooper was unable to control the unstable vehicle.

Finally, the rear end of the jeep lifted up in the beginning of a roll. I blacked out at this point. Awakening, I found myself on my back beside the road, with blood running down my face from a shallow cut at the hairline. In the daze of shock, I looked around, spotting Cooper to my right. Blood oozed from a large gash in his forehead, exposing white bone beneath his black skin. More bone protruded from his forearm. A goose-egg was throbbing on my arm, but the skin was unbroken. I tried to sit up, but dizziness forced me back down. Off to my left I saw the lieutenant. He too was in worse shape than I was, with an arm bent at an unnatural angle.

Another Army jeep came by shortly after the accident and called in a medevac. Someone kept telling them they could send the slick (unarmed chopper) in without waiting for gunship escorts because this was a traffic accident, not a hostile fire zone incident. Somebody gave us all a jolt of morphine before the chopper got there, so I was feeling fine flying into 24th Evacuation Hospital in Long Binh. I don't remember much of the flight, other than the medics loading me in the chopper and slicing up my pants legs. I guess the blood from my head wound had dripped on them when I sat up, so they were just making sure my legs weren't injured.

The next thing I remember is Stubby coming to visit, on the second day I think, of what my medical records show was an eight-day stay in the hospital. I thought my stay was only three days until I got the records from St. Louis in 2003. I wonder now what went on those other five days that I don't remember.

Wearing his usual bushy-mustachioed grin, he quickly moved through the obligatory "How are you feeling?" to "Who was driving the jeep?"

"Cooper," I told him.

"Are you sure?"

"Yes. You can ask the lieutenant."

Clearly disappointed he couldn't lay the accident on me, he left with a perfunctory "OK, I'll see you back at Bearcat when they let you go."

Cooper wound up getting evacuated all the way back to Hawaii. With a skull fracture, concussion and compound/complex fracture of the arm, his Vietnam tour was over. I would have liked to go there with him, without having the injuries he had, but I had to stay. My hard head, and possibly my helmet, had saved me. Tossed out of the flipping/rolling jeep, all I got was a scalp laceration, a mild concussion and a bruised arm. But the jeep accident provided a welcome respite from duties as usual. The injuries from the accident were quick healing. Most annoying about the accident was its timing. I missed out on Bob Hope, Raquel Welch, and all the rest of the USO show. They were at Bearcat while I was in the hospital and then at Long Binh after I got back to Bearcat. Once I returned, I did have the benefit of two weeks of exempt duty. That really galled Stubby. I got to spend time at an above ground pool that Recreation Services put up and I could loaf around listening to music. The effect it had on Stubby made my time off so much more enjoyable.

Once exempt duty was over, it was back to the detail work. Sometimes I was filling sandbags. Other times it was maintaining the berm, a 12-foot high mound of dirt 6-8 feet thick, around the perimeter of Bearcat, designed to keep the VC out. Whether sandbags or the berm, it meant fighting the laterite. In the rainy season, laterite was soft mud, ankle deep or more. In the dry season, thick dust covered a surface barely yielding to a well-swung pick. There was no in-between—it was either rock-hard or it was swamp-soft.

Each day of detail work was like every other day, an unremitting sameness. It was then that the next phase of my corruption began. During my first three months spent in Vietnam, I remained an observer of the nightly escapes so many of the other soldiers made. Either they were smoking dope or they were drinking alcohol. In the morning, the boozers (mostly the NCOs and other lifers) were cranky and sluggish from hangovers. When we had alerts during the night, they had a hard time getting up and out of the hooch. The dopers didn't seem to suffer any ill effects in the morning, could make it out faster in alerts and seemed to be having more fun. Having resisted my corrupting friend Roberts's entreaties up until now, one night I gave in. I think doper's are, by nature, more evangelistic about their vice than drinkers. In any case, it became my means to escape the monotony.

I had already been a cigarette smoker for four years. Now I had to learn the traditional techniques and rituals peculiar to dope smoking. No simple puffing and exhaling of marijuana, like a regular cigarette. There had to be more style and finesse, not to mention conservation of the more valuable product. We went out to the perimeter road, near the berm surrounding the camp. In the dim moonlight, out of sight of NCOs and officers, Roberts pulled out a joint, marijuana wrapped in rolling paper.

"OK, here's the deal, we just have one joint and pass it back and forth. You don't need your own. When you take a hit, take it deep and don't exhale right away. Hold it in." Roberts explained, as he lit the joint and proceeded to demonstrate—taking a large lungful before passing the working end of the joint to me.

"That stuff smells weird, man," I said.

"Hey, don't worry about it. Just take a hit and pass it back," Roberts whisper-hissed, thereby letting out the least amount of dope possible with the air needed to move his vocal cords.

"OK," I said, taking a deep drag on the joint before passing it back.

A few hits later, I was already feeling its effects—a giddy giggling euphoria I had never felt before. By the time we finished the joint, time had perceptively slowed down. The fifteen minutes we were there seemed like an hour. Other altered perceptions were scary in an amusement park sort of way. Walking back, I stopped in alarm before a yawning chasm in my path back to the hooch. It was so deep and wide I needed a running start for a broad jump! Roberts laughed at my fear of the drainage ditch, only two-feet wide and not much deeper. But to me it was a chasm! I couldn't just step over it, or so it seemed.

Smoking dope made life in the hooch much more bearable. While stoned, the simplest pleasures became intensely enjoyable. We played hearts or spades, most nights. We seldom played poker or other games for money. That was not a wise thing to do if you were stoned. For some unknown reason, Roberts began calling me "Ace" during these occasions. So I began calling him "Jack." Every now and then, for the sake of variety, he would be Ace and I would be Jack. Then there was Weir, the surfer. Weir didn't smoke dope. He was a boozer not a toker. He played cards just the same, along with other irregular cast members. Weir had the peculiar habit of referring to the trunk of his beloved and profoundly missed Pontiac GTO as a "turtle hull." As in, "We'd put a case of beer in the turtle hull and then hit the beach."

To some extent, the dope culture bridged the rank gap among smokers. E-1s through E-5s smoked and hung out together, up to a point, without rank being an issue. There was a spec-5 (specialist, grade E-5) in the Service Battery of our battalion, for example, who was happy to share his dope with me. For no apparent reason, more of the guys in Service Battery were boozers, so he probably thought it was safer to smoke with an EM (enlisted man) in the HQ Battery, rather than someone in his own battery. As an E-5, he had separate quarters in a hooch divided into four rooms. Burning incense partially obscured the smell of dope openly smoked in his room. While there one evening, he bragged about how he got over on his unit, being Jewish.

"I got to spend three days in Saigon last week," he laughed. "There's no rabbi at Bearcat. The closest one is in Saigon. I told them I had to observe the High Holy Days with a rabbi, so the CO had to let me go. It was great man! I scored some great shit. The dope there is way better than what they sell around here."

"I thought the stuff here was pretty good," I said, revealing my status as a dope-smoking novice.

"Well it is good compared to the States, but Saigon's got the better dope here."

It would be somewhat disingenuous of me to fault his religious sincerity, inasmuch as I was enjoying that very good weed here in his hooch. Not only did he have good dope, his girlfriend back in San Francisco sent him all the current music. So here I was, in a combat zone, getting stoned and listening to Cream, Electric Flag, Jefferson Airplane, and other great groups. To add to the mood, she even sent him a pair of glasses with two different colored lenses, each faceted like an insect's eyes. The glasses provided a pseudo psychedelic view without the aid of acid. For all I know, maybe she sent him some of that too, on the back of a stamp. If she did, he didn't share that with me, which was fine. I was fearful of altering my consciousness much further than the dope had, especially while here in Vietnam.

The somewhat tranquil times and dope-augmented joys of January didn't last. The Tet Offensive staged by the NVA and Viet Cong beginning January 31, 1968 and lasting several days, jolted us back to the reality of war. The offensive struck targets throughout the country. The attacks produced large losses and few tactical victories for the NVA/VC. Despite the losses incurred, the fact that they were able to coordinate the attack and have it splashed all over American television gave the (ultimately correct) impression that the U.S. was not in control of the situation in Vietnam. Bearcat itself had not been a major target, receiving only a few hits. One RPG (rocket propelled grenade) round landed in the dirt between several hooches in our part of the base camp, leaving a six-foot wide crater about 3-feet deep at the center.

"Damn," I said to Roberts, "they missed Stubby's hooch. Another 15 feet and they would have got that mother-fucker."

"Yeah, it's a shame isn't it?"

"Damn!"

Roberts laughed, thinking it a joke. He was right. I didn't really wish Stubby were dead, at least not then.

The military cut back MEDCAP trips significantly after the Tet Offensive. Maybe the higher-ups didn't want to spend the money or maybe they thought it too risky. I had seen the fire-snake of red tracer rounds slither from gunships over Long Thanh the night of the incident. More likely, they just figured it wouldn't work or they didn't care. Either way, it left me one less alternative to life with Stubby, sandbag or berm details. So I would volunteer for the ammo run to Xuan Loc, near where one of the firing batteries was located.

It was crazy, volunteering to ride shotgun on a 5-ton truck hauling a load of 105-mm howitzer shells. Sure, the trucks ran with the windshield down and no top so you could scramble out faster if the truck caught a round from the VC—but how likely is it that you could get far enough away, if at all, if the ammo got hit? But when you're 20 years old and bored, what the hell. Besides, sex and drugs (if not rock and roll) was readily available in Xuan Loc. Unlike the guys fighting in Iraq 35-40 years later, nobody was complaining about a lack of armor for the vehicles; we were all too crazy to care. Many guys didn't bother to wear the heavy and hot flak vests (very inferior to those in use today), of which there weren't always enough to go around anyway.

For the guys from Service Battery, driving the trucks hauling ammo was part of their regular duties, which may have explained why they were so wild. They always ran a jeep escort in front of the ammo truck, providing a couple extra guns in case of problems. On one run to Xuan Loc, I watched the driver and passenger in the jeep passing a pint of whisky back and forth. As I said before, the guys in the Service Battery were mostly boozers, not dopers. The driver of the ammo truck squawked on the radio that he wanted a swig. So the jeep driver slowed down, closing to within 15 feet of the truck. Then his passenger flipped the bottle up in the air and back over the jeep, where it hung briefly in mid-air—allowing the ammo truck driver to move the truck under it. He caught it with one hand. It would have made a great slo-mo in some movie.

After dropping the ammo to C battery, we stopped in town for short-times and dope. Marijuana could be had at low prices (even at a private's low wages) in 1967 Vietnam. Five dollars scored a bag of dope the size of those pre-shredded salads now sold in the produce section at the supermarket. Or you could pay two dollars for 20 joints repackaged in a regular cigarette pack. I don't know why, but they were always Paxtons. The original menthol cigarettes came in a crush proof pack. It was difficult, nearly impossible, to tell a pack of 20 joints from a pack of regular cigarettes. Somebody had to have carefully unsealed the cellophane at the bottom, pulled out the pack and removed the 20 cigarettes. Then they had to have gently massaged out the tobacco below the filter tips, before restuffing the former cigarettes with marijuana and twisting the ends shut. Then all 20 joints were put back in the pack, the top foil replaced, the pack slid back into the cellophane and the cellophane resealed. It must have taken a great deal of patience to be so meticulous. Why did they go to the trouble? I don't know who did the work, the kids who sold the packs, saying, "You buy pot, GI?"—or someone older, but it was always quality work.

At times, the quality of the dope itself was almost too good. Maybe it was the cheap, oversized glasses the Army provided for prescription lens wearers. Or maybe it was my genetically provided oversized head. Or just part of the usual weird thoughts that come from stoned minds. Anyway, one night in the hooch, somebody said I looked like an owl. I readily agreed, standing up and flapping my wings. This gave me the nickname Owl, to go along with Ace. This almost led to serious injury while on guard duty one night.

Guard duty generally was an uneventfully boring (thankfully for us) regular task. Our base camp's location due east of Saigon was apparently not high on the target priority of the VC nor on their way elsewhere. It was a three-man 24-hour rotation at the corner tower on the berm. There was a cot in a small room cut in the berm below the tower, but it was tough taking a turn sleeping. The sheltered area was perfect for mosquitoes and we didn't have netting at the berm. If you kept a poncho over yourself to keep the mosquitoes from biting, you got too hot. The repellent provided to us smelled so nasty and got into everything that most of us didn't use it. People handled the boredom of guard duty in their own way. For Andre, "I done found you out. You ain't shit, first sergeant" Labeau, it was drinking Canadian Club. For me it was smoking dope. Thus it was, when he said, "Hey Owl, I bet you could fly back to the world!"

"Yeah man, I could do it," I said as I stepped up on the tower railing.

Moving more quickly than his alcohol-impaired state would seem possible, Andre put an arm on me, "Whoa, man. You sure you can do that?"

Reluctantly, I came back down. I'm not sure, now, whether I was just goofing then or if I really thought I could fly. It was just as well I didn't try, since the tower railing was at least 25 feet off the ground.

Chapter 10 — Killing Stubby; Killing Time

WHILE THE DOPE-ENABLED EVENINGS of frivolous pursuit made life bearable, each night had to end in sleep. It was then, lying in my bunk, that the specter of Stubby darkened my thoughts. I had taken an extra year of service in the Army to go to radio repair school, primarily to keep myself safe if they sent me to Vietnam. Despite being the best in my class, I couldn't work on radios, thanks to Stubby. So instead of staying safe in camp, I volunteered for hazardous duties rather than do tedious detail work and further expose myself to Stubby's mindless rages. Never before, and never since, have I hated anyone as much as I hated him.

Perhaps they were only drug-induced fantasies, but as I lay on my bunk at night, I pondered ways I could kill the man. If we were sharing a ride in a helicopter (preferably a smaller one like a UH-1 Huey) for some reason, I could accidentally push him out the chopper door. It was unlikely we'd ever have such a ride together or that I could succeed, but it was such a delightfully refreshing image. Or I could roll a grenade into his hooch some night after he was well anaesthetized with booze (actually, that would have been most any night). But the grenades were kept locked up in the ammo bunker. Even assuming I could somehow get the key and grab a grenade, I probably couldn't toss one in Stubby's hooch and get back into my own bed before it went off. Running back *into* the hooch after the explosion instead of out would look much too suspicious. I didn't want to end up in Long Binh Jail, en route to a firing squad. If we had gone out on one more trip in the field together, where I had easier access to grenades and C-4 and more opportunities to avoid blame, I might have taken my shot at fragging him. Fortunately, for both of us, that never happened.

How strange it seems now, except in Buddhist terms of cause and effect, to realize that eleven years later and half way across the world, George Harrison would be thinking the same way about me! I had forgotten all about my deadly intentions toward Stubby by then. It took many more years of Buddhist practice before connecting the dots. At the time he made the threat to kill me, I could not figure out why my future father-in-law could feel so strongly toward me. Once I began writing this memoir, the reason became clear: it was simply an effect and planning Stubby's demise the cause.

Meanwhile, with the half-way point of my 12-month tour approaching, I began planning for R & R, a week's escape from Vietnam provided to relieve the stress we all faced. It was Hawaii for married guys. Single guys had a choice of Singapore, Kuala Lumpur, Penang, Bangkok or other such places. The military flew us or paid our way to and from the destinations, while the airlines and hotels had special deals for spouses. Not only would I get to spend time with Gloria, I would be away from Stubby *and* in a safe location. Even better, he would be getting ready to leave when I returned. He had already been there almost six months when I arrived in the unit.

It was very strange interlude for me, though it must have been stranger still for the guys spending their days in the jungle. We all went from jungle fatigues to polyester. About the only thing the two places had in common was the lush foliage, but the Hawaiian version looked a lot better since no one had sprayed it with defoliant. Instead of Armed Forces Radio, the entertainment du jour was Don Ho. Aided by discounts for the military, Gloria and I did all the popular tourist activities. We went outrigger canoe surfing and snorkeling at Waikiki beach with its white sand and clear water. Out a hundred yards from shore, the water was maybe 12-15 feet deep and clear all the way to the bottom. Needle-nose fish that I might have taken for barracuda, but assumed were not, swam circles around me. Gloria suggested we take in a movie, a more Mainland type of activity we were accustomed to doing.

We went to see *The Graduate*. An odd choice for us, it turned out, given the content of the movie. I could identify with the clueless innocence lost by Benjamin Braddock (Dustin Hoffman) sowing his wild oats, although my own circumstances were quite different. Gloria's reaction to the single-minded pursuit of Elaine Robinson (Katherine Ross) differed from mine. I found it romantic, the ideal of pursuing the true love. Gloria was taken aback by the sexual escapades, especially Benjamin's romp with Elaine after the affair with her mother. The aborted wedding scene prompted Gloria to inform me, after leaving the theater, that the marriage of her best friend had broken up after only a few months because it turned out her husband was gay. He apparently thought he might be able to kick the homosexual habit if he got married. Her friend's marriage wasn't the only one entered into in ignorance, for the wrong reasons. Neither Gloria nor I knew then, how mistaken we too had been.

We made the requisite visit all Honolulu tourists must make to Duke Kahanamoku's club. The club was famous for its Polynesian floorshow, singer Don Ho and, of course, Hawaiian food. Don Ho had the night off the evening we were there, not that I missed him. He wasn't exactly my kind of singer. Before the waiter came, I looked at the drink list on the table and joked to Gloria, "Hey, you want to get a Mai-Tai?"

"I'd never drink. That's evil!" Gloria snapped in disgust at my suggestion.

"Just kidding, just kidding. You know I don't drink either. You know my brother Doug is an alcoholic." *Whew, no sense of humor.*

"OK."

Despite taking in the attractions, I didn't come to Honolulu only with tourist intentions. I had hoped that absence would make more than Gloria's heart fonder, so that the R & R week would be like a honeymoon. It did not turn out that way. The sex was desperate and intense only for me. She was never quite as excited about sex after her mother's visit to our humble apartment in Odenton the year before, soon after we had first begun our married life together. In this, as well as other things, time and the very different circumstances we found ourselves in were already sharpening divergent perspectives between us. I had borrowed a Polaroid camera from another guy to take some nude pictures of her, in lieu of having the real thing. I was hoping to resist further encounters with the prostitutes back in Vietnam. As she was undressing, with her bra and panty girdle still on, I pulled out the camera for a quick shot.

"What are you doing?" She exclaimed, startled as the flash went off.

"I just wanted to get some pictures of you to have for me to remember you by when I go back to Vietnam."

"Well you don't need pictures of me in my lingerie!" She sputtered. "What if somebody else saw them?"

"Actually, I wanted to get pictures of you nude. I'm not going to leave them laying around or show them to other people."

"Absolutely not! That would be dirty. You should be ashamed of yourself!" How could I tell her that I wanted the photos to focus my desires on her and not be looking for sex among the women in Vietnam? I couldn't. I went back with one startled shot of Gloria, reminding me not of intimacy but of obstinacy.

While Gloria and I were on our anxious interlude in Honolulu, things were not going so well for the rest of America either. LBJ announced on April 1, that he would not seek reelection. His approval rating for handling the war had dropped to 30% in national polls. Johnson had pushed the Civil Rights Act of 1965 through Congress, but America was in conflict over the scope and pace of its implementation. Three days later, as I was boarding my flight back to Vietnam, Martin Luther King was shot and killed. This resulted in riots in over a hundred cities across the country. When I got back to Bearcat, I quickly learned how much more tense the relations were in Vietnam between white and black soldiers. A dumb redneck, unhappily doing KP, got into a heated discussion with a somewhat stoned African-American cook about the prospects of life back in America.

"Well at least I have a place to go back to. Where y'all gonna live after the ghetto been burned down?" This prompted the cook to knock aside the fiery-hot chimney of an immersion heater with a bare arm in trying to get to the man.

"Where's my rifle? I'm gonna kill this muther-fucker!" He shouted.

Thankfully, he couldn't get to his rifle, since our weapons were kept locked up. It would be a few uncomfortable days before things blew over in our unit. I wished that Alford was still in the unit, but he was long gone by then. Worse, Stubby was *not* gone. He had extended his tour for another six months. We would remain together all but a few days of my time in Vietnam. That seemed like another good reason to keep getting stoned.

It was late one night when Jackson and I lit up behind the commo trailer. We were careless and indiscreet in not going all the way out to the perimeter road, 100-yards away. Sgt. Harris, an E-5, noticed what we were up to and took the opportunity to scare the shit out of us. From out of sight around the corner, he did a passable impression of Stubby's voice, "Maberry, Jackson! What are you doing there? I smell marijuana!"

"Just coming back from the latrine, Sgt. Seagram," Jackson said unconvincingly in a shaky voice.

"Just getting some air. It's hot in the hooch," I said, with my stomach rising halfway to my chest.

Coming around the corner, Harris revealed himself in a fit of laughter, "Whoa, had you guys goin', didn't I?"

"Hey man, don't be playin' like that. You nearly gave me heart failure," Jackson said, still shaky.

"Look, you guys should be more careful where you're smokin' weed. That could have been Sgt. Seagram instead of me," Harris said.

"Yeah, you're right," I said.

"Yeah, thanks man. We needed a reminder," Jackson agreed.

Meanwhile, with no Polaroids and a less than enthusiastic response from Gloria, I was soon back to visiting the local ladies for service, more frequently and with less attacks of conscience for going beyond oral sex. The sex was mechanical and never very satisfying. Sometimes it happened behind some bushes in the laterite pit. Other times we did it on a floor, sometimes covered by a thin mattress, surrounded by pine crate walls stamped with descriptions of the U.S. Army ordnance they once contained. Even at the church-run steam bath and massage parlor, we all expected sex. Why else would anyone go to a steam bath in the tropics? We didn't always get what we were after. Only some of the women working there would provide sexual services and those who did stopped short of full intercourse or even oral sex. They limited themselves to massaging the privates' private parts.

The month after my return from R & R, May 1968, more than 2,000 American soldiers died in combat, the highest monthly loss of the war. Fortunately for me, the VC were generally busy elsewhere, not at Bearcat. The scary thing was that a major part of the 9th Infantry Division was busy elsewhere as well, leaving us and the few other units there to fend for ourselves. Guard duty came around more often because we now had responsibility for more of the perimeter berm. I soon became able to sleep anywhere or anytime, even atop the cement hard sandbags of the guard bunkers elevated above the berm. Nobody wanted conversation on guard duty anymore. We just got our chunk of sleep, did our shift and went back for breakfast at the mess hall. It was safer that way anyway, less distraction from keeping an eye on the ghostly shadows cast by the moonlight on the tree line, some two hundred yards of cleared ground away from the berm. It was a time when the imagination could run rampant. Were the shadows moving in tandem with the breeze in the trees, or was that a black pajama clad VC out there?

On darker nights, it was a time to resent the fool two bunkers away, with the glowing tip of his cigarette visible to the tree line and beyond. If there *were* any VC out there, he could attract a sniper round, putting your position at risk as well. He should have waited until his shift ended, smoking behind the berm instead of on top. But the VC were not there. At least we could find no evidence of them. At daybreak, the last duty of the berm guard was the morning sweep. Out as far as the claymore mines with their convex faces like a reaper's scythe lying on the ground, connected to trip wires. At the slightest tug by an errant ankle, the wire would trigger the claymore's blast of shrapnel through the flesh of any intruder. The sweeps never revealed footprints or other signs of activity near the wire. We made sure to stay behind the mines and the wires.

Despite the fright Sgt. Harris gave Jackson and me about smoking weed, as the days wore on, it seemed like nobody cared if we did anyway, not even Stubby. Jackson told me of a strange conversation he had one night in the NCO club. Jackson tended bar there for some extra cash (he really had become a virtual Rochester). "Stubby comes into the club, throws his money down on the counter and says, 'Hey Jackson, give me a pack of Camels.'

'OK, Sarge, here you go,' I told him and handed him a pack. Then he says to me, with kind of a sly grin on his face,

'I guess you smoke Paxtons, huh, Jackson?'

'Uh, no. I smoke Kools,' I told him. But from the look on his face, I figure he knew the deal with Paxtons. He knew I smoked dope, but he wasn't making nuthin' of it. It was scary weird, man."

"Sounds like it! You think he knows I smoke?"

"I don't know, man. What do you think?"

"I think if he did, and he could catch me at it, my ass would be out."

"Yeah, most likely," Jackson laughed.

Oddly enough, my remaining days with Stubby didn't turn out as bad as I expected they would. Perhaps he knew how I felt or grew bored with me as a target. He let up on me the last few months we spent together in-country. I kept busy on my usual details, staying out of his way and marking time until I would get on the big bird once more for the trip home. Looking back on it now, I can also imagine that the purpose of our interaction had already been accomplished. The conflict that led to my wanting to kill him had already set up the conditions for strengthening and developing my Buddhist faith, many years later.

With only two months left to go on my tour, I had a religious experience of a different sort in the village of Long Thanh. My instructor, a masseuse at the church-run steam bath and massage parlor that soldiers frequented, forced me to confront the sins that I had been ignoring until then. After exiting the steam room, I took my place on the massage table. Lifting the towel covering my groin, I signaled my desire for a hand job. In response, pointing first to my wedding ring and then to her wedding ring, she asked in broken English,

"Why you ask me this? You married man. I married, too."

"Uh, uh, ..." I made no further reply. I could only lay there in guilty and embarrassed silence. I began to think about how I was dishonoring my marriage, my wife and myself. Worse, I was complicit in the dishonor of the Vietnamese. Women, young and old, lived in ammo crate shacks because their villages were getting destroyed or made unsafe by the Viet Cong, the ARVNs or the Americans. Wartime poverty drove them to sell their bodies to us American soldiers. But not to this soldier anymore. My remaining trips to the laterite pit and to Xuan Loc omitted sex.

Meanwhile, political violence continued in America. Armed Forces Radio reported that Bobby Kennedy was dead, shot and killed while campaigning for president, June 5, 1968. In August, we heard reports about the 1968 Democratic Convention. Even in Vietnam, we were able to see what was happening back home. While we were supposedly protecting the democracy of Vietnam, what became known as the "Chicago Police Riot,"[2] was happening on the streets of America.

Over the course of five days, members of the Chicago Police Department chased unarmed protesters, local residents and members of the news media for blocks through the streets—clubbing them senseless, spraying them with mace, kicking and pummeling them. Cops-out-of-control appeared on live TV as well as on taped news reports. Even newsman Dan Rather, trying to interview a delegate, was knocked to the floor inside the convention hall by security guards, who no doubt were employed by the first Mayor

Daley. U.S. Senator Hubert Humphrey of Minnesota got the Democratic nomination, despite refusing to support a platform plank to end the war.

With only a month left in-country, I stopped volunteering for the road trips. Now that I was a short-timer, it made no sense to take any more chances on getting blown away by the VC. Besides, I wasn't buying sex anymore and I wouldn't risk trying to smuggle dope back into the U.S. As much as I enjoyed smoking the dope, I had no plans to continue doing so on my return. Gloria wouldn't understand. With my time winding down, my stash was almost gone. To make it last until I got on the plane and to make sure I lasted until then, I stopped smoking dope while on guard duty.

Without the haze of marijuana diverting my attention to trivia, unbidden doubts and questions began dominating the moments of silence I spent on the berm at night. *What the hell am I doing here in Vietnam and what the hell is going on back in America? If democracy is so good, how come we Americans can't even respect each other? How can we keep South Vietnam "free" when we treat the women like whores and look down on the men as cowards or sissies? How can we accomplish anything positive when the people running the war are drunks, corrupt, mentally incompetent or all of the above?*

I did make one last "shotgun" run with two days left in Nam. It was definitely an unwise risk, but I was kind of shamed and dared into it. The staff sergeant in charge of our hooch wanted somebody to accompany Jackson to Long Binh for his out-processing. Reluctantly I went, riding along in the ¾-ton truck, armed only with an M-79 grenade launcher. It was a weapon good enough for enemies nearby, but no help against a sniper at a distance. The trip was uneventful, a dry run for my own exit to come.

My own ride in the prison-barred bus between Long Binh and Tan Son Nhut was a very different one than what I experienced 12 months before. Now I had a fear of the known, rather than the unknown. In a mix of wary anticipation and excitement, I now knew how the guys waiting on the tarmac felt when they saw me and the other new arrivals get off the plane. Once aboard the World Airways plane (a contract charter on the government payroll) it was "let the party begin." We were the happiest bunch of passengers a flight attendant could ever have.

---

[2] So labeled by Daniel Walker, director of the Chicago Study Team, in a report to the National Commission on the Causes and Prevention of Violence—formed by President Johnson in 1968 to study urban violence.

Chapter 11 — Back to the World

HOME FROM VIETNAM, I HAD a month's leave in Minneapolis before reporting to my next duty station at Ft Knox, Kentucky. A strange mix of relief, shock and pleasure awaited me in Minnesota. Back in the safe and familiar civilian world I had grown up in, there were no more berms or bunkers. There were no officers to salute, no sergeants telling me what to do and no formations to stand in. I used flush toilets again in bathrooms with indoor showers. I slept in a real bed with sheets and no mosquito netting. I ate real food in restaurants. Minnesota's cool fall weather ended my year of sweating. Finally, being back with Gloria brought an end to dope and psychedelic music.

Gloria had stayed with her parents while I was in Vietnam. Squeezing me into the Nelson's apartment, along with her, would have been out of the question. Instead, we stayed in a short-term apartment/hotel, near downtown Minneapolis. My lusty intentions, sated only slightly by my indiscretions in Vietnam, were blunted by Gloria's response to some unexpected reading material left behind by the previous occupant of the room. Apparently, he or she had both a bad back and a sexual fetish. Curious about the stiffness of the bed, Gloria discovered a plywood sheet placed between the mattress and the box springs. She had to run an errand, so I said I would remove it. When I lifted up the mattress, I found several graphically illustrated booklets on spanking—including extensive discussion on the relative merits of various implements such as willow, ash, cane, hemp or silken rope whips. I read a few pages in the booklets that had a narrative and looked at the illustrated discussions of the tools. I found it all quite amusing. It was not to my taste, just oddly funny that someone should be so into something like this.

"Look what I found between the plywood and the mattress," I said, handing Gloria a couple of the booklets when she returned.

"This is filthy! It's disgusting!" she said, handing it back to me as if it was a soiled diaper.

"Hmm, very strange. Can you believe people really enjoy stuff like this?"

"No! Stop looking at it. It's dirty. This stuff should be burned. Get rid of it!" She demanded.

"OK, I'll put in the trash," I said, trying hard to keep from smirking at her distress over what I thought simply silly.

"Not in our room! Somebody will think it's ours!" She said more insistently, looking seriously concerned about the prospect of discovery.

"OK, OK. I'll take it away. Don't worry." I dumped the stuff down the trash chute a few doors down the hall from our room. I think she somehow blamed me for the material being there, or at least faulted me for not sharing her level of disgust. The experience further widened our libido gap.

By late October 1968, we were on our way to Ft. Knox. I had ordered a new Chevelle Malibu through the Army Post Exchange (PX) before leaving Vietnam. Despite remaining a PFC the entire year in Vietnam, thanks to Stubby, the addition of "combat pay" to base salary gave me enough extra cash for a down payment on a new car. The total cost of the car was only $3,000. The car was supposed to be ready for pick up in Minneapolis when I got home on leave but the Chevy dealer taking delivery of it said it hadn't arrived yet, so we had to take a Greyhound to Louisville. We still didn't have any furniture and not much else besides clothes anyway, but it was annoying. The dealer lied or was confused about the delivery. My brother Doug kept checking on it for me. Eventually he went there in person and found it on the showroom floor. Doug drove it to Kentucky for me, in exchange for a return bus ticket.

Before leaving for Kentucky, I had voted by absentee ballot for Hubert Humphrey, a homegrown hero to Minnesotans. Election results came in soon after we arrived. Richard Nixon eked out a victory of half a million votes over Humphrey, with the third party candidacy of George Wallace complicating things. Nixon ran on a platform of "Law and Order" (referring to clearing the streets and neighborhoods of criminals and punishing them severely, while indicting "Liberals" as being soft on crime). Nixon also claimed to have a "secret plan" to end the war in Vietnam.

My final year in the Army was a welcome relief from the hassles of Vietnam. I had no more worries about VC. I had no crotch-rot. My clothes stayed dry all day. Most importantly, I had no more Stubby. I had a real job to do, although there was enough waste of time and resources to confirm the military life as a paradigm of inefficiency and incompetent irrelevance. I worked with sane, rational people, for the most part. I tried in vain to reclaim the innocence that I lost in Vietnam. I smoked no more dope, drank no booze and had no sex outside the marriage to Gloria. Once gone, I soon realized, my innocence could never return. I no longer was the callow youth my straight and narrow wife married.

Despite being "back in the world," there were still austerities. Most military installations are not in urban or even suburban locations. They are usually way out in the middle of nowhere. Married housing on post was not available for a short-term, low-ranking enlisted man like me. Even if it were, it would not have made sense to live there because Gloria couldn't drive and we needed her to get a job to help us make ends meet. Now that my combat pay had ended and Gloria was no longer living with her parents, money was tight. We rented a furnished apartment in Shively, a suburb of Louisville. Ft. Knox was 25 miles to the south. She got a job as a nurses' aide in Louisville, 25 miles to the north. I dropped her off there in morning, backtracked past our apartment and continued on to Ft. Knox every weekday morning. She got a ride back home with a coworker.

It was a dark and dangerous trip every day, taking Gloria to Louisville and driving on to Ft. Knox along Dixie Highway. The road was nicknamed "Dixie Dieway" for all the traffic deaths along its route. I stopped for coffee and a donut at a diner a couple miles south of our apartment every morning, to make sure I didn't fall asleep at the wheel. But it wasn't Dixie Highway that almost got me. It was the interstate near the nursing home. As I sped along in the right lane in the pre-dawn hours one morning, another car suddenly appeared half a car length in front of me. He had entered the road from a ramp beside me, hidden by the darkness and apparently without looking. At 60 miles per hour, there was no time or point in honking. Instinctively, without having had any training in the maneuver, I executed a four-wheel drift— letting off the gas and cutting the wheel sharply to the left, then cutting the wheel back to the right and stepping back on the gas. The car slid to the left lane and kept going forward, saving us from almost certain death. It still wasn't my time to die. I had other things to do yet.

I had to make morning formation in my company at 6 a.m. It made for a very long day for both of us and, like the first few months we lived together at Ft. Meade, for a very short evening. At my rank and at the prices back then, a small television was two month's take-home pay, so we didn't have one. With dinner done at 7:00-7:30, we only had an hour or so until bedtime anyway if we wanted to get 8 hours sleep. With the little time we had to talk, we touched on her day and mine. She had some adjusting to do. Most of the other nurses' aides were African-American. She had never worked with or around so many blacks before. The job itself was more demanding, in a morbid way, than her previous stints in nursing homes. When a resident of the Louisville facility passed away, the nurses' aide responsible for that person's room had the responsibility to pack large quantities of cotton in all of the deceased's bodily orifices, to prevent any messy leakage before removal of the remains by a mortuary. That certainly rivaled the shit-burning details of Vietnam. My days at Fort Knox were not nearly as bad as that.

I was "permanent party" (as opposed to being a trainee or on TDY) at the Armor Training Center, Ft. Knox, working in the tank park fixing radios. During that extra year I had volunteered for, I would finally be doing what I was trained to do. Although nominally assigned to a company in the training battalion, I worked in a radio shop with two civilians and three other Army radio mechanics from other companies. Remarkably, for the military, the efficiency of having all the mechanics together at one site was not only recognized but actually put in place, although not without some rancorous resistance from some company commanders who wanted to possessively exert control over "their" mechanics. Somehow, Staff Sergeant Singer, the E-6 overseeing the radio shop, managed to keep the companies off our backs for the most part. He even got us excused from regular rotation at company assignments like guard duty and CQ runner. I think he must have had some friends in the battalion HQ. During the winter, however, all of us who worked at the tank park had to share a rotation stoking the coal-fired furnace that heated our warehouse-sized shops. We didn't feed the furnace directly, as in the days of the steam engine trains, rather we kept a large hopper filled with coal. A continuously running auger carried coal from the hopper to the burner box.

SSgt. Singer was an easy-going likable guy who just wanted to see that the job got done right and on time. This was probably the only example of such rational thinking I encountered in any NCO during three years in the Army. He had no use for sycophants, laughing loudly along with the rest of the shop when Joe, one of the civilians working with us joked, "Gray (another Army radio mechanic) one of these days Sergeant Singer is going to turn a corner too fast and break your nose!" Joe was a hillbilly from Appalachia, who enjoyed telling tales (fictitious we all hoped, but I was never sure) of how wonderful sheep were for sex. "They're real patient and just the right height, much better than cows. You have to watch out for cow pies with them or them stepping on your feet. With sheep, you just hook their hind feet in your pant's cuffs and hold onto the wool on their loins. There's nothing like it, feeling that lanolin on your hands when you're coming."

For some reason he never made quite clear, SSgt. Singer had first spent six years in the Air Force and later joined the Army, slowing his career movement upward. I too had a slow advancement, but I wasn't making this a career. My problems with Stubby had kept me a PFC my entire year in Vietnam while others, like "Rochester" Jackson, were promoted. Although the actual approval and paperwork had to come through my company, SSgt. Singer finally got me promoted to specialist, E-4 by convincing the company that I was doing a good job on their radios.

The Armor Training Center, one of two in the U.S. at the time, trained tank crews. This was AIT (advanced individual training) for the four-man crews consisting of a driver, gunner, loader and tank commander. Permanent party did the training, administration and kept the equipment running. Along with radio mechanics, the tank park had other repair crews responsible for working on tank engines and the track that moved them (track mechanics) and for working on the electrical system that allowed the turret and cupola to rotate and power still be supplied (turret mechanics). We worked on our respective equipment in the shop. There were always tanks and jeeps due for maintenance or down for repairs. When the trainees went out on bivouac, a three-man crew (track, turret and radio mechanics) from the tank park went with them during the final part of their training when they would be firing the main gun.

While the trainees had to sleep in shelter halves in their fart sacks (sleeping bags), we slept on air mattresses in the back of the deuce and a half we drove out to the field. A cooler of sodas, sandwiches, chips, etc. made our brief stay more pleasant than theirs. But things could get difficult for us. The training officer could get very testy if we couldn't quickly get malfunctioning items working. I had a few spare radios to exchange with ones that went bad but couldn't do extensive repair in the field and the training schedule didn't allow much time for repair delay. Working radios were essential not only to communicate between tanks but also to provide intercom within the tank. The roar of the huge engine revving up, the rumbling clatter of the track reverberating through the hull and the booming concussion of the main gun firing made it impossible to communicate person-to-person other than by intercom.

For the most part, the equipment was reliable, sufficiently so that we had excess time on our hands. Excess time is a common thing in the military, generally in inverse relation to the rank of the individual. This is not a good thing. It's associated with the phenomena of "hurry up and wait," which is what typically happened when a unit was told to assemble and prepare to move out on a moment's notice. The moment often expanded interminably from minutes to hours as impending orders are delayed, revised, cancelled, re-imposed, etc. by officers up and down the chain of command. Reading a history of the First Maine Cavalry's exploits during the Civil War (a unit in which my great-grandfather had served for four years), I was not surprised to see that this was also a common occurrence then. I suspect it was common among the Pharaoh's armies in ancient Egypt as well. Annoying as it may be to the enlisted man, waiting is probably an unavoidable thing in moving troops around. Equally common and annoying were the meaningless tasks assigned again and again, tasks which were undoubtedly avoidable had those in charge not insisted they be done.

If there is a point to having a standing army, it is readiness. How can you tell if the army is ready? Conduct inspections and drills to test readiness, of course. Does the equipment work? Are the men well-disciplined soldiers? Do they respond quickly and correctly? Most inspections we had went way beyond readiness. They focused more on appearance. Maintaining the training equipment didn't require 40 hours a week. To fill out our days, we spent time polishing things that didn't need polishing or repainting things that didn't need fresh paint. After all, it was important to our unit commander's career that his equipment had a higher gloss or his paint a sharper line than some other unit's stuff. Woe unto you if you were in the lower-rated unit. That meant you were tasked with removing the deficiency. A painted line that deviated by a half-inch over a 20-ft run would have to be repainted to make the deviation no more than a quarter-inch. How could the Army function properly if these requirements were not observed? It was unclear to me how this related to winning the war in Vietnam or any other war. But then I wasn't a field-grade officer, who undoubtedly could have explained this to me had I dared to ask such an impertinent question and he deigned to answer.

It may be unfair to tar all career military officers and NCOs with this brush, but that is all that I saw. Given the small cost of paying low ranking enlisted personnel, it may well have been counterproductive to exert much effort to avoid their wasting time on useless tasks. Yet from the standpoint of improving both morale and productivity, rather than having us perform useless tasks, why couldn't the Army have used us to perform some community-based activity? Like Christmas in April/Habitat for Humanity kinds of home repairs or roadside cleanup off the military reservation? I don't know when Toys for Tots started, but I don't think the Army had anything like this Marine Corps program during my three years in the service. Perhaps now, with the all-volunteer Army, things are different; I don't know. As frustrating as it was wasting so much time, the experience convinced me never to accept a civilian job with so much busy work. If I somehow mistakenly began one, I would quit or be fired rather than tolerating the busy work.

As little as I found to like about military life, I didn't find much to look forward to at the end of the day, when going home to Gloria. We had spent only a few months together before I went to Vietnam. Now, after several months of short evenings interspersed with weekends dedicated to shopping, laundry and other essential tasks, marriage had yet to become the wonderful life I had anticipated two years before. It now became apparent to me how different we were, from the outset of our marriage. Our own, quite opposite family backgrounds colored our expectations of the role of husband and wife. While her family was far from well off, they had never been as affected by poor finances as had mine. Gloria's mother wore the pants in the Nelson house. To the contrary, my mother was at a loss without my father. Conflicts in expectations led to conflicts in communication.

"You better wear your boots, it's supposed to snow," I said to Gloria one morning, during what passed for winter in Louisville.

"I don't want to wear boots. It's too much trouble."

"But your feet will get wet"

"Don't tell me what to do!"

Then there were the arguments about money. Like the one we had about buying a vacuum cleaner (for our hardwood and vinyl floored apartment).

"Wait a few months, 'til we get a little more in the bank," I said.

"Why do we have to do that? We can charge it."

"But we *still* have to pay for it!" I said, a little too strongly.

"You're just tight!"

Gloria wasn't entirely wrong. Given my family's experience with money, I squeezed pennies almost as flat as did those souvenir-making arcade machines with the pressure rollers. Still, it didn't keep me from renting a TV to watch Neil Armstrong and Buzz Aldrin set foot on the Moon, July 20, 1969. My interest in space had begun in grade school, culminating in a report for a school project in 11th grade on the number and purpose of satellites then in orbit. I was also a science fiction fan. So I couldn't miss seeing this, despite the extravagance of renting the TV. Gloria, of course, would have preferred that we own a TV.

As the astronauts ended their journey on the path from Earth to the Moon and back, I continued my own more mundane travel. I drove daily from Shively to Louisville to Ft. Knox and returned, one day blending into the next until it was time to say goodbye to the Army. I also said goodbye to the kindly ladies at the diner on Dixie Highway, where I stopped every morning for lifesaving coffee and a donut en route to the tank park. The ladies gave me a going away cake. What the army gave me was my remaining leave pay, discharge papers and much to think about. Away from the immediacy of war and without a TV providing continuous updates, the year at Ft. Knox had already given me time to reflect on the surreal experience of Vietnam and military life.

At Ft. Knox, there were pointless tasks pursued to perfection and red-necked civilians enamored of sheep. Time and resources wasted, both human and physical, were the norm of daily life there. It seemed to bear little or no rational relation to keeping the Communist domino from falling in Southeast Asia. Vietnam couldn't be that just war I learned about in the public schools.

We were supposed to be protecting the local population from the predation of communism. We were supposed to be preserving the benefits of democracy we enjoyed in America, for them to enjoy in the same fashion. At least that is what I had thought. What I saw and experienced was something entirely different.

We couldn't tell the VC "bad guys" from the South Vietnamese "good guys"—there were no uniforms or insignia identifying the former as such. They were all Vietnamese, the same in physical appearance. Bad consequences flowed from this. By treating all the civilians as friends, American troops risked being killed by a VC, but treating all civilians as potential VC made us no better than the VC. MEDCAP programs were curtailed and American troops began using the local people much like the VC and NVA did, as pawns to be played. Villagers were fucked over by us if they helped the VC and fucked over by the VC if they helped us.

Even if the war itself could be justified, the effect on American youth could not. We were corrupting, wounding and killing our own youth. Individuals were remolded into disciplined combatants, taught to follow orders and not to think. We were sent far away from the stabilizing influences of friends or loved ones, especially from the watchful eyes of mothers. Having reshaped the malleable minds of young men, the military failed to restore a semblance of morality to replace what was lost in the process. Instead, officers and NCOs at least tolerated and often actively encouraged the notion that the people of Vietnam didn't matter. Go ahead and fuck 'em, kill 'em or do whatever you want. So you never drank, you never smoked? That was easily cured. Booze was readily available. Drugs were cheap and easily found, even by those who knew nothing of them before coming to Vietnam.

It took a religious woman working in a massage parlor to remind me of my own moral shortcomings—pointing first to her wedding ring and then mine, chastising me for requesting a hand job. I couldn't blame the Army, the Vietnam War or the politicians for my own lack of integrity. All of them did, however, play a major part in my corruption. The politicians and the military provided the venue, the opportunity and a lack of virtually any detectible leadership to the contrary. Given the age and maturity of the young men sent off to war, this lack of moral leadership was a fault of no small measure.

During basic training, I had laughed (silently) at chaplains concerned with profanity and other evil doings by the drill instructors. Where were the objections to killing? The religious impression that remained embedded in my mind from Vietnam is of a chaplain exalting General Westmoreland, holding up religious services waiting for his arrival and treating him with all the respect and courtesy one might afford royalty. A man who, I later learned, thought that to the Oriental, "life was plentiful and cheap."

Now it was time to make sense of all this, as a free man again, on October 10, 1969.

The Quest

Chapter 12 — Transitions, Endings and Beginnings

THE DAY AFTER MY DISCHARGE, we were on the road to Minneapolis, returning to an interrupted life. But just as all the king's men couldn't put Humpty Dumpty back together again, nor could the innocent young man that went off to "serve his country" resume the life he had planned. I had seen too much, heard too much and felt too much. I was no longer an innocent. Before Vietnam, my immediate goal was to enter college. College had a nebulous purpose to it, mystically connecting my writing aspirations with a generalized development of knowledge. I had few, if any, specifics in mind beyond learning how to ensure a dependable living.

When I went to Vietnam, I naively believed that the objectives of our system of government not only should be, but actually were associated with the ideals I learned in school. The ideals came from the noble statements found in the Declaration of Independence, the Constitution and its amendments. I thought that ethical or moral imperatives implicit in those ideals would guide the behavior of our leaders. That is not what I saw in Vietnam. That is not what I heard in the U.S. Army. Racism, sexism, jingoism, alcoholism and drug abuse are what I saw. Black marketeering and other criminal activity are what I saw. Were we bringing the inalienable rights to life, liberty and pursuit of happiness to South Vietnam? Not that I could see. Nor did it seem that we who spent a year there had our own fair shot at any of these three noble goals.

Although my body had left the war in Vietnam a year before, my mind could not escape this conflict. News of the impending Vietnam Moratorium Day inundated us as soon as we got to Minnesota. October 15, 1969 would be the first nationwide antiwar rally, calling for an end to the Vietnam War. This could not be a coincidence; coming just five days after my leaving Ft. Knox and military service behind. My outrage at three wasted years had reached critical mass. Something had to be done. Common sense demanded that America stop sending young men to Vietnam. I joined Vets for Peace in the Minneapolis observance of the Moratorium, along with an estimated five million people throughout the United States.

The fighting in Vietnam was essentially a civil war, much like the one that we had fought in America a hundred years before. In Vietnam, too, it was a war between North and South, albeit a different North and a different South. I didn't recall learning, while in my American history classes, that any Asian or European countries sent troops to fight on American soil in support of either the American North or the South during our war.

At best, the government in South Vietnam was corrupt, oppressive and unstable. If anything, the North appeared more concerned about the welfare of *all* the populace than did the South, with Ho Chi Minh having led the fight to independence from the exploitation of colonial France (who we had backed against the Vietnamese).

We had no strategic objectives in the war. We just wanted to kill as many VC and NVA as we could in hopes that the South could survive, but in so doing we were ravaging the country. B-52 bombs, Rome Plows and defoliant were destroying rice paddies, rubber plantations and other productive lands. Even if we didn't assume they were VC, most of us were condescending toward the people. We treated the women like whores, the men like wimps or fags, and the children as suppliers of drugs or other contraband.

It was more than difficult to talk to Gloria about this. I simply couldn't talk to her about this. Gloria was essentially the same person in the fall of

1969 as she was when we married in the spring of 1967. It was I who had changed. It was I whose illusions about American rectitude and morality had been shattered. It was I who had dreamed of killing a drunken psychotic making a career in the U.S. Army as an NCO. It was I whose consciousness had expanded through the auspices of marijuana.

Gloria had no frame of reference with which to understand my new perspective on life. She had no college aspirations. She couldn't understand my attitude about the war. Even if she could understand, we didn't have the time to talk about it. We had to get back to work almost immediately on our return. Our paychecks from the Army and the nursing home in Kentucky wouldn't last long. Eight days after getting out of the Army, three days after the Moratorium, I was already working from 4 p.m. to midnight at the Post Office. She was working from 7:00 a.m. to 3:30 in a nursing home. We saw less of each other than we did at Ft. Knox. That was just as well.

By the end of the year in Kentucky, I had begun enjoying the time spent at Ft. Knox more than the time spent at home with Gloria. Since I cared little for the Army, clearly there was something very wrong with this marriage. We were all too often in conflict. We were not well suited for each other anymore, if we ever had been. I cannot honestly say that the marriage would have lasted long anyway, as different as we were from one another at the outset of marriage, but the Vietnam experience accelerated the process of dissolution.

Having forsworn smoking dope for over a year, a few months into the Post Office experience, I started again. A couple of young college girls (at 18 or 19-years-old, they seemed much younger than me at 22; due, I expect, to the experiences I had had) working as temps at the Post Office offered me a buzz as we left the building together. I couldn't resist the temptation. They were through for the night but it was my lunch break. I enjoyed the smoke with them, but it made the rest of my boring time sorting mail pass excruciatingly slowly. The next time they offered to turn me on, instead of getting high with them, I just scored a dime bag ($10) of dope. They offered me some blotters of acid as well but I declined. My hold on reality was too tenuous to risk chemically altering my brain, perhaps forever. I felt that marijuana posed no peril to an evolving consciousness. Smoking dope did pose a threat to the waistline however, with a severe case of the munchies happening all too frequently.

Smoking dope stimulated other appetites as well, which could not so easily be satisfied. On the few occasions I came home stoned, I tried to initiate sexual activities that Gloria wanted no part of. It left us both frustrated. Concerned about my behavior, she talked to our old mutual friend, Bill Casbohm, about my "marijuana problem." He had since found the religious truths he was seeking back in his time at the YMCA. He had become a Mormon, adopting the religion's strict prohibitions on drugs and alcohol. He told her he knew several members of law enforcement who were fellow Mormons, including one FBI agent. The FBI agent suggested speaking to the local police, explaining that if I weren't transporting dope across state lines, the Feds would have no jurisdiction. So Bill informed the Minneapolis police about my illicit activities. According to Gloria, the local police responded by telling him, "We don't have time to follow around every hippie in Minneapolis just to catch one smoking a joint."

Hah, saved by insignificance! I thought to myself.

This dysfunctional marriage could have dragged on interminably, like a comatose patient in a persistent vegetative state. I didn't want that. It could just as easily have been Gloria that filed for the divorce; instead, I did, in mid-March. We agreed on this at least. Fortunately, we had delayed having any children. There would be no alimony either. She kept the few pieces of furniture, linens, furnishings and other household goods we had acquired by then and I kept the car.

The spring of 1970 brought major changes to my life: A marriage ended, while college and an exciting but ultimately traumatic affair began. I finally started college near the end of March, almost five years after high school graduation. After Vietnam, I saw college in a different light. The year in Vietnam rid me of my naiveté and my illusions. I was skeptical and arrogant, but not cynical in my idealism. I looked to college for the tools needed to reclaim my ideal of a just and noble America. I intended to take it back from the dishonorable men, posing as right-minded patriots, who had stolen it from their unsuspecting fellow citizens. It wouldn't be that simple, of course. I gave college more credit and myself more hope than either could deliver. But I didn't know that then.

I wanted, I needed to know how and why had we got into the mess called Vietnam. So I began exploring the history of American involvement in Vietnam even before classes started. I read *Beyond Vietnam: The United States and Asia,* a book by Edwin O. Reischauer. Reischauer was an expert on the Far East, having spent his first 17 years in Tokyo. He served as a lieutenant colonel in Military Intelligence during WW II. For many years, he was a professor of Japanese History at Harvard University and later served as Ambassador to Japan from 1961 through 1966. The book made clear that at each fork in the political road, the U.S. consistently chose the wrong path, leading to the war in which I served. President Roosevelt, in 1945, was initially inclined to support independence of Vietnam from France. It had been the Viet Minh, led by Ho Chi Minh, which fought the colonial French. Like the Vichy French government that collaborated with the Nazis during the German occupation, their colonial counterparts in Indochina cooperated with Japan during WWII. The British argued against dispossessing France of its Asian prize. The British were still clinging to the colonial mindset even as their own empire faded into the sunset, so they must have had sympathy for France as a fellow member of the club.

When the Vietnamese rebelled, the U.S. sided with France as well. How ironic that we, as former colonies ourselves, should take the colonial power's side. We supplied 80% of the money France spent on battling the Vietnamese. But it wasn't enough. Following the French defeat, the Geneva Accords of 1954 artificially divided Vietnam into North and South, ostensibly only on a provisional basis. The treaty promised free elections in 1956, to reunify the country. When it became clear that Ho Chi Minh would win a free election, President Eisenhower supported Ngo Dinh Diem's decision to hold no election. Subsequently, Diem and his greedy family cronies oppressed all but his Catholic supporters. When the regime became unsupportable, President Kennedy's administration, which I naively had thought so highly of, apparently acquiesced in Diem's assassination in 1963.

Once I began classes, I soon learned that Vietnam was not the only hot issue on campuses across the country. Civil rights, women's rights, human rights and the environment were all items on the college agenda. Busing students to achieve integration had mushroomed in the sixties and seventies. So too had law suits and complaints to federal agencies by people seeking vindication of rights granted under Civil Rights Act of 1964. The Act barred employment discrimination based on race, sex or other protected classes. Congress passed the National Environmental Policy Act in 1970, creating the Environmental Protection Agency and a variety of laws to prevent or remedy pollution. The first Earth Day was April 22, 1970. Roe v. Wade was decided on January 22, 1973. While the issues were national in scope, Minnesota was in the forefront on many of them. In fact, like the University of California at Berkeley and the University of Wisconsin at Madison, Minnesota was a breeding ground for radicals both on and off campus.

While I had some sympathy for many of the advocates for these causes, I wasn't inclined to be a radical. Even if I had been so inclined, I didn't have time. As a "regular" at the Post Office, I was required to work a 40-hour week. I couldn't simply reduce my hours to attend college. So I continued working the 4 p.m. to midnight shift 5 days a week at the Post Office. Given my work schedule, I didn't take a full load, just three classes: communications (a substitute for Freshman English for those qualified for it), physical geography and an introductory sociology class. Still, the first quarter of college was an exhilarating, tumultuous and confusing time for me.

During the first week of classes, an attractive, but married, woman started hitting on me. Jill was trim and fit, with short, natural blond hair framing a pixie face. Over the course of a few weeks, during between-class coffee-fueled dialogues, she went on to explain, "Dave and I have an understanding, he doesn't mind if I go out with other men."

"Are you sure? It just doesn't seem right to me to go out with a married woman."

"John, it's OK. He doesn't have time to do all the things I would like or take care of my needs. If it's OK with him, why should it bother you?"

The attention was flattering, but I was trying to reclaim my ideals, not corrupt them further. I was hooked when she casually provided a peek at a model portfolio a photographer had created for her, including an array of classic nudes.

Why me? I asked myself. The photographer was a previous flame. His own promotional photo accompanying the portfolio showed a hunk who, unlike me, suffered not a bit in comparison with Tom Selleck. I had been on a bland diet of repressed sex from Gloria's limited menu. How could I refuse Jill's offer of haute cuisine hinted at in the glossy gallery?

"All right," I said. "But not until my divorce from Gloria is final; I don't want to do anything that would mess that up and I wouldn't feel comfortable with it."

While pondering Jill's felicitations and adjusting to being back in school, there was the war to contend with. Protests and rallies were frequent on college campuses. Less than a month into classes, I joined a small antiwar march on April 18. As I soon learned, Vietnam War protestors were a diverse group. Radical types like the NLF (National Liberation Front, AKA Viet Cong) supporters who chanted "Ho-Ho-Ho Chi Minh" were among them. Then there were the SDS (Students for A Democratic Society, a radical left group) factions that wanted a revolutionary change in "Amerika." The only common denominator among the groups was their opposition to the continuing role of American forces in Vietnam. For some, it went further than that, an opposition to war in general. That was the case for the American Friends Service Committee (Quakers) who were dedicated pacifists. I didn't have a political or religious axe to grind like many of the others; I just had a recognition that we were in the wrong place at the wrong time and weren't going to be successful. Therefore, we should leave before more Americans died.

In the meantime, I puzzled over my three classes. We didn't see the physical geography professor in person. He appeared only on a satellite-fed television screen in a large auditorium once a week. We did see a graduate assistant once a week, who led a small section of 25 students. I found it nearly as exciting as watching paint dry. But it was part of the science distribution requirement for liberal arts. At least the introductory sociology class had topics that were more interesting. I always associate this class with a conversation I had, perhaps a year later, with another antiwar veteran. We had been smoking dope for a long time that day. Bill had smoked so much that the blood vessels in his eyes resembled red roads from an inset map of Los Angeles. We got to talking about sociology class, about how simple or commonsensical the concepts were.

"The central thesis of Talcott Parsons [a noted sociologist]," Bill said, "is that things are pretty much what they seem."

"Yeah, man. That's it exactly." In this instance, the pseudo-profundity often experienced by the dope smoker was truer than typically the case. In looking back at our time in Vietnam, we had concluded things were pretty much what they seemed there too, not at all what they were said to be by the politicians and generals that had put us there.

The communications course was the most profound. From it came the tools for a self-scrutiny and a paper analyzing my own failed marriage. I received an A on the paper, "Conflicts in Role Expectations and Their Effect on Marital Communication." *I was hip to marital bliss now,* or so I thought.

Chapter 13 — Love and Death, Here and There

ON APRIL 30, 1970, THE court entered my divorce decree. That same day, with Jill in tow, I tossed my wedding ring into the Mississippi River from the pedestrian bridge joining the East and West Bank campuses of the University of Minnesota. The ring that a Vietnamese woman had pointed to in giving me a lesson in morality, two years before, now served a different purpose. Tossing it in the river was a spontaneous rite, symbolizing my freedom from the self-imposed shackles of my too-young marriage.

It would be a little longer before we could consummate Jill's intentions. That same day, President Richard Nixon announced a major escalation of the war, including an invasion of Cambodia. Four days later, on the campus of Kent State University, 12 members of the Ohio National Guard fired 67 rifle rounds into an unarmed group of students protesting Nixon's actions, killing four of the students and wounding nine. Some of the victims were not even protestors, just students on their way to classes. Television and newspaper coverage graphically informed America of the tragedy. Massive protests quickly spread to campuses throughout the country, including the University of Minnesota.

Striking students took over the University of Minnesota's Coffman Union, occupying it for the next week. The mayor of St. Paul wanted the Minnesota National Guard to come on campus to quell the protest. After the

Kent State debacle, Malcolm Moos, president of the university would allow the Guard on campus only if they were unarmed. Eventually things quieted down. For the remainder of the quarter, Friday classes were canceled as a time of reflection. ROTC drills were prohibited on campus. Rallies, protests, canceled classes and much dialogue about the war would continue for the remainder of my undergraduate education.

On May 8, 1970, I joined a large march (there were over 300 parade marshals alone) to the Minnesota State Capitol. Before the march could start, an initial organizing hassle began about who would be in front. Would it be the SDS, the Alliance of University Workers or Vets for Peace (VFP)? Ultimately, VFP won out, carrying a flag-painted coffin replica and the Minnesota Vets for Peace banner. I was among them. To the right of the banner was a partial amputee in a wheel chair, pushed by another war-disabled veteran. As in all such marches, the participants chanted one slogan or another: "What do want? Peace. When do we want it? Now!" Meanwhile, along the parade route, the onlookers added choruses of peace songs. Even the watchful police smiled and occasionally flashed a subdued peace sign at a march that was totally non-violent, quelling the anger and the pain of feelings about Kent State. But the war continued, unabated.

Finally, on June 13, 1970, Jill and I went on our long-awaited first date, a Neil Diamond concert at the Minneapolis Auditorium. I picked her up at her home, still wondering whether I should be doing this and why she had picked me out of a university crowd. Despite my doubts, I couldn't help being excited about it anyway. Nearly to the open car door, she turned back to wave goodbye to her husband Dave, an average-looking guy perhaps a few years older than she or I. He was standing in the doorway, leaning down a little to get a look at me, waiting behind the wheel. It would be 2:30 a.m. before I brought her home. While the agreement with Dave did not extend to sleepovers, apparently it didn't preclude wild sex. In the face of my earlier self-doubts, Jill assured me that I had nothing to fear in future amorous adventures with women. How encouraging.

Then it was on to a summer of sex. It was the best sex I had ever had, not that I had had so much sex by the age of 23. I sublet the attic apartment of another anti-war veteran that summer, in a house on Clarence Avenue Southeast, near the campus. He had painted the entire apartment in monochrome black—the walls, the trim, the bathtub and sink, the pipes, everything. It was an interesting, but not very inviting color scheme. So I livened up the wall with a life-size poster print of Jill in a two-piece swimsuit, posing on the grass at Lake of the Isles. We went to other Minneapolis lakes that summer as well, Calhoun, Harriet and Cedar, where we could swim or sun. With Dave working during the day and Jill taking only a few summer classes, there were plenty of free days for hitting the beaches. There were also opportunities for afternoon delight before I went to my job at the Post Office. Other times we met between classes, making out in one or another of the lover-friendly alcoves of Coffman Union, once the student occupation ended.

I even got comfortable going out together with both Dave and Jill or spending time with them at their home. Not that we all went to bed together, since none of us were into group sex. We all went to Wisconsin one weekend, to visit her family, including her parents, brother and sister. They introduced me as a friend of the family, which, of course, by then I was. I made an inept attempt at waterskiing, towed behind her brother's boat. He wasn't too patient about beginners and I wasn't too keen on swallowing too much lake water or having a high-pressure enema. At times, I was perhaps a little *too* comfortable with the open relationship. Jill scolded me one day for familiarly but negligently patting her behind in view of another family friend. She didn't want him to feel he had the same prerogatives as Dave or I. That would have been too complicated for all of us and perhaps a little too much for even the understanding Dave. Dave really was very understanding. He was quite sympathetic on one occasion when I had a bad chest cold.

"You don't want to go home by yourself with that bad cold. Stay here and sleep on the sofa. It pulls out into a bed. Jill can rub some Vicks on your chest and I've got an old t-shirt you can put over it," said Dave.

"Sure, Dave, why don't you get the Vicks while I make up the bed. Just sit down over there, John, until it's ready," Jill added.

"OK," I coughed.

Life was good, too good. It had never been so good. Five years later, when I first heard Brian Ferry sing, "Love is the drug," my time with Jill immediately came to mind. Like a drug, my attachment to Jill was an intoxicating addiction. It left me in a state of withdrawal when I didn't get my fix and made me willing to do whatever I had to, to get it. I surrendered control of my heart and my life to Jill, playing by her rules, keeping nothing of myself in reserve. She could be flighty and moody, but *soooo* exhilarating. With Jill at the center of my life, I spent my days and nights riding a teeter-totter. Sometimes I was up and sometimes I was down. When things were going well with Dave, Jill had less need of me. If I pressed, she retreated from me. She wasn't *my* wife, after all, so she had no obligations toward me. I had gotten in way too deep, infatuated with and dependent on, someone to whom I was only a friend and a good fuck. Worse was in store by the fall.

I had to be out of Bob Anderson's apartment by the time school started at the end of August. During an odd rapprochement with my brother Doug, we rented an apartment together. It was fortunate for me, in more ways than one, as it turned out. I took a bigger load of classes in the fall, 15 credits, and I was having trouble handling a 40-hour workweek with school. Besides the hours, the mind-numbing task of sorting mail for 8-hours was getting so bad that my supervisor counseled me about abusing sick leave, which I took to escape the monotony. So I quit on September 18, shortly after the fall quarter started. It was a risky financial proposition but I did at least have the GI bill to pay for my tuition. Like most students, I would have an intermittent succession of low-paying jobs thereafter, through the end of college.

In October, Jill gave me the news, over coffee at Coffman Union. "It's over," she said.

"What do you mean, over?"

"I'm leaving Dave."

"So," I began, optimistically "Does that mean you'll be spending more time with me?"

"No. It means I need space to consider what I really want, what I really need."

"OK. So where does that leave us?"

"There is no *us*. There is you and there is me. If I continued seeing you now, it would remind me of Dave. It just wouldn't work."

"So you're leaving him and me."

"Yes. We've had some great times together, which I will always treasure, but all good things must end. This is the end."

"But—"

"Don't worry, John, there will be other women after me," she said as she stood up to walk away.

I sat in shock at the table. I had put too much of myself into our relationship. Jill had left me bleeding raw, ripping away the tendrils of heart and soul I had foolishly attached to her. Jim Morrison's voice ran through my head, singing the Doors slow dirge, "The End." I felt sure that Jill was wrong. I felt certain that there would be no other women after her. Driving back to my apartment, I concluded that in the game of life, I had already achieved all the positive points I would ever achieve. The negative so outweighed the positive that I could never win. *I should just forfeit, that's what I should do.* In a futile effort to do so, I downed about 30 Sominex tablets. Over the counter sleeping pills were not really the best choice for a successful suicide; perhaps inwardly I didn't want it to be. I left a note for my brother, who was not home at the time. Frustratingly, after a few hours, I was still not asleep, although my vision was double and my head felt odd. My brother had since come home, but failed to notice the note scrawled on a paper bag. I began having second thoughts about my decision and made some semi-coherent noise, attracting Doug's attention. He looked in on me and was alarmed at my appearance. I pointed to the bag on the table.

Reading the note, he panicked, "Why? Why!" he asked.

"Jill," I said, "but I've changed my mind. Help me!"

He had the presence of mind to grab the paper bag, with the empty pill packages, as he dragged me out to the car. We made a frenzied trip to the emergency room at Hennepin County General Hospital.

Holding up the packages, an emergency room resident asked, "How many of the pills did you take?"

"All of them."

"When did you take them?"

"A couple hours ago."

"It's too late to pump your stomach. They're well on the way to being dissolved at this point."

"Get his weight and get some charcoal in him," the resident said to an intern.

The intern and an orderly walked me over to a scale.

"Activated charcoal will absorb the drug that's still dissolved in your stomach; how much we give you depends on your weight," explained a nurse.

"Is there an antidote?" I asked.

"No! And if there was, I wouldn't give it to you!" the intern replied, turning away. I guess he was tired of treating would-be suicides.

They put me on a gurney. I started getting delirious and angry. I don't remember what I said, I just remember yelling and cursing. Orderlies quickly put leather straps around my wrists and ankles. I woke up in a hospital bed, with a friendlier orderly. He seemed impressed, regaling me with the prowess of my drug-induced convulsions.

"Man, you were really out there! It took three guys to hold you down! You ripped a quarter-inch thick ankle strap in half! A guy had to sit on your leg 'til we got a heavier strap on you."

"So I'm OK?"

"Oh, I don't know about that. You look OK to me. I'll tell the nurse you're awake."

Doug and the resident who had seen me earlier came by shortly.

"You're lucky you didn't come in here any later. Sominex wouldn't kill you by itself, but you took enough of them to put yourself in convulsions that might have," the doctor told me.

They kept me overnight. They wouldn't let me go until the resident psychologist came in and interviewed me—why did I do it, was I going to try again, etc. I told him about my game theory, giving only an abridged version, skipping over the losses I had incurred. I didn't mention that my parents were both dead before I reached adulthood. Or admit my too-willing participation in devaluing Vietnamese people. Or how I unwisely married Gloria, then discarded her. I did tell him about foolishly falling for Jill, putting my emotional health and happiness in her hands. Having survived my clumsy attempt at forfeiting the game, I assured him I would not be trying suicide again.

"I realized that no matter how bleak things may seem, they could possibly improve if I was still alive. But not if I was dead. I won't be doing this again," I said.

"OK, you seem to have resolved this episode on your own. I'll sign off on your release orders. But if you have any issues you would like some help with, we have an outpatient program here. Just give us a call."

My response to the psychologist presaged the Buddhist perspective I would later acquire. While one is alive, one can always make causes that will change karma for the better and that will alleviate suffering. I had dodged death in Vietnam when thrown from a moving vehicle. I had escaped again on a dark interstate highway in Kentucky, performing a racecar maneuver I had never seen or practiced. Now I had survived an aborted suicide. In the hospital, I thought I was simply fortunate or lucky in my escapes. Now I know better. The cause for a current phenomenon may exist an interminable distance in the past, making it difficult to discern. That distance doesn't make an event any more random than today's weather is random. Just ask the nearest physicist about chaos theory. Still, I now know I need to be meticulous in the causes I am making today, to better appreciate and preserve this life.

A couple of days after my Sominex trip, I was back in class. It amazes me now, to think how resilient I must have been, bouncing back so quickly into class work. So unlike my high school days, my college classes and my personal life were closely intertwined. In the first quarter, I had analyzed my failed marriage as part of an assignment in communications class. Now, I used the aborted suicide experience as the topic for an extemporaneous talk assignment in my speech fundamentals class a couple weeks later. I don't recall now what I said, but I do recall being pissed off that I only got a B for my efforts. Perhaps I didn't render the trauma sufficiently vividly. But it was one of those tight-assed graduate teaching assistants running the class. They were hard graders anyway compared to associate or assistant professors.

Along with taking the speech class, I was also on the debate team. Debate provided a clear contrast of the academic to the real political world. We were debating wage and price controls, an active political controversy in 1970, given the costs of funding the Vietnam War. But academic debates are conducted in a rigid format, alternating affirmative and negative arguments, followed by timed rebuttals. Judges score the debate. Winning means more succinctly and more clearly articulating the essential arguments supporting your position, pro or con, than your opponents. In the real world marketplace of ideas and policy choices, the outcome is not an academic matter. In the political arena, I learned that debate is less likely to be honest. More often, the facts are hidden or distorted and the public misled on both the objective and the outcome. Should the United States have had its armed forces in Vietnam, for example? Or more recently, Should we have sent troops to Grenada, Haiti, Bosnia, Afghanistan, Iran or Iraq? Legitimate criteria can be found to make important public policy decisions, but all too often are ignored for political reasons.

With apologies to Melville, don't call me Ishmael, call me Candide. The winter quarter (January of 1971), broadened my intellectual quest to make sense of life, a quest demanded by my Vietnam experience. The government was doing the wrong thing and the majority of the American population didn't seem to notice. If they did, they didn't seem to care. But what could I do? What should I do? My humanities class offered a starting point, by introducing me to an 18th Century kindred spirit, Voltaire's *Candide*.

Professor Pangloss had instructed Candide, "everything is for the best in this best of all possible worlds." If God is perfect, then how could his created world be otherwise? That we do not see the world this way is only because we do not understand God's plan. So all the sufferings people experience, like war, pestilence, starvation, crime, and poverty are all part of that grand plan—which we do not understand. Voltaire goes on to expose

Candide to all manner of horrors inflicted by armies, political and religious authorities. He graphically disabuses the naïve Candide of the foolish notions taught by Pangloss. Voltaire's purpose is holding up to ridicule, views of some other prominent writer/philosophers of the time. I certainly hadn't seen as much evil as had Candide, but I was every bit as naïve as he was before my time in the military. I actually believed that the seemingly well-intentioned politicians had only the best interests of the American *and* Vietnamese people at heart when they sent us all off to Vietnam. Voltaire savagely satirized not only the religious thinkers of his day, but the political philosophers as well, for failing to make real world assessments.

Although written more than 200 years before, *Candide* was still timely for me in 1971. I soon learned, while seeking music on my car radio, that the notion of God's will satirized by Voltaire lived on. I paused overly long on one station between the presets. I heard an evangelist commenting on the "audacity" of a so-called believer in asking, "Why the good, such as innocent children, should suffer an early death through war or starvation. This is none of our business," said the evangelist—"it is only God's business!"

"Okay, that explains it!" I laughed out loud, talking back to the radio. It was at this point, I believe, that I began drifting back toward agnosticism. It wasn't so much that I was unsure of God, as it was that I was sure that the religious leaders who purported to know Him so well must either be mistaken in their beliefs or intentionally misleading believers for their own purposes. If God did exist, I too had the audacity to want to know why all the innocents had to suffer. It made no sense to me. If God did exist, surely He couldn't be like this. If He were like this, I would take my chances on hell and damnation. This was a God I didn't care to worship. If I were to worship God, it would be a God I could understand and appreciate free of the claptrap so-called Christians used to control weak-minded believers.

With all the variety of Protestant denominations, with their varying interpretations of how best or most correctly to worship God, it seemed that picking a church was somewhat like picking an item from a menu. Or maybe it was like choosing a style of music, or clothing on a rack. In all cases, what it amounted to was finding a professional intermediary to inform you how to practice a belief in God. Once you found one with which you could feel comfortable, all you had to do was show up at the designated place and time and receive your blessings. I had begun my religious life as a Methodist, faithfully going to Sunday school as a boy and later MYF as a teenager. My mother's unrelenting suffering left me doubtful about God for a time, until my ill-fated attraction to Gloria. Then I accepted the tenets and practices of the Lutheran church, with little concern or question for what it all meant. Then came Vietnam.

Having seen the shallow observance of dogmatic beliefs practiced and preached by pastors denominated as chaplains, including the Westmoreland episode, I found it hard to accept organized religion as either comforting or believable. Doing violence to other human beings, in God's name, had to be wrong. Killing for Christ couldn't be morally correct. Perhaps there simply wasn't a God. How could I be sure about the existence of a God in a world where Protestants and Catholics killed each other in Northern Ireland, Jews and Moslems killed one another in the Middle East, Buddhist monks burned themselves up in protest in Vietnam and America happily embraced capital punishment—with prison chaplains administering spiritual soporifics to the death bound. If there was a God, it was up to me to find Him in my own way. I was confident about one thing, living a virtuous life, with concern for others, was important.

Meanwhile, having sufficiently recovered from the exciting but ill-fated affair with Jill, a flippant flirt attracted my attention. She usually sat near the window during my communications class, alternately looking out and gabbing with the guy behind her. One day, my gaze lingered a little long.

"Take a picture—it lasts longer," she said with a mocking grin.

"Are you sure you want to be in it?" I asked.

"Sure! You got a camera?"

"No, not right now. We'll have to make it another time," I said, leaving it at that for the time being. Not long after this exchange, we unexpectedly met in the lobby of a repertory theatre near campus, where students could see classic movies cheaply. She was coming out of the movie with the guy that sat behind her in communications.

"Hmm, looks serious," I said, looking in her direction.

"Why, are you jealous?" she asked.

"No, should I be?"

"Nah, it's just that assignment from Franklin. We're not here on a date," he said, looking back and forth at us, wondering what we were talking about.

"We're going to Dinkytown for some pizza, want to come along?" she asked.

"Sure, why not." I said.

The other guy didn't stay long. He said he had to get up early to study. Soon enough she was gabbing in class with me. I suppose it was the quirky smart-ass nature we had in common.

In a continuing quest for the security of serial monogamy, I quickly got serious with Liz. Perhaps my ancestors were herders or farmers rather than hunters. Chasing women might be exciting fun for some guys, but not for me. Having caught one, it seemed much simpler to hang on to her rather than go back on the prowl. Later on, I would realize there was more to it than that. I came to rely on the refuge, the emotional security I could find in a woman's bed. I sought a safe port where the stormy seas of daily life were calmed in a secure but soft embrace. For now, it was the convenience of copulation close at hand.

While exploring the world of learning and the world of women, I continued exploring the antiwar movement. Given the frequency of classes interrupted for rallies, protests and demonstrations, becoming more involved was almost inescapable. By the spring and summer of 1971, love and learning were on the back burner, while the war boiled over on the front.

In late February 1971, I traveled with a busload of fellow students to Washington, DC for what I thought would be my first national protest. It didn't amount to much. A couple thousand people got together at Catholic University to hear a variety of speakers. I recall nothing anyone said or even the names of who spoke. I do remember that it was a surprisingly warm day, even by Washington standards—70 degrees. That was a shocker, coming from Minnesota. The group I traveled with were mostly members of the student contingent of an amalgamated group called the MOBE (Mobilization to End the War). I was going as a member of Vets for Peace. The MOBE was planning what they hoped would be a large protest on April 24, in Washington. As it turned out, I would be there, but not with them. What I remember most vividly about the February trip, were the conversations on the bus. I had assumed that Nixon was lying through his teeth about leftists being behind all the antiwar protests. I had assumed J. Edgar Hoover was just being his usual self, looking for Communists behind every bush. So I was surprised to find how many leftists really were involved in the protests. The odd relativity of politics was an amusing insight I gleaned from the trip.

On the bus with me were Socialist Workers Party members, Rosa Luxembourg fans and other varieties of left-leaning youth—including one who had been to Cuba to help bring in the sugar cane crop for Fidel Castro. Arguments would ensue among the differing factions represented. Unable to persuade one another, they would hurl stern accusations at each other. "Stalinist!" Said the blond short with short hair.

"Revisionist!" Retorted the curly brown haired one.

I had no clue what they were talking about, never having read any of their tracts. I knew who Lenin and Stalin were, but I had never even heard of Rosa Luxembourg. From what each of these heavy political thinkers said, as near as I could tell they seemed very similar in their respective opinions. They, on the other hand, could see no significant difference whatsoever among the members of Congress. To them, for example, Barry Goldwater on the right and Eugene McCarthy on the left might as well have been of the same political party and viewpoint. Nonetheless, my fellow travelers (a double entendre from before my time) were all in favor of quickly ending the war in Vietnam. The fact that their reasons were very different from my own was not of major import to me at the time. I had barely begun my college education, but I already knew that much about politics and bedfellows.

Chapter 14—Vietnam Vets Against the War

BY THE SPRING OF 1971, Vets for Peace was moribund. I was looking for ways to get it moving more strongly. In March, I learned about Vietnam Veterans Against the War (VVAW) from Bob Anderson, the guy whose monochrome black attic apartment I had sublet the summer before. It was a national group just gearing up for action in Minnesota when I joined. When I told him about my trip to Washington, DC with the MOBE people, he wasn't sure he wanted to let me in. I explained I had gone as a member of Vets for Peace and assured him I wasn't a far left politico. VVAW, I soon learned, had less to do with radical politics and more with radical pacifism, if there were such a thing. Because I had not been on the frontlines, I hadn't seen the worst of the war. Now I heard about the daily evils and occasional atrocities committed by Americans, from the mouths of the veterans involved. They added new reasons to the ones I already had for opposing the war.

In February 1971, VVAW had conducted hearings in Detroit. About 150 Vietnam veterans spoke about the acts of violence they had either committed or witnessed during their tours. VVAW called the hearings, "The Winter Soldier Investigation," inspired by the famous words of Thomas Paine's pamphlet, *An American Crisis,* written during the American Revolution:

"These are the times that try men's souls. The summer soldier and the sunshine patriot will, in this crisis, shrink from the service of his country, but he that stands it now deserves the thanks of man and woman."

Remaining silent would have been easier. More than the time they spent in Vietnam, revealing the truth about the conduct of the war was their real service to our country. The vets described the effects of napalm on a child's flesh. They revealed how Agent Orange destroyed crops and not just jungle hiding places of the Viet Cong. They told of the common use of free fire zones—where anyone found within could be killed on sight, without warning or challenge. Since the Viet Cong didn't wear uniform insignia, we Americans could not tell by looking who was or was not an enemy. Therefore, the rule of thumb for determining enemy body counts was simple: if they were Vietnamese and they were found dead, they must have been VC. That the NVA and VC committed more atrocities on their fellow Vietnamese than did Americans is probably true but also beside the point. There was no excuse for corrupting American youth into doing the same. Our soldiers needed to leave Vietnam. We should send no more young men there. We had to speak up.

The local Vietnam Veterans Against the War "headquarters" was co-located with "Vet's House," an alternative service organization for Vietnam era vets who couldn't relate to the VFW, DAV, etc. The latter groups couldn't understand why we wouldn't want to fight for the mystique of American military service, which they held dear. The answer was simple: They had experienced an age of events that supported the mystique and we hadn't. World War II was a different war. So too was Korea. Once confronted with the essential realities of the situation in Vietnam we could do nothing else but express our sorrow, our disgust, our outrage—and demand an immediate end to the U.S. involvement in the war. So going to the VFW or DAV for assistance in getting VA benefits was not a viable option for many Vietnam Vets.

Vet's House was an actual two-story house in Minneapolis, owned by Ed Lambert, a social worker who—along with several other veterans including myself, incorporated a non-profit organization on the site. The co-location of VVAW on the same site had both problems and benefits, however. We had to be willing to assist people who, while not comfortable with the old farts at the VFW, weren't entirely comfortable with the VVAW political posture either.

Paranoia ran rampant among antiwar and counterculture groups throughout America. It may seem an apocryphal legend perpetuated by "radical" types everywhere, but we actually did wonder why our telephone service stayed on, despite months going by without paying the phone bill. Was it due to FBI wiretaps on the phones? Based on what we later learned about the illegal COINTELPRO operations run by the FBI, it may well not have been paranoia.

We did try to be careful, at least in discouraging the use of drugs in Vet's House. This was no small feat, since many members—myself included, smoked dope and some used a variety of other drugs as well—symptomatic of the Vietnam experience and its continuing effects. On the other hand, I don't recall that Bob Anderson did. He was the Twin Cities Coordinator of VVAW when I joined the group. Bob was very sincere in his efforts to end the war and I don't think he needed or wanted drugs clouding that objective.

Up to this point, VVAW had not had a great deal of visibility in Minnesota. That changed quickly on March 16th, when it initiated an around the clock vigil in front of the Minnesota State Capitol. We were there supporting a bill that would make it illegal for the federal government to compel a serviceman from Minnesota to fight in an undeclared war, i.e., Vietnam.

Two-man teams stood on either side of over a mock coffin, draped in an American flag. Before the coffin, a pair of jungle boots sat in the snow, with a rifle stuck bayonet down in the frozen ground between them. A steel pot helmet topped the rifle butt—the symbol of a dead soldier and prominent part of the VVAW logo. The bill's sponsors, veterans of the Korean War or World War II, joined Vets for Peace. Moved by our vigil, Governor Wendell Anderson asked us into his office and he joined VFP as well. Following the bill's passage by the legislature, the governor signed the bill. The attorney general of Minnesota brought suit in Federal District Court based on the law, despite knowing full well he would not likely prevail. The symbolism of the suit conveyed an important message from the people of Minnesota nonetheless. During the legislative process, I angrily harangued one representative from a suburban Twin Cities district. He had made several negative comments on the bill, before registering his nay vote.

"I hope for your sake if you have a son, he doesn't have to die in Vietnam!" I yelled at him in a capitol corridor.

"Get outta my face, you Commie sympathizer!" he replied.

"Fuck you, asshole," I said in parting, an early manifestation of the rage I felt at politicians who persisted in supporting the war. Were they too simple-minded, I wondered, to realize that they had duped not just the public but themselves as well, into actually believing the foolish positions they espoused?

Shortly after our lobbying success, I took over the task of coordinating speaking activities in the Twin Cities. There was a lot to do; fortunately, I found that I would be able to earn ten quarter-credits from a history professor for writing a report on my VVAW activities. This left me only two regular classes in the spring quarter. I began calling pastors to solicit talks at area churches, as well as calling colleges, other veteran's organizations and peace groups to get us on their agendas. Since VVAW was not that well known, we got only a weak response. To change that, we decided to have a mock search and destroy mission in Minnesota, which we referred to as a RAW—for Rapid American Withdrawal and war spelled backwards.

After hearing Vice President Spiro Agnew refer to American antiwar critics as "homefront snipers," we immediately adopted the moniker for our RAW, calling ourselves the "Minnesota Homefront Snipers." Along a 104-mile route from Little Falls to Minneapolis, jungle fatigue garbed vets carrying toy M-16s pretended to interrogate and torture or kill prisoners. We passed out leaflets telling the people what would have happened to them had they been Vietnamese:

"A U.S. Infantry company has just passed through your
area. Had you been Vietnamese, we might have burned your
house, raped your daughter, shot your dog, or shot you."

We also gave out replica "Chieu Hoi" passes (which were guarantees of safe passage to a refugee center) and replica "Free Fire Zone" notices. The notices warned villagers that we (the U.S. soldiers) had declared the area hostile; anyone remaining within it could be shot on sight without any provocation on their part or any opportunity to present identification. Many refused to take the notices. Of those who did, some found it hard to believe that American troops would really be fighting like this. We must have been making this up, they thought.

Back at Vet's House, I answered the phones, keeping the media informed on the whereabouts of the "Minnesota Homefront Snipers" and providing updates on the progress of the RAW. This succeeded in "bringing the war home to the people"—which was our intention, yet without seriously disrupting their lives. Some people on the street in Minneapolis were not sure that this was guerilla *theater*—not real guerilla activity. One man pulled a vet off a "victim" and kicked him in the groin. Another threw his wife and child against a wall and covered them with his body. Of course, that was exactly the point. The people in Vietnam were living like this on a daily basis.

John Bortner and I recorded a PSA at KQRS, a "Progressive Rock" station in Minneapolis. We thought the PSA was great. A couple choruses of "When Johnny Comes Marching Home Again," fading into two guys whistling the tune in the background, with a voice-over "Will **your** Johnny come marching home? Let the president know you want the troops home now! A message brought to you by Vietnam Vets Against the War." The station manager wouldn't play it, calling it "too controversial." This was, after all, a commercial and not a public radio station. Hah! They were, we concluded in the parlance of the day, "*hip* capitalist pigs."

The next month, from April 19th through the 23rd, VVAW staged Operation Dewey Canyon III—"a five day limited incursion into the foreign country of the Federal Government to end the war." Minnesota sent three busloads of vets to DC. I spent my 24th birthday camped on the Mall, only a few blocks from the U.S. Capitol. We were there to lobby Congress and to put pressure on Nixon to end the war. Of course, Nixon didn't care what we thought and treated us as shabbily as we had expected him to.

Government officials stopped a delegation of Gold Star Mothers, disabled veterans and clergymen at the gates of Arlington Cemetery, preventing the delegation from laying wreaths commemorating soldiers who died in the war. Adverse publicity forced the government to relent, allowing the delegation into the cemetery the following day. An administration spokesman reported that Nixon believed that no more than 30% of the people in our camp were actually veterans. Given the amount of surveillance that the FBI and other intelligence services were conducting under white House direction, it seems likely he should have known very well that almost all of us were Vietnam veterans. In response, VVAW collected 1,200 forms of documentation of veteran status from persons then in the encampment for display to the media, thereby confirming that over 90% of the individuals were indeed Vietnam vets. In protest of the war's continuation, most of the vets threw medals they had earned in Vietnam over a high chain-link fence that surrounded the Capitol during our visit. Conjoining that protest with Nixon's reported doubts about our service, Denver Post editorial cartoonist Olliphant portrayed a dismayed Nixon looking at a pile of medals with the caption, "How about those for credentials."

We had some support in Congress, however. Twenty-five Congressmen opened up their offices for us to sleep in if necessary. Others offered us places to shower. Two secretaries from Congressman Donald Fraser's Office (5th District, Minnesota) opened their apartments to Minnesota vets, giving them a place to shower. Senator Eugene McCarthy, who came to visit us on the Mall, did the same. McCarthy was an ironic reminder to me of General Westmoreland. One was a dove and the other a hawk but both had the same gray plumage, with no feather out of place in a strong breeze. Sharing the politician's presence of detached conviviality, they both failed in their most important quests: victory on the battlefield of Vietnam for Westmoreland and victory for McCarthy on the floor of the 1968 Democratic Convention in Chicago.

Despite the seriousness of our purpose, the trip was not without its light moments. The excellent relationship we enjoyed with the U.S. Park Police as the days wore on was surprising. No doubt, orders from on high guided them in ignoring the aroma of marijuana and the open bottles of liquor in the hands of some in the camp. Still, they seemed happy enough about the duty. Meanwhile, other Caucasians like me were walking about the mall and the Capitol area with upraised fists, exchanging salutes of "Power to the People!" with the local brothers. Then there was the oft-heard refrain in mock radical speak, "Free John Kerry's maid!" Not said to his face, of course. Word had spread throughout the vets that Kerry came from a well-to-do family. That was long before he married Teresa Heinz, adding even more wealth.

Finally, there was my visit to Senator Hubert Humphrey's office with half a dozen other vets from Minnesota. The very month I arrived in Vietnam, October 1967, Humphrey had said about the war, "This is our great adventure and a wonderful one it is." A real latter day Professor Pangloss, I thought, after having read Candide. He later regretted the comment, but not in time to support the peace platform offered at the 1968 Democratic National Convention. Things were going along reasonably well during our visit with HHH until one of the vets said, "We can put you in the White House if you'll end the war."

"I would be grateful for your support in the next election," Humphrey replied as only a true politician would, hopeful he would get a rematch against Nixon in 1972.

"No, you don't understand, we mean right now!" the guy insisted.

Humphrey's face paled and he looked around the table nervously, trying to figure out if we all were of the same mind. We quickly changed the subject, hushing the guy up before he could freak out Humphrey any more. I don't know whether it was Post Traumatic Stress Disorder (PTSD), too many drugs, or maybe just impatience with the political process (which most of us had every reason to feel strongly about) that prompted the suggestion. Humphrey's discomfort didn't really matter much to me anyway. I didn't think he was up to the task of ending the war, which is why I supported the ill-fated candidacy of George McGovern in the next election.

Following the trip to DC, it no longer was necessary for me to solicit speaking engagements. Everyone was calling us, wanting to see and hear someone from VVAW. I went out on many talks myself and we had six other people going out as well. With the increasing reports of atrocities on all sides and the continuing American casualties, it seemed that the tide of public opinion was turning. A "Dump the War Rally" was set for the sports center in Bloomington, a Minneapolis suburb. Sponsored by the Bi-Partisan Caucus to End the War in Vietnam, the event featured John Kerry as the keynote speaker. Local VVAW members would serve as ushers/security.

We asked them to let us sell "I Support VVAW" buttons. We needed funds to pay the bills at Vet's House, print flyers, etc. But the Caucus leaders didn't want individual groups fundraising separately at the event. Bob Anderson, John Sherman (Vets for Peace leader) and I met with a few of the Caucus leaders to hash out an agreement.

"Look, Mr. Fisher, we are the credible people here in the antiwar movement. We were there. We saw for ourselves. People need to hear us." Bob told him.

"I know you are. I understand how you feel, but everyone wants to raise money at the rally. We have already told all the other groups they could pass out literature but not sell anything. All the proceeds will go to pay for more TV and radio spots. We have to get more people speaking up."

His face reddening, Bob said, "We can do that. But we need funds to operate. This is the ideal time for us to sell buttons. We are not everyone else. We're not some political fringe group or religious organization. We're the people who were there. **Either you let us sell buttons, or we'll have to tell John Kerry not to come!**"

"Wait a minute, we didn't make arrangements with you guys to bring him here. We dealt directly with the national organization!"

"You think if we told him you were jerking us around about selling a few buttons he wouldn't pull out?" Bob added, a shade redder.

"You wouldn't really do that would you?"

"If you leave us no choice."

"All right, all right. You can sell your buttons, but I don't like being pushed like this."

It was an ugly and uncomfortable reminder of the power politics within the antiwar movement. We probably couldn't, and wouldn't try, to make good on the threat—but it worked. We netted $2,400 selling 2,700 buttons. Not a lot of money but it would keep us going a few months. A crowd estimated at 27,000 attended the rally. A burst of optimism buoyed my spirits. Perhaps the people would demand the president end the war and bring the troops home. I find it amazing, now, realizing that there was still that much naiveté remaining in me. Vietnam and the aftermath of that experience had yet to eradicate it completely.

People did ask for the war to end. A majority wanted it to end soon. But soon was a relative term. To the Nixon administration, soon appeared to be a very long time away. Congress seemed unwilling to hasten our departure from Vietnam. VVAW kept going on talks, but the problem was not convincing the audience about the war, but convincing them not to believe the BS coming from the White House about winding down the war and about "Peace with Honor." Bob Anderson was pessimistic, seeing little more that we could do. His girl friend Zibby, a loyal supporter of antiwar efforts until then, was more so.

"You can keep protesting if you want Bob, but I've had enough. If you want me, I'll be backpacking across Europe," she told him. A couple weeks later, Bob resigned from VVAW, saying he was going to find Zibby. It wasn't that he was giving up on America, he was just looking for something more positive. He went looking for a loving relationship instead of death, which was occurring in Vietnam and America as well, dealt out by politicians who could find no better way of resolving problems. I can't say I had much more optimism than Bob, but I took over when he left. The members elected me Twin Cities Coordinator of VVAW in May 1971.

Shortly thereafter, I attended a national conference of coordinators held in St. Louis on the 4th, 5th and 6th of June, where we came up with strategies for the coming days. Two veterans from each state would again go to the Mall in Washington, DC to camp out and fast until passage of the McGovern-

Hatfield Amendment (which would have mandated total U.S. troop withdrawal by December 31, 1971). I'm not sure the camp-out fast got very far. The bill was defeated 55-39 on August 31. We did set up a lobbying staff of three in DC. And upon our request, the Veteran's Administration authorized VVAW to represent veterans in VA benefit claims cases.

The trip to St. Louis had its amusing moments. Perhaps I had now become a radical. If I were a radical, I decided to be a hip one. I boarded a commercial flight wearing a knit tank top, blue and white denim hot pants, tire-treaded sandals and a wooden-beaded necklace. The flight attendants were ogling me, I thought. Then again, maybe they just thought I was odd, getting on a plane like that.

On the ground that afternoon, it was my turn to ogle. We were skinny dipping at dusk in a well-off VVAW supporter's backyard pool. I tried my best to keep from staring too long at a pair of bare breasts bobbing in the water. That would be uncool, if I wanted to remain in solidarity with the Women's Rights Movement. Before "politically correct" became either vogue or a cliché, this was called "raising your consciousness." And if I didn't stop looking, more than my consciousness would be rising. Later, at a fund-raiser populated by well-to-do, liberal ladies of advancing age, Mike McCusker, a VVAW leader from Oregon, was explaining how it came to pass that he volunteered.

"I joined the Marines to get a gun. I was afraid my penis wasn't long enough." A potpourri of puzzled, startled and a few knowing looks appeared on the faces of the blue-hairs. I just shook my head, thinking to myself, *Mike, why are you talking about penises in front of these old ladies? We need their money. It's OK to shock them about the war but don't make them think we're rude and crude.* Ultimately, it seemed to do no harm. If they didn't know how much of an extension some guys thought a gun barrel made to their manhood, they needed to. Without the power of testosterone, how could you fuel a war?

A week after my return to Minneapolis, the Pentagon Papers were released. Within a short time, the U.S. Supreme Court had ruled, 6-3, that the Nixon Administration could not prevent their publication. While the government could prosecute Daniel Ellsberg, the Rand Corporation consultant who had leaked them to the New York Times, they could not keep from the public a top-secret study that no longer was a secret. I found it ironic that everyone was making such a big deal out of it. Now that a *Defense Department study* explicitly details government policies and deceptions, we're all supposed to be shocked to find out what opponents have been saying is really true? Much of the same information had already been published four years before, without controversy, in Reischauer's book, *Beyond Vietnam: The United States and Asia.* The Pentagon Papers just provided more details, describing how successive presidential administrations gave lip service to democratic principles while supporting, aiding and abetting dictatorial excesses.

Meanwhile, on September 3, Howard Hunt and G. Gordon Liddy, both later of Watergate fame, coordinated a break-in of the office of Dr. Lewis Fielding, Daniel Ellsberg's psychiatrist, in Los Angeles. They were looking for information that would be damaging to Ellsberg. At the time, most of America, me included, didn't know that they were responsible for the break-in. They covered their tracks, making it like the work of addicts looking for drugs. The local police apparently didn't know otherwise. They were acting at the behest of the Nixon administration, part of a group within the White House known informally as the Plumbers.

Chapter 15—More Love and More War

VVAW HAD MADE ITS VOICE heard. Other groups had made their voices heard as well. Yet the war continued, without cease. Speaking requests began tapering off. Veterans eager to be activists were dwindling away. I was running out of ideas to motivate them or myself. Meanwhile, Liz wanted to get a teaching degree in elementary education, with a focus on special education. Her mother cared for a couple foster children, one of whom was severely retarded and barely trainable. The other one, if I recall correctly, was moderately retarded and hence educable. Mankato State College, about 80 miles south of Minneapolis had a strong program for teachers, including special education, so she transferred there for the fall quarter of 1971. I admired her dedication and fortitude. I couldn't have handled that particular challenge. Whether it was my heart or my gonads, I chose to follow her there. More likely, it was the subconscious recognition that I needed the refuge, the security of a relationship where my psyche could receive restoration whenever needed. Liz was fun and a relief from the seriousness of the quest and the anti-war protests.

Mankato was a big change from Minneapolis. It was a small town about the size of Midland, Michigan. When the 12,000 or so students were there, the town swelled to nearly 40,000. A little more scenic than Midland, Mankato straddles the Minnesota River, 85 miles southwest of the Twin Cities. The campus overlooks the river valley from high atop a hill. When I went there, it was one of five campuses scattered about the state, as part of the state college system. Originally, it had been a teacher's college but had expanded to business and liberal arts curricula by the time I arrived. Now, as have most other aspiring institutions concerned with image, it has moved from a mere college to become Minnesota State University, Mankato. "A rose by any other name ..."

Through a help wanted ad posted on a bulletin board at the college, I got a part-time job as a nighttime janitor, cleaning a bowling alley and a storefront office/appliance showroom for the local natural gas company. With that small salary and the GI Bill, I rented a one-room apartment at the base of the hill. With the able assistance of her cooperative roommate, Liz maintained a fiction for her parents that she lived in the dorm room they were paying for. Her roommate always said she was at the library, in the shower or otherwise unable to come to the phone whenever they called. She would call back from my place, where she spent most nights. It turned out later that they suspected what was going on, but they appreciated her effort at disguise, which avoided their having to acknowledge our cohabitation.

Shortly after our arrival in Mankato, I decided to have Liz pierce my left ear. In the words of David Crosby, it was now time to let my "freak flag fly." On a campus like Mankato, you had to be clear about who you were. I knew I was an antiwar veteran. Most of my friends smoked dope. It was clear I wasn't a jock, a business major or a Greek (which often seemed to be one and the same thing). To me, most of the Greeks (fraternity and sorority members, that is, not emigrants from the Mediterranean) were the enemy of sorts. They were politically unenlightened, indifferent to or in support of the Vietnam War. They were frivolous beer guzzling hedonists as well, unconcerned about any other political or social issues. They were misogynists or worse. As had happened around the country at one frat or another, the local TKE chapter was accused of having passed around a retarded girl for sex ("What's wrong with that? She consented and enjoyed it" they reportedly demurred). So long hair, a beard and an earring (Liz had a handful to spare, ones that once were part of a pair) would identify my political culture to all.

For the first time in my life, I felt a part of a group—a dope-smoking, anti-war, pro-freedom and pro-equality group.

Like most four-year liberal arts curricula, those of Mankato State required a variety of subjects during the first two undergraduate years. Because I began in the spring of the previous year, I was still a sophomore, with more distribution requirements to satisfy. The fall and winter quarters included introductory math, art, biology, chemistry and music classes. I remember none of them, although I earned A's in all—except for art, which I took Pass/Fail and passed. I had some opportunity for intellectual discovery, however, with an introductory psychology class and Professor Walker's alternative American history class, "Red, White and Black—an Historical Perspective."

In Walker's class, I learned much about the "Trail of Tears," the forcible removal of the Cherokee from the Carolinas and Georgia to Oklahoma. The Cherokee published their own newspapers in the East and had a higher literacy rate than the whites who wanted their land. I learned how a guild system, predating the American union movement, was imposed in the pre-civil war North to elevate whites into skilled trades and exclude free blacks who were then strongly competitive and even dominant in some crafts. I learned about Reconstruction and Jim Crow. This eye-opening history hadn't been a part of my elementary or high school courses. History writing seems, like other spoils, to belong to the victors.

Despite my new historical perspective, I never got into "White Guilt"—the belief that whites were and always have been the foremost oppressors in the world. Therefore, those of us who happen to have been born white in modern times must accept and pay for these sins of our ancestors as if they were our own. Perhaps I didn't fall into that trap because I learned from another class, in sociology, that neither white America nor whites elsewhere in the world have a lock on the oppression of minority populations. Dominant majorities, of any variety of colors or ethnic backgrounds, have subjugated indigenous populations across all continents of the world. In most countries, some politically or economically powerful segment of the population has found it convenient or advantageous to identify other segments as different in some way. Having done so, they use the difference to justify giving the others a smaller slice of the reward pie, a bigger burden of work or less freedom. Whatever the method of segmenting people, the results were the same. It didn't matter whether the criteria was ethnicity, religion, race, or some other characteristic. Rather than feeling guilty for my "race", this knowledge spurred me to look more broadly for solutions. How could I help stop this way of thinking, this behavior, and this unwarranted discrimination I wondered?

Meanwhile, another presidential election season approached. Summer would bring nominating conventions. Now, at the end of winter quarter, early March, 1972, it was time to put my recently learned American Government knowledge to work. While I held strong views about ending the war, I wasn't ready to join the Weathermen or any other revolutionary group. They didn't have solutions that I could see. All they had were destructive fantasies. I went for the political mainstream instead. Along with many other Mankato students, I attended the Democrat-Farmer-Labor Party (DFL, the Minnesota subset of the national Democratic Party) precinct caucuses. With the large number of students, we controlled several precincts, leading to the embarrassment of favorite son Humphrey. I and other McGovern delegates outnumbered Humphrey's supporters. For those of us radicalized by Vietnam, Humphrey wasn't sufficiently contrite about his past support of the war. He had lost to Nixon in 1968 by only 500,000 votes, but that was probably thanks to George Wallace. Running for president as an independent, Wallace received 10 million votes. A great majority of those votes were likely to have gone for Nixon had Wallace not been running.

Despite the efforts we made to dump Humphrey, the local party regulars welcomed our continuing participation. Compromise and attaining consensus are essential to political success. So I became a member of the Blue Earth County Executive Committee, an alternate to the state central committee and editor of the local DFL newsletter. If I wanted to steer the political boat in a different direction, it would be easier being on board than on the shore yelling at the crew.

Spring quarter, late March 1972, I was finally out of lower level distribution requirements. *Now what? How could I synthesize all this information I was taking in and make something of value out of it? What would I do with my life?* Among other things, my high school yearbook caption said of me, "perfect lawyer." Maybe it was my overly analytical and argumentative nature that made the yearbook editor think so. It had never occurred to me as an actual occupational choice while in high school. I don't recall now how it was that it entered my mind the spring of 1972, but I started thinking about it. Maybe the judicial branch would be a better place for righting some of the wrongs I saw in society than the executive and legislative branches of government. Maybe as a lawyer, I could be a part of that battle and still earn enough money to be a writer on the side.

I didn't expect to have a problem gaining admittance to law school. Despite the protests, cancelled classes, and recreational dope smoking, my cumulative grade point average (GPA) stood at 3.81. That was quite a change from the Cs and Ds of high school, which put me in the bottom half of my graduating class in 1965. The difference between those academic achievements reflected the motivation I now had. I hadn't given up laziness or procrastination entirely, I just got better at demonstrating to instructors that I understood what they were teaching while learning what I really wanted to find out.

There was no prescribed "pre-law" curriculum. I wanted classes that would further my dual quest of enlightening myself and of finding the levers to change America and the world for the better. An "Open Studies" major offered the flexibility I needed. Studying political science, I hoped, would tell me why the reality of the political process differed so much from the theory. Adding sociology would help me understand how organizations, institutions and other groups affected the behavior of American society, within the political process and outside it. Psychology would explain the formation and expression of individual beliefs. And philosophy would provide a methodology to make sense out of all this and life itself, or so I thought. I took lots of courses in all of these subjects, along with some English classes to give me a better handle on writing about life outside of academia.

From political science, I learned the mechanics of the American political process and the respective roles of the three branches of government—legislative, executive and judicial. I also learned that while the mechanics of passing laws or adopting regulations should be value-neutral, they often are not. Similarly, while the content of law or policy should be based on how well it serves in achieving a desired, valuable outcome, this too is often not the case.

Even when honest and well-intended government officials tackle a problem, the sheer difficulty of reconciling too many competing interests can make a cost-effective or sensible solution unattainable. Working through the political system seemed to be the right thing to do, just not the easy thing to do. What, if anything could be done to make it work better, I wondered? Perhaps finding answers to this would be one of the things I could work on.

Never far removed from my everyday life, the Vietnam War came front and center again during spring quarter. On April 30, 1972, Nixon escalated the bombing of North Vietnam, targeting the civilian population areas of Hanoi and Haiphong. It appeared to be at the behest of Henry Kissinger, his secretary of state, in hopes of extracting desired concessions at the Paris peace talks with representatives of North Vietnam. At best, Kissinger was an amoralist, to whom any means justifies the desired end. He was an erstwhile Machiavelli to a president who would be his Prince (not that Nixon needed any instruction in deceit or misuse of power, as we all later learned through Watergate). The bombing of civilian, not military targets, sent a message. The message had the same purpose as the atomic bombs dropped on Hiroshima and Nagasaki and the firebombing of Dresden, a non-military target, during World War II. There were no military objectives in these attacks on civilian populations, only political pressure of the most extreme kind. Antiwar protests erupted on campuses throughout the country following the massive bombing in North Vietnam's largest cities.

So it was, that on May 9, 1972, hundreds of students (including me) from Mankato State abandoned classes and surged through the streets of the city, protesting Nixon's actions. When a truck driver persisted in trying to drive through the crowd, someone tossed a bottle under his front tire, infuriating the hapless driver as he moved forward on a flattening tire. A segment of the crowd continued up the ramp, onto the Main Street Bridge to U.S. Route 169, blocking the roadway. I thought this was a mistake and stayed off on the embankment to the side of the bridge. The bridge could not long remain blocked. While the president of Mankato State negotiated in vain with protest leaders, a contingent of State Police wearing full riot gear assembled on the bridge, facing the protestors across a 50-yard open space. Inevitably, the order to disperse came from the officials. When it went unheeded by the road-blocking but otherwise peaceful students, the State Police moved against them with tear gas canisters flying and batons swinging. Watching a young man stagger back, blood streaming from a cut above the eye where a baton had impacted, rage engulfed me.

Unthinking, I picked up and threw a rock, striking a trooper in the groin. He doubled over in pain, unaware where the missile had come from. Another student standing beside me yelled, "What are you *doing*!" I immediately regretted the angry response. It was unexpected, coming from the anger coiled like a cobra in my gut, waiting to strike. I wanted to strike out at the many people I blamed. I wanted to strike out at the pissant politicians unwilling to take a stand to stop the war, strike out at the hip capitalist pigs who talked progressively but were interested only in profit, strike out at the so-called "Silent Majority" of Nixonian mythology, sporting "America— Love It or Leave It" buttons and bumper stickers, and strike out at the police and military who knew no other way of controlling people except beating them down.

I didn't want to be like them, yet here I was responding in kind. I should have known it was there, when I snapped at the punk politician in the corridors of the state capitol a year earlier. Having seen the beast more clearly now, I knew I had to focus on peace, not on violence. If I gave in to my anger and to violence, I would be no better than Kissinger and Nixon were, which was a most revolting thought.

The next day, we held another rally. There were hundreds of students, dozens of faculty members and some college administrators there. Flush with success at blocking, if only for 45 minutes, the Main Street Bridge, many students wanted to continue to wreak havoc to "bring the war home" to the citizens of Mankato. They were encouraged by SDS members and Mitchell Goodman, a poet and draft resistance crusader invited to the campus by the college president to occupy a "Chair of Ideas." Abbas Kessel, a popular professor argued against it. I agreed with Kessel, so I stepped up to the mike.

"This is bullshit! If we block the streets, keep people from getting where they are going, who are they going to be pissed off at, Nixon or us? This war needs to stop! The bombing needs to stop! I was there in Vietnam. We are not going to win. All we are doing is killing more people— Vietnamese and American. Nixon doesn't give a shit what you or I think, but he might give a shit what the townspeople here think. If you want them on our side, let's just march and not block the streets. If you're with me, let's line up and go!"

There were still those who insisted on confrontation, but I helped convince a couple hundred students to peacefully march. It would be my last organized protest against the war, although I didn't know that then. The next day, the Dean of Students saw me walking on campus and called me into his office. "Please, sit down. You saved me the trouble of trying to find you. I wanted to thank you for your efforts yesterday. I was very impressed with your help in redirecting that crowd of students from blocking the streets again."

"Well, it just didn't make sense to me—messing with the townspeople again. I just said what I felt," I replied, wondering where this was going.

"I'm sure they were as moved as I was by your sincerity. You really seem to know what's on student's minds. You know Mankato State could use somebody with your kind of influence with fellow students. I'd like to talk to you about that. I'm sure we could make it worthwhile for you." He continued with a wolfish grin.

"Uh, yeah—I'm sure you could. But I'm not really interested. I need to get to class." I got up quickly to go. This sounded too much like becoming an informant. As far as I was concerned, narks and undercover agents were just about as bad as the people they worked against.

"Well, if you ever change your mind, just come see me. The door is always open." He said, shaking my hand as I was heading to the exit.

It was ironic that the college administration was now looking for student informants after inviting somebody like Mitchell Goodman to teach there. I wondered why was he there. Goodman was a poet, but that didn't seem to be the point, since he was doing no readings or instruction in poetry. Perhaps it was his celebrity antiwar status. Goodman had been convicted, a few years before his invitation to Mankato, of conspiring to subvert the Selective Service System. He and four others, also convicted, were encouraging young men to burn their draft cards and resist induction. The convictions were later set aside. His reputation would certainly appeal to activist students and attract attention to the college. As far as I was concerned, the only appropriate chair for him to occupy was made of porcelain—from which his neo-anarchistic ideas could be flushed down the drain. I said exactly that in a letter published in the campus newspaper. For Goodman, draft and war resistance had become a rationale to tear down the system. He offered nothing with which to replace it. I found the prospect of anarchy an unwelcome alternative to the Nixon administration.

Since I didn't have a political construct in mind to replace the one under which Americans lived, it seemed wholly irrational and morally unjustifiable to tear down what was in place, even if it was flawed. To many radicals of the time, the starting point of rhetoric was the phrase, "Come the revolution..." The assumption was not if, but when. I thought such an outcome unlikely at best, even if Richard Nixon's band of buggers and burglars continued their dirty deeds. Too few members of the American public were sufficiently outraged to spawn a revolution. Some radicals read Franz Fanon's *The Wretched of the Earth* and found in it a thrilling call to action. I found in it a startling confirmation of the corruptibility of man. As Lord Acton's admonition says, "Power tends to corrupt and absolute power corrupts absolutely." Fanon himself cited examples from around the globe of former leaders of revolutionary movements becoming just like the dictator they overthrew, oppressing their people and sending off the financial spoils to a Swiss bank account.

Rather than raising the consciousness of John Q. Public to align with their radical views, the confrontational and often violent protests that some factions pursued in the late sixties and early seventies only made the Nixon administration more palatable. Their foolishly risky strategy was the mistaken belief that if they caused the government to come down oppressively on radicals, the rest of the population would flock to their side in opposition to the government. So the rhetoric continued with the question, "Which side are you on?"

Unable to rationally support the radical agenda and with peaceful protest having no obvious effect, my antiwar activities were ebbing. They were replaced with the Democratic Party's political efforts to turn Nixon out of office in November. In June 1972, Nixon's henchmen broke into the headquarters of the Democratic Committee in the Watergate hotel. Of course, it wasn't immediately apparent that they were, in fact, Nixon's henchmen, due to the cover-up by white House senior staff and by Nixon himself. There were plenty of other instances of corruption already publicly known, however, including large illegal contributions by corporations to Nixon campaigns, bribery and kickbacks. So besides Nixon's continuation of the war, there was plenty of reason to throw him out of office. At the same time, I wanted to see local Republican elected officials, who supported Nixon, ousted as well. So I continued my involvement with the state and local Democratic Party. As editor, with the help of several other party members, I put together the Blue Earth County DFL newsletter. In the fall, I helped with voter registration.

In the meantime, Liz and I made wedding plans. We weren't so countercultural that we didn't see the virtue in marriage, financial and otherwise. We got married September 9, 1972, a few weeks before the fall quarter started. The Nilsens welcomed me into the family. They looked beyond the beard and the long hair that one of the grandparents said made me look like Jesus Christ, and the earring that fit in the hole Liz had pierced the year before in my left ear. Like Gloria's mother before them, they evidently saw a brighter future for me than I did for myself. Perhaps Liz did too. I didn't consider it at the time, but my planning on law school surely played a part in us getting married. Liz must have figured I wouldn't be a dope-smoking activist the rest of my life, although she said nothing of the sort at the time.

We rented the basement of a house, not far from the north end of the Mankato campus. It was drab and a little dreary, with a tiny bathroom under the stairs and a small kitchen on the other side. We did have a bedroom separate from the decent sized living room. The lighting was surprisingly good for a basement. While the windows were small and high on the wall common to the bedroom and living room, they at least were on the south side. The old woman who owned the house lived upstairs with her grown son. She had no objection to my plastering the windowless west wall with a 10-foot wide, floor-to-ceiling 7-Up poster, styled by Peter Max. I wasn't crazy about Max or 7-Up, but it brightened the otherwise dull room. The woman was friendly enough and not too nosy.

The son was middle aged and somewhat addled. He had been on a destroyer torpedoed during WWII. He was one of only a few survivors rescued from the sinking ship. Many Vietnam vets and those who have served in subsequent conflicts suffer from PTSD. For the WWII vet, doctors called the same disorder "Shell Shock." This man clearly had it. Although liberal and idealistic, I felt uncomfortable around the man and found interacting with him very difficult. I envied my friend Bob Corbett's ease at conversing with him. As a fellow Vietnam Vet Against the War, Bob was a more hands-on idealist than was I.

In November, it became clear on which side was the American public. Nixon beat McGovern in a landslide. I could not understand how the American people could have been so stupid, so mindless as to be taken in yet again by Nixon. Yet I should have seen it coming, foretold by bumper stickers: "My country, right or wrong." "I support the President." "America, Love it or Leave it." These were the popular slogans, political shorthand for the millions of Americans delegating decision making to the president. It made *some* sense. Individual citizens don't have the time or the access to all the pertinent information on national security. Making decisions on those kinds of issues is what we elect a president to do. But presidents shouldn't betray the trust voters give them. Presidents shouldn't be lying to and misleading the American public about what they are doing and why. Uncritically accepting Nixon's blandishments, the public was more concerned with the often-longhaired protestors. The Nixon administration succeeded in identifying the long hair as a sign of the protestor's anti-establishment status. We were malcontents, troublemakers and didn't share mainstream American values thought the electorate. Many union members, typically reliable Democrats, joined "Democrats for Nixon" in support of the war and of Nixon. Oddly enough, in another one of the imponderables of American culture, only a few years later, the construction workers began sporting long hair beneath their hard hats.

My last year of college was an eventful one, with the Nixon administration securing my cynicism for the next few years. Following the massive "Christmas bombing" of North Vietnam in 1972, the U.S. position in the Paris peace talks was apparently sufficiently strengthened to result in the signing of a cease fire to take effect January 28, 1973. In an address broadcast on January 23, 1973, President Richard Nixon told the American people that, *"Throughout the years of negotiations, we have insisted on peace with honor.... In the settlement that has now been agreed to, all the conditions that I laid down then have been met. All American forces will be withdrawn from South Vietnam.... The people of South Vietnam have been guaranteed the right to determine their own future, without outside interference."* This then, must have been that "secret plan" to end the war, which Nixon had campaigned on before winning his first term in 1968. Unfortunately, in the four years it took that plan to take effect, nearly 21,000 more Americans (and hundreds of thousands of Vietnamese) had died in Vietnam.

I can only assume that the Nobel award committee members suffered from diminished mental capacity in 1973, when they awarded the Nobel Peace Prize jointly to Le Duc Tho (of North Vietnam) and Henry Kissinger later that year. At least Le Duc Tho was honest enough not to accept the award, because he felt "peace has not yet really been established in Vietnam."

Of course, he undoubtedly knew then, that North Vietnam wasn't planning on living up to the terms of the agreement either. And the terms of the "Peace with Honor" agreement trumpeted by Nixon were not much better than the terms found in the agreement on the table before his election in 1968.

During the Vietnam War, American planes dropped over 7 million tons of bombs on Southeast Asia, 3 ½ times the tonnage we dropped in all of WW II. Most of the bombing came during the Nixon years of the war, including the secret and illegal (we were not at war with them and Congress had not authorized it) bombing of Laos and Cambodia, as well as on civilian targets in North Vietnam.

Meanwhile, throughout 1973, investigation of the Watergate break-in cover-up dominated the news, ultimately adding the "gate" suffix to virtually every political scandal that came after it for at least the next 30 years. No political scandal since then has ever approached the Watergate debacle in the degree of abuse, the numbers of people involved and the corruption of the president himself. How truly corrupt Nixon and the men who populated his administration were, became clearer as time wore on. In the midst of all the sordid details, the irony had escaped me. The Democratic National Committee was broken into and bugged by Nixon's henchmen. The conspiracies to cover it up were proven by conversations in the White House and Executive Office Building recorded on a secret taping system, which had been installed at Nixon's own request to preserve for posterity the history of his administration! The tapes certainly succeeded at that.

I had spent three years in the military, so I was well accustomed to profanity. I was surprised and revolted however, in listening to discussions among the president of the United States and his most senior advisors. Nixon's language was uncommonly crude and vulgar. Profanity may have a place in communicating strong emotion, but when it is routine and frequent, it implies a limited vocabulary or a laziness of thought that shouldn't be associated with the presidency. As much as I detested Nixon for his policies and behavior, I never expected that he would remind me of sheep-loving Joe, my civilian coworker at the Ft. Knox tank park. Of course, profanity was the slightest offense captured on the tapes. Once the existence of the tapes became known, the downward spiral accelerated for Nixon, pleasing me greatly.

Nixon did not want to turn over the tapes, of course. He had Archibald Cox, the Special Prosecutor appointed to investigate the break-in and cover-up, fired for persisting in a request for the tapes. In the end, the Supreme Court told Nixon to turn over the tapes, which revealed that Nixon was in on the cover-up of the Watergate break-in from the very beginning. Seven top White House aides were indicted for various crimes. Four of the aides were convicted or pled guilty (including the former attorney general, John Mitchell). An additional seven men were indicted and sentenced to jail for the break-ins at the Watergate, including the infamous G. Gordon Liddy.

Nixon's White House Plumbers also infiltrated agent provocateurs into VVAW, leading to an indictment of eight VVAW members from Gainesville, Florida. Everyone in the antiwar movement was familiar with the admonition to "just walk away" when pressed by a fellow demonstrator to commit acts of violence during a protest. It was more difficult to do when they were part of the inner circle planning events. The "Gainesville 8," as they came to be called, allegedly were planning to violently disrupt the 1972 Republican National Convention. At trial, the jury acquitted all of them after brief deliberations. From the Watergate Special Prosecutor's report, it became clear that government conspiracy and misconduct was the far more serious offense. FBI agents installed electronic devices, trying to monitor conversations between the defendants and their attorneys.

I took only one more political science course at Mankato, administrative law. I did this as a preview to see if going to law school really was a good choice. I had had enough political theory to go along with the supposed *realpolitik* of the Vietnam War. If the American people had no more sense than to vote Nixon back in, politics was not the answer to any questions I had about making changes happen. Instead, I began searching, without realizing it, how to connect the inner self to the world ostensibly outside myself. Psychology, philosophy and popular science in the late sixties and early seventies were all very much about discovering who you are. Finding the means to "self-actualization," as described by humanistic psychologist Abraham Maslow, seemed like a good goal. Unfortunately, arriving at that pinnacle required satisfying a whole hierarchy of needs beforehand. Whew! Wasn't there some kind of a shortcut, I wondered?

I read the first few of a series of popular books written by Carlos Castaneda: *The Teachings of Don Juan: A Yaqui Way of Knowledge; A Separate Reality; A Journey to Ixtlan* and *Tales of Power.* Living the life of a warrior, being "impeccable" and conquering fear seemed reasonable enough. "Finding a path with heart" sounded fine too. Doing these things by making allies of datura (Jimson weed) and peyote, however, seemed not so wise. Was *seeing, stopping the world, not-doing* and other mystical techniques of deconstructing reality necessary? Probably not, I thought. Cannabis was mind augmenting enough for me. I didn't want to try the drugs Castaneda described nor experience his otherwise altered states.

I also read a powerful book by Viktor Frankl, a Jewish psychiatrist who had spent several years confined in Auschwitz and other Nazi death camps during World War II. His captors could not defeat him. While his body was confined, his mind remained free. His book, *Man's Search for Meaning,* reinforced the conclusion that finding meaning, even in suffering, is essential. Quoting Dostoevsky, "There is only one thing that I dread: not to be worthy of my sufferings," Frankl goes on to explain that even in a concentration camp, a man has a choice on how to respond to his predicament. Frankl says, "It is this spiritual freedom—which cannot be taken away—that makes life meaningful and purposeful."[3] So I assimilated the two concepts I viewed as useful from Castaneda and Frankl: to accept the eventual reality of death without fearing it and to strive to live a life of value.

Through two summer sessions at Mankato, I added literary courses to my exploration. I thought they would come in handy later, once I became a writer. The extra credits would allow me to graduate at the end of December, an advantage for stashing away a little extra income before heading off to law school the following year. My last quarter of college included an internship at the office of Consumer Affairs for the City of Minneapolis. Working there made for a lengthy commute each week, because I still had two classes in

Mankato, 80 miles from Minneapolis. The internship entailed completing the last two units of a consumer education curriculum guide, on buying automobiles and shopping for groceries. The internship also included lobbying the school board to include some of the consumer items within the curriculum. Having come from a financially challenged family, in today's parlance, teaching the guide's functional competencies to high school students seemed critical to me. Conveniently, the office was able to continue paying me through June of 1974, six months after I graduated from Mankato. Working there also enabled me to work off the bad karma I had created while being an encyclopedia salesman. Of course, I didn't think of it in those terms then. I just knew that I had suckered some people into buying books that might not have been the best use of their financial resources. Working in Consumer Affairs didn't do anything for those people, but at least I could help protect others from making the same mistake.

Working in a consumer protection office also further developed my anti-corporate sentiments. Clearly, there were plenty of other unscrupulous businesses besides door-to-door hucksters. There were the used car salesmen, rip-off repair shops of all sorts, driveway sealers, among others. But even the "legitimate" businesses misled or deceived people. There were the bogus markdowns like those I saw at the department store at Southdale, bait-and-switch ads and warranties weaseled out of, for example.

Still, I had no desire to impose unnecessary or impractical burdens on business. Others in the office found it difficult to understand why I chose to test consumer use and knowledge of unit-pricing. If we were going to require grocery stores to go to the trouble of making the labels and putting them on shelves, I thought we should at least know that shoppers knew why they were there and understood how to use them. The lack of interest in cost-effectiveness and practicality among government officials and the public continued to astound me years later, as I proceeded on to full-time jobs.

Part of my perspective about the business establishment and corporations was guilt by association. The corporations and business in general were most often supporters of the Republican Party. The Republican Party was the party of Nixon. It was the party of the right wing, which supported the war. And it was the party that cared for the rich, not the poor. Of course, it all wasn't that simple. My analysis was imperfect and perhaps unfair. After all, the owner of Fisher Nuts had been one of the major planners and sponsors of the "Dump the War Rally" in Minneapolis. But as shorthand, it didn't seem all that far from the truth and convenient for quick judgments. It was also a part of the cynicism that had now become full-blown, thanks to the Nixon administration.

By the end of my undergraduate studies, I had become a cynical idealist. I still held the ideals that I had had from my early school days, but it had become much harder to believe that they could be realized. The conduct of the Vietnam War, the abuses of Watergate, the impotence of organized religion in affecting the worst of human behavior, the apathy and the ignorance of the populace had all combined in a morass of doubt. How could optimism survive? My college studies confirmed that after thousands of years of so-called civilization, war was still endemic, with only brief respites. Political and economic systems of all shapes and sizes had had their day in the sun, falling by the wayside upon some new scheme devised by the best or most powerful thinkers of the new day. Some book or some professor, I had supposed when I began college, would provide all the answers I needed to make the world a better place and to reclaim America from those who had led it astray. But the more answers I received, the more questions I had. Expanding the radius of my knowledge had indeed enlarged the circumference of my ignorance.

Politicians proudly parroted America's democratic ideals, insisting we not only honor these ideals here but also export them abroad. In truth however, they trampled them underfoot at home when the needs of political power suited them. Abroad, presidents and members of Congress supported dictators and oppressive regimes so long as they advanced American economic or political interests—the common people be damned. I knew now, how foolish that I had been before going to Vietnam. I knew now, how naïve I had been in thinking that those wonderful American ideals taught in school were intrinsically linked to foreign policy and government operations. How much like a child's belief in Santa Claus or the tooth fairy, had my thinking been. Politicians populate and run government. Generals run the military, but the politicians tell the generals what to do!

The denouement of Watergate occurred near the time I started law school. On August 8, 1974, Richard Nixon announced his resignation from the Presidency, effective the next day. NBC commentator John Chancellor said words to the effect that no one was celebrating this announcement. It may have been a well-intentioned commentary on the tragedy of the moment for America, but it was quite an erroneous misreading of popular opinion. I'm confident I was not alone in rejoicing at the news. Try picturing the Herbal Essence shampoo commercial airing on television the first few years of the 21st Century. You must have seen it, the one where the woman moans in virtual orgasmic delight, "*Yes, Yes, Yes!*", as she rubs her fingers through sudsy hair. That would approximate, but still understate how I felt at hearing Nixon's announcement. It was not simply a case of schadenfreude for me. It was a sense that karmic justice had been rendered, long before I knew anything about karma from a religious or philosophical perspective. Nixon profoundly deserved the ignominy, the disgrace of having to resign. Yes, it was painful and embarrassing for America—but it should have been. All of those fuzzyheaded "Democrats for Nixon" and the reprobate Republicans that had given Nixon a landslide victory in 1972 had this coming. I, and others like me, had told them so but they were too dumb to understand his true character or didn't care to listen to us. Still, Nixon too contributed to my eventual pursuit of Buddhism, by confirming that placing faith in political solutions was a foolish notion.

---

[3] Frankl, Viktor E., *Man's Search for Meaning,* p. 87, Washington Square Press, 1985, copyright Frankl 1984.

Chapter 16—Law School

DESPITE MY CYNICISM—OR PERHAPS because of it, I still planned to go on to law school. I had a small quantum of hope that I could discover some just principles of law upon which to rely, earning an honest living by fighting for the things I believed in. I even had hopes of possibly remedying some of our government's abuses. I had sent my Law School Aptitude Test results to Harvard, Georgetown, Willamette and the University of Minnesota. Based on my grades and the LSAT, I thought I had a shot at Harvard, but they turned me down. After seeing my scores, Willamette urged me to apply. After seeing my scores, I declined their offer. Georgetown and the University of Minnesota also sent acceptance letters. I jumped at the invitation to Georgetown. Liz and I bought a beat-up old telephone company van, with only two front bucket seats, to move our few meager belongings to Washington, DC.

First year students were required to arrive at school a few weeks early, for orientation and an early start on a legal writing course taught by an upperclassman. Called "Law Club," it would continue throughout the first year to ensure that we all learned how to lay out fact patterns, legal issues, properly cite authorities, and perform other tasks essential both for law school and for legal practice. I dropped off Liz and the contents of the van at her brother's place in Virginia Beach. Carl was a Navy corpsman, stationed there. I went on to DC to attend law club and to find us a place to live for the coming year. Liz kept in touch with frequent little cutesy cards, expressing her love without words, except for the occasional plea she made, to find a place quickly for the two of us to live.

Through the law school, I connected with an assistant U.S. attorney who owned a tourist home on Capitol Hill, in the 600 block of East Capitol Street. He was offering an apartment to a law student in exchange for managing room rentals. Tourist homes on Capitol Hill are like "Bed and Breakfasts" but generally without the breakfast and not nearly so nice. Typically, they are old rowhouses with ten or twelve rooms for rent on a nightly, weekly or, rarely, a monthly basis. Although part of Georgetown University, the Law Center was not in the Georgetown neighborhood. The Law Center is near the Capitol. The tourist home would be a convenient place to live, from which I could walk to classes. So at the end of the pre-school summer session, I retrieved Liz and our belongings from Virginia Beach.

Our Georgetown life started inauspiciously, a harbinger of many difficulties to come. The first night there, we left most of our things that were not immediately essential in the van behind the tourist home. During the night, someone broke into the van and pilfered some items. The stuff taken was not particularly valuable to anyone else but us. The items lost included a cheap bicycle, a sewing basket belonging to Liz, a briefcase containing a variety of undergraduate work I was saving and a few other items. We reported the theft to the DC police, but they offered little hope we would ever get any of the stuff back. We didn't. This petty crime was not high on their priority list. We never heard from the police again. It bothered Liz greatly and left a long-lasting pain. It was her pain, but I felt it indirectly, in a less amorous Liz.

After the pain of this loss, the convenience of being able to walk to class paled. Then, less than a month after classes started, we had to find another place to live. The attorney had expected to be able to rent out a couple rooms in the basement, as the previous owners had done. Without the rental income from those units, the cash flow would be insufficient to cover his mortgage payments. Only after purchasing it, did he learn from the local building inspector told that the existing basement rental units didn't meet current building code requirements for ceiling height. Rentals by the prior owners had been "grandfathered" under the previous code. Once the property changed hands, it had to meet the new code requirements. For an assistant U.S. attorney, he hadn't done a very thorough legal review before closing on his investment. He couldn't afford the cost of remodeling, to meet current code requirements, so he wound up selling it back to the prior owners at a loss.

From the tourist home, Liz and I had taken on another apartment-in-exchange-for-service deal. Although it lasted longer, through the end of the first year of school, it worked out no better. A woman with a moderately retarded, hyperactive pre-teen son needed an expertly qualified nanny. Since Liz had focused on special education in college, she was equipped to handle him. In exchange, we lived rent-free in the English basement of the woman's large rowhouse in the 500 block of C Street N.E., still on Capitol Hill. It was an odd efficiency. The large open kitchen had a high ceiling, with the old-fashioned tin painted a dull white. The large living room had a sofa bed furnished by the landlady, along with our old rocker and a blue-mirror-glass topped end table that had survived the thefts at the tourist home. The tiny bathroom fit under an inside stairway to the main floor above, along the west side of the living room wall. We had our own private entrance, in front of the stairway.

Like her son, the woman who owned the house was somewhat hyper. In her frequently scattered state, she was an intrusive distraction, interrupting whatever we were doing by opening the door at the top of the stairs to say that she had to be somewhere and requesting Liz to watch her son. While the economics were good, the lack of privacy and on-call nanny arrangement were less than satisfactory.

In the spring, a flight of termites emerged from the window frames in the front of the house, swarming in search of new wood to colonize. The owner was shocked and dismayed, unaware of the termite's presence before then. Damage was extensive and the house needed repairs. I suspect the repairs cost more than she could afford. Soon after, she announced that her grown daughter needed to move in and we needed to move out. Whether it was her daughter or someone else moving in, I'm sure it had to do with cash flow. We had expected the arrangement to continue into the next year. Once again, we had to find another place to live on short notice and Liz needed to find a job to pay the rent.

She took a job as a claims representative at the local Blue Cross/Blue Shield affiliate. It was an unpleasant job in an unpleasant workplace. Claims reps worked desk-to-desk and row after row, with not even a cubicle wall to separate one worker from another. In a telephone-intensive line of work, the warehouse-sized open floor plan made every day an ordeal. Subscribers calling the office were frequently dissatisfied with claim decisions they had received in writing. So the front-line claim reps all used phony names with the callers—just in case someone wanted to target them for an after-hours personal reprisal. Teaching might have been better, but it was not an option. Most elementary schools were not on bus routes and Liz still didn't drive. Perhaps her Minnesota teaching credentials were not fully acceptable either.

We gave up on finding another place on Capitol Hill because rents were high and parking a hassle. We found yet another basement apartment. This one was in upper northwest near Chevy Chase, Maryland. Basements were getting to be our regular habitat. First, we had rented the one in Mankato, then the woman's home on Capitol Hill and now on Livingston Street. This basement was in a detached home, at least 30-40 years newer than the row houses on Capitol Hill and newer than the house in Mankato as well. The house was in a nicer neighborhood than the one we had left and just a block off Connecticut Avenue N.W., where Liz could catch a bus to work. I rode the bus too, and the Metro subway, to get to classes at the Law Center. It was far easier and cheaper than trying park to anywhere near there.

The summer I started law school was the year after *The Paper Chase* came out. The movie depicted the pressures of first year studies at Harvard Law School. I thought it funny and probably apocryphal. *I* wouldn't have put up with the sarcasm and intellectual humiliation that the movie portrays the author, James T. Hart, taking from Professor Kingsfield. Hah! I soon learned that while the movie might be a little overdrawn, it wasn't by much. I couldn't help thinking of the Red Queen's instruction to Alice in *Through the Looking Glass,* "Now here, you see, it takes all the running you can do to keep in the same place. If you want to get somewhere else, you must run at least twice as fast as that!" Virtually *everyone* at Georgetown was near the top of their undergraduate class and very sharp. I would now be a small fish in a very large pond. At Mankato State, my upperclass courses generally had no more than 20 students and often had far less. In contrast, each of the first year required classes at Georgetown Law included about 200 students, seated stadium style in auditorium-sized classrooms.

Classes were taught in the Socratic Method a la *Paper Chase.* Professors would ask a question, get a partial answer and ask another question based on the first response. Soon even students from the deepest and slowest drawling Southern states were talking at the pace of a Manhattan native, lest impatient classmates glare at them. We covered prodigious quantities of intellectually demanding textbooks each week. Research, analysis and writing requirements were equally demanding. I dedicated nights, weekends and virtually every waking moment to study. I had not expected to work this hard. During my undergraduate years, I had easily breezed through classes with little exertion. At the University of Minnesota, I had single-handedly polished off a pitcher of beer and a medium pizza, before taking and passing a final in Spanish. Later at Mankato, I had managed a B on a history final, taken while stoned on marijuana. I soon found that law school required a radically different approach.

The month before my first year of law school ended, Vietnam made news again. The last two deaths of Americans in Vietnam came on April 30, 1975. They died in a helicopter crash during the evacuation of the U.S. Embassy in Saigon. The evacuation had come because the government of South Vietnam had surrendered to the Communist-led North. According to Kissinger's Nobel Prize winning treaty of 1973, there were supposed to be free elections to reunify the country. Neither the Viet Cong nor the North Vietnamese were supposed to use military force to take control. Not surprisingly, things did not work out quite that way. The South had had little chance of success at forestalling the North's eventual victory while U.S. troops were there. After the U.S. left, they had none at all. Having removed all troops two years before, the United States did not intend to return to enforce the treaty. Or in the parlance of the day, the refrain of "Peace With Honor" from pardoned ex-President Nixon and his calculating crony Kissinger was clearly "no longer operative." The decent thing to do would have been for Henry to return his prize and for Nixon to apologize. That of course did not happen.

I regret not one minute of the time that I spent in protest of the war. I only regret that my efforts appeared to have had little effect at ending the war sooner. Despite Nixon and Kissinger, South Vietnam fell to the Communist North anyway. This war could have ended with the same result well before the 1973 cease-fire, if Nixon had not persisted in his patently false quest for "Peace with Honor." It could have ended in 1969 had Nixon not sabotaged the peace process underway in the fall of 1968. It could have ended in 1964 or 1965, before I went to Vietnam, if Lyndon Johnson had not managed to get the Gulf of Tonkin Resolution adopted and U.S. involvement escalated. The war could have been avoided altogether if Eisenhower had simply allowed free elections in 1956, 20 years before. Had Eisenhower done so, the Vietnamese would undoubtedly have elected Ho Chi Minh president of a combined Vietnam then. That would have saved millions of dollars and spared hundreds of thousands of human lives, Americans and Vietnamese. But that would have taken more than political vision. That would have taken a more realistic worldview than ideological imperatives allowed. It would have taken the perspective of an enlightened person, who could see things the way they really are and acted humanistically. I didn't know that then. I had yet to acquire a fuller understanding of life's essential realities, including the causes of war. That came only when I began studying Buddhism, two years later.

I had little time for such reflection in the spring of 1975; I had too much studying to do for final exams. In May, my first year of law school concluded. My grades were a rude awakening, shocking in their mediocrity. All but one of the first year classes were yearlong courses. In that one half-year class, I had managed to earn a B grade. In May, one additional B would be my highest grade. The other grades were a B-, two were C+ and one a C. The grades were not *terrible,* but I hadn't received a C or even a C+ since high school, back in my lazy and troubled days. It was a blast from the past that I didn't enjoy, especially since my ego had grown so much larger during my four successful undergraduate years. I was not alone in my suffering of course. Most of my fellow students would get over their disappointment, in plenty of time to cultivate the arrogance and intellectual conceit common among lawyers.

While unsettled by the rigor of law school, I remained secure in my own self-constructed religious faith. The Vietnam experience and then Voltaire's savaging of organized religion had convinced me to resist dogma and reject what I viewed as spurious claims of organized religion. Continued observation of the nonsense peddled by self-anointed religious leaders confirmed my conclusion that I should follow my own path of simply trying to do the right thing, working to create a better world. I routinely brushed aside the various proselytizers that typically hit me up on the street or knocked on my door. So it was wholly out of character that I sat still for a twenty-minute spiel about Buddhism soon after school ended. Perhaps I let the person continue because of boredom, as I waited for Liz, off shopping somewhere at Springfield Mall (a large shopping center in Virginia, 20 miles south of Capitol Hill). I listened only half-consciously, paying little attention to a description of some mumbo jumbo I needed to chant in order to be happy and create world peace. The obviously fervent believer invited me to a meeting in Springfield the very next night, to learn more about it. Living on Capital Hill, I saw no point in returning to Springfield for anything of such dubious value. I soon forgot the encounter entirely, at least consciously.

With the first year of law school ended, I made a brief foray into public interest law. During the summer, I volunteered at the Commission for the Advancement of Public Interest Organizations. It was small group, consisting of Claire Nader (a physician and the more famous Ralph's sister), Carl Clark (one of the inventors of the automobile air bag) and a couple other staff members. Sid Wolfe (from Public Citizen Health Research Group—another entity under the Nader umbrella) came around from time to time as well. Liz was not thrilled with my choice. She thought I should be working for pay, particularly since she had to be working at a job she didn't like. So I added a paying job for the bulk of the summer, working as a research assistant. It was a strange job, working with the lawyers at a congressionally mandated study commission with a typically ungainly title: The National Commission for the Review of Federal and State Laws Relating to Wiretapping and Electronic Surveillance. G. Robert Blakey, well-known law professor and drafter of the RICO (Racketeer Influenced and Corrupt Organization) Act, was a member of the Commission and a frequent visitor.

The contrast between the two groups couldn't be starker. The public interest group was a diverse bunch of activists. They ranged from the absent minded professor/pocket protector engineer Carl Clark and the methodical and dedicated Claire to the loopy but good hearted public interest staff there to do the grunt work. The wiretap group members were prosecutors from organized crime strike forces and their groupies, law students like me and people like Blakey. The prosecutors delighted in telling war stories and playing wiretap recordings from their strike force work.

I wasn't thrilled with the idea of using undercover informants and electronic surveillance to eavesdrop on people. While this might be the only successful way to prosecute the mob, I didn't like it and I didn't see it as a career option for me. I couldn't trust the government to spy only on organized crime figures or other real criminals. J. Edgar Hoover and the Nixon administration had made that "perfectly clear" during their time in office. I was relieved to be done with this group at the end of summer.

The summer wasn't all serious. Like me, the upperclassman who led our law club was a big Pink Floyd fan. Before school ended, he got us tickets for a show coming up on June 10, 1975, at the Capital Centre in Landover, Maryland—just outside Washington, DC. We had seats high up on the sides of the arena, but with a great view of all the props Floyd was using as part of the mammoth road show they put on during their 1975 tour. The problem was the stairs. Also like me, my mentor smoked dope. Not surprisingly, for a concert like Pink Floyd, the smoky haze of burning marijuana hung thickly in the air. We were so stoned, that the cascade of stairs seemed perilously steep. I hadn't suffered such spatial distortion since my first time smoking dope in Vietnam. The people nearer the floor appeared the size of ants. The way some of them scurried around on unseen trails, they might well have been ants. I stayed put, avoiding the challenging descent until the concert's conclusion. Finding the right seat was itself a challenge for some and a memorable part of the evening.

"Can I see your ticket please?" the usher, with four other concertgoers in tow, asked the first person in my row.

"Huh?"

"Can I see your ticket please?" he asked again.

"Huh?"

"Can I see your ticket please?"

"Oh, my ticket. Uh, yeah, here." The first guy finally put it together.

"You belong in the next section, over there" said the usher, pointing across the aisle.

"Uh, Ok."

"Can I see your ticket please?" the usher asked the second guy in the row.

"Huh?"

"Can I see your ticket please?"

"Huh?"

"Can I see your ticket please?"

"Oh, yeah, my ticket. Uh here." The second guy got it together.

"You belong in the next section, over there." Said the usher, pointing again across the aisle.

"Can I see your ticket please?" the usher asked the third guy.

At this point, we couldn't take it anymore and fell out laughing, so I didn't hear the rest of this scene. Eventually, the patiently insistent usher penetrated the hemp-induced brain-fog of the foursome next to us, replacing them with some slightly less stoned folks.

In the fall of 1975, the second year of law school began. It was more frustrating than the first, for a number of reasons. Watching lawyers on television or in the movies makes it all look very glamorous and exciting. But the entertainment industry does little justice to the day-to-day workings of the legal profession. By the end of the first year, I had learned to read a fact pattern and deduce what the outcome *should* be when applying applicable law. That was the easy part. That was not what lawyers get paid to do.

What lawyers and law students alike must do is to provide persuasive legal authority for the outcome they believe is correct. That entails researching all sides of a case and supplying citations to other cases to prove your position correct. Analyzing, organizing, synthesizing and summarizing cases or proceedings are what lawyers must do. Closely scrutinizing facts, issues and decisions to determine whether they fit a given precedent or are distinguishable from it, is what lawyers must do. That is essence of the intellectual labor and work product law firms pay their lawyers to provide. Not only did I find this tediously boring, I found it to be very hard work.

In addition to class work, I now had real work as well. As the school suggested, I didn't even attempt a part-time job during the first year at Georgetown. By the second year, our finances demanded that I work. Besides, I needed to pick up more credentials to put on a resume for the future. For most of the second year, I was a research assistant to Professor Victor Kramer. Kramer had been a senior antitrust attorney at the Justice Department and later a senior partner at Arnold and Porter, one of the major DC law firms. He was a very demanding boss, sort of a type-A 65-year-old Napoleon.

"Maberry, come into my office," he would say abruptly, in preparing to issue a work assignment.

"Close the door. Sit down," he would continue, pacing rapidly back and forth within the distance walkable in an eight by ten foot office. He was almost identical in height to Stubby but without the muscles, the mustache or the psychosis. Instructions flowed from his lips machine-gun style, matching his gait.

"You got that?" he always added, a split second after the last word of instruction, in about the same amount of time that elapses after the traffic light turns green before the driver behind you honks the horn.

"Yes."

"Well, why are you still sitting here? Get to work!" He wasn't like that all of the time—just most of the time. *Was this what I had to look forward to, if I became an associate at one of the big law firms?*

Through the spring of 1976, I spent most of my waking hours at Georgetown. If I was not in class, I was in the library studying—including Saturday and Sunday from morning well into the night. If not in class or studying, I was working for Professor Kramer. I was so busy, that if I had any idea what Liz did while I was away, I no longer recall. I do know that we spent some time with friends when I wasn't in the library. I felt mentally saturated at times, intellectually incapable of absorbing any more information. Having learned to "run very fast" by the end of the first year, during the second I felt the need to be able to slow back down. In a variation on the proverbial executive of the 1950's coming home to his martini, I regularly came home to a joint after a hard day and night of law school. With a few puffs of smoke, I would escape to "Corpus Collosum" or one of many other shows on my favorite radio station, WGTB. The station played only progressive rock, what I wanted to hear. During the day, the political radicals staffing the station ran Pacifica news and offered anti-Catholic commentaries that embarrassed the FCC license holder, Georgetown University.

I was only one among many law students of the 1970s getting stoned. I attended one party where the person passing me a joint was reportedly the valedictorian of the American University Law School. Apparently, she and my law club leader managed marijuana and legal studies without difficulty. That was not so true of me. My escapes into the haze of marijuana proved only partially successful and came at a steep price. I could still get into the music moments, but with the consequence of being unable to do further study. If my brain was incapable of legal analysis before getting stoned, it was less so afterwards. By nature a lazy person and a procrastinator, a cannabis induced enhancement was not helpful. Instead of relieving stress, as smoking usually had in the past, it compounded stress by adding on guilt from making the ill-considered choice of escape. It didn't make life with Liz any easier either. High and horny go together. With me high and she not high, it meant for some frustrating nights.

More than marijuana, sex was a psychic salve, for relieving my stress. The climax of sex counted as a victory even if all other daily activities were unsuccessful struggles. Sex refused, for whatever reason, became a double whammy. I felt rejected, compounding my unrelieved school stress. The physical union was a substitute for an emotional bond, the one interpersonal outreach connecting me to the world outside myself. I was still too needy, depending on this act to confirm my self worth.

Continued uncertainty about my future added to the other stresses and frustrations that marked my second year of law school. Many of my fellow students were very secure in their plans. They knew exactly what courses they would be taking this year and the next because they had already decided what type of law they would practice after graduating. I still had no clue what I would do with this legal education I was working so hard to get. So I took a potpourri of environmental, land use and legislative drafting classes in hopes that a compelling interest would develop, ordering my life. Alas, that would not happen this year either. Well, at least I could get a legal job during the summer to earn more money than I did the previous summer and maybe a place to work after graduation.

At the close of the school year, I finished my servitude with Kramer and moved on to clerking at an actual law firm. The firm did administrative law, primarily before the Interstate Commerce Commission (ICC). The job paid reasonably well, but it was hard to get excited about. Which tariff classification applied to a given commodity could mean a difference of six or seven figures in transportation costs to a shipper over the course of a year. The far from thrilling task of researching and writing memoranda on which of the possible classifications should apply, fell to me. I guess the thrill of tariff classifications is gone for everyone now, because Congress abolished the ICC in the 1980s during the wave of economic deregulation that swept across America.

My uncertainty about a future direction, after two years of law school, was becoming a problem for Liz. I had to confess to her that I was less than thrilled with the law firm at which I now worked. I still held out hope that the final year of school would produce a magic bullet of clarity, producing a charmed path through my confused mind. Liz expected that at the conclusion of law school, I would earn a good income. Perhaps she even figured she would no longer have to work. The fact that I even considered low-paying public interest law was bothersome to her. With protests against the war no longer necessary and the Nixon regime ended, it seems she felt that I had paid my dues making noble causes. Now I should be focusing on making money. We had a serious talk about it in early July, 1976.

"I hate it here. I hate working at GHI. I have been supporting you for two years while you went to law school. Now you say you don't know what you want to do. I don't like this apartment. I don't like this town. I'd rather be back in Minneapolis," Said Liz.

"I know. I'm sorry, but law school isn't what I expected. I thought I could just learn how to practice law and then it would become obvious what I should be doing. It just hasn't happened yet."

"Other people seem to know what they're going to do. Why can't you figure it out?"

"You know I'm not like a lot of them, especially the ones that work for the fat cats. Criminal law, from either side is too ugly. I thought public interest or environmental law would fit me but it doesn't pay shit. Besides that, most of the people who work in public interest law are just as arrogant or conceited as the people working for the corporations are. The whole legal profession is full of people that are *assholes* and I don't want to become one. I don't want to be somebody's hired asshole."

"I understand that, but what are you going to do with yourself? You've had four years of college and now two years of law school. It's time you start figuring out what you're going to do."

"I know. I'm trying my best but it's just not coming together. I don't really know. I want to do something I believe in, something that needs doing. I spent three years in the Army doing busy work. I want to do something that's right for me and for some good purpose. I wouldn't mind working for the FTC or some of the other federal agencies. But now I'm finding out that they have these regional quotas that put me at a disadvantage because we're living here."

"Well, can't you apply anyway?"

"Yes, but last year they had 1,200 applications for 60 jobs at the Federal Trade Commission. It's harder getting a job there than it was getting into Georgetown. I'm probably in the top third of my Georgetown class, but that's not even good enough to get an interview there."

"Whatever. You think about it. I want to go home and visit my parents for a while. I have vacation time."

"OK. You know I need to stay here and work. They won't let me off and even if they did, we couldn't afford it."

"Sure. That's all right."

A few days before Liz left for Minneapolis, the engine in the van gave out. We weren't supposed to *have* the van anymore. The plan had been to sell it after we got here. We were supposed to replace it with something newer and more reliable, not to mention more comfortable. But we weren't exactly rolling in money so I hadn't sold it. When it broke down, I had it towed to a service station. Stressed out, freaked out or just trying to be happy, I foolishly smoked a joint while considering what to do about the van.

The shop told me they could put in a rebuilt engine for $900. We had paid $600 for the van two years before. Paying $900 to put in an engine should have seemed obviously idiotic. But we didn't have much more cash than that to buy something to replace it. Since the rest of the van was a known entity, there was a modicum of sense to go ahead and have the engine put in, but only a modicum—*a dumb, dope-enhanced modicum.* This decision probably was the straw broke the camel's back, pushing Liz away. She was furious when I told her.

"You spent *$900* to fix that stupid van! How could you spend that kind of money on that damn van? . . . . It's 'cause you were *stoned* wasn't it?"

"Well, yeah, I mean I did get high. I was waiting for them to fix the damn thing. I had this book I was reading. I just needed to relax. I was stressed out. . ."

"You can't just go through life in a haze of smoke. You gotta … It's crazy. We didn't have that kinda money to spend on that stupid van! I hate that damn thing. I know we needed it to move out here, but we don't need it anymore. We need a car, not an old telephone company van. You only paid $600 for the thing. Now you paid $900 to put an engine in it? It doesn't make any damn sense!"

Liz went on to Minnesota, leaving me to put my time in at the law firm and listen to "Corpus Collosum" in the nighttime. In August, Liz called from Minneapolis to announce a change of plans.

"I'm coming back to town next week."

"Great."

"You probably won't think so after I tell you the rest of it."

"What do you mean?"

"I'm going to move in with Barbara temporarily, until I can find a place of my own."

I probably should have seen it coming. Maybe all the work of law school kept my mind too occupied to notice. Maybe it was the dope occluding my senses. Or maybe it was just a man's cluelessness of how his wife sees his shortcomings. After her return, we talked again on the phone. I clung to the hope that she would change her mind, but she apparently had done all the thinking about the relationship she cared to. In her mind, it was over. She allowed me to visit her at her coworker Barbara's apartment a couple of times but it was far from reassuring. I was there visiting her, a month or so after she had returned from Minneapolis, when she took a call from another guy. I don't recall what she said, only how she said it. She spoke in dulcet tones, that intimate voice she had reserved for my ears alone during the five years before then. Despite having been through it before, it amazed me how quickly a woman's heart could turn stone cold toward a man she had loved, and just as quickly warm to another. Like flipping a switch—love on, love off. I drove home shaking, as if an icy vise were squeezing the breath from my chest.

With Liz gone, I couldn't afford the basement rental on Livingston Street in northwest DC. When the lease expired in October, I moved to a tiny furnished efficiency on North Scott Street in Rosslyn, Virginia, which I shared with the resident roaches. Rosslyn is a neighborhood in Arlington County, just across the Potomac River from Georgetown via Key Bridge on the north and from the Kennedy Center and Constitution Avenue on the east via the Theodore Roosevelt Bridge. From there I could walk to the Rosslyn Metro station for a quick subway trip to school and work. I had been used to humble abodes during my student years, but this one brought back my not-so-fond memories of the dump I briefly shared with my brother Doug in Minneapolis. Perhaps this was something like getting to the part of the movie where I came in. Doug had been present for my aborted suicide attempt at that Minneapolis apartment. His willingness to sleep in the walk-in closet there enabled the start-up of my relationship with Liz. Now that relationship was ending.

Another call from Minneapolis came early next year, signaling another ending. The phone's insistent ring woke me from a sound sleep. The call came around 2:00 a.m., January 18, 1977. "This is the Hennepin County Medical Examiner's Office. Am I speaking to John Maberry?"

"Yes," I said, adrenaline-laced dread quickly clearing my head.

"Are you related to Douglas R. Maberry?"

"Oh no! Yes, he's my brother," my dread nearly confirmed.

"We found your name and number in his wallet. I'm sorry you have to hear it this way, but your brother has passed away."

"What happened?"

"He appears to have suffered a heart attack. We'll be conducting an autopsy to confirm the cause of death. Will you be making funeral arrangements?"

"Yes, I'll get there as soon as I can."

"All right. Just tell the funeral home to call us. They know what to do. Again, I'm sorry to give you this bad news."

Sleep came back slowly that night. Another death, so many deaths, deaths of people and relationships marched in a funeral parade through my head. My marriage to Liz came first in the procession. The near-fatal fling with Jill followed close behind Liz. Then came Gloria, from a marriage long gone. Even the deaths of my mother and father, who remained only as dim images, pained me that night.

I called my other brother Bill, who now lived in Miami, to give him the news. Bill and Lorraine had moved to Florida when Bill became pharmaceuticals manager for Dow Chemical's Latin America accounts. I didn't reach Bill, I awakened Lorraine instead. She told me Bill was in South America, so he wouldn't be coming to the funeral. Lorraine would not be attending either, since she still had small children to take care of. I waited until morning to call Liz with the sad news. She expressed her condolences but declined to travel back to Minneapolis with me for the funeral. Besides me, only some aunts, some uncles, and a few friends of Doug would attend the funeral.

By the time I got to Minneapolis, the autopsy was complete. The report confirmed atherosclerosis, as well as cirrhosis of the liver, which was no surprise after 25 years of alcoholism. Doug had succeeded at a slow suicide where I had failed at a quick one. He was just 3 months past 48 when he died, 4 months younger than our father had been when cancer ended his life. I made all the arrangements: writing the newspaper obituary, pulling our mother's minister away from his administrative duties back into active ministry to deliver a eulogy and setting up the military burial at Ft. Snelling National Cemetery. As little regard as I had for the military, Doug had been a lifetime member of the DAV, so I expected this to be what he would have wanted.

Liz called a few days after I returned to Rosslyn.

"My mother said I should go back to you—that at a time like this you really need me," Liz told me, with no discernable tone of agreement in her voice.

"So, should I start looking for a larger apartment then?" I replied, tongue-in-cheek.

"No, I don't think so," she laughed, "it's over. I'm not getting back together with you just because your brother died. I'm sorry about him, but that doesn't change anything."

"You're right. I didn't expect it would."

I had changed my feelings about Doug by then. He had come out to visit Liz and me once, after we went to DC for law school. He was proud of me, proud that I had made it all the way to law school. I could find no way to say I was sorry how I had hated him before—for his weakness at escaping into the bottle and his other shortcomings. Still I think he realized and recognized my change of heart. During his last year of life, he had cut back some on the alcohol. He had tried to quit before, having had periods of sobriety as long as 18 months. This time it was the influence of a long lost love, a girl friend he had been involved with during his college days. She had happened to come back into his life the year before, 20 years after they were last together. It was good that he had a little love and joy in his final year. I wish his or my timing had been just a little better, so that I could have learned of and told him about Nam-myoho-renge-kyo before his death.

Back to the Future

Chapter 17—A Seed Sprouts

FROM DEATH COMES LIFE. TWO weeks after returning from Doug's funeral, I attended a party. It was like most parties. People were standing around with a drink in one hand, a cigarette in the other, holding forth inanely on topics of little or no consequence. The more intoxicated they got, the more animated (but no more meaningful) the conversation became. *Borrrrrrinnng.* It was Lorna's party. She was a legal secretary, at the law firm where I clerked. I wasn't obliged to go, from the self-interest perspective, as would have been the case if the invitation had come from one of the law firm's partners. I went anyway. How could I turn down free food and booze? It was fortunate that I did. I met Leslie there, a member of Lorna's carpool. They all commuted from Virginia to the K Street business district in DC.

Amidst the dull peoplescape of the party, Leslie sparkled like a mirrored ball above a dance floor. *Who is that person? Why is she so alive, so different from the rest?* I had to talk to her. I asked what it was about her that accounted for her obviously higher state of being than the rest of the partygoers. She explained that she was a Buddhist and she chanted.

"Oh, what do you chant—Nam-myoho-renge-kyo?" I asked.

"Yes! How did you know that?"

"Somebody told me about it two years ago at Springfield Mall. They invited me to a meeting but I didn't go. When you said you were a Buddhist and chanted, it just popped into my head."

"Do you remember who it was?"

"No."

"Well, they planted a seed. Once you hear it, you never forget it."

A seed may have been planted, but in 1975, the ground surrounding and supporting my life was compacted too hard for it to sprout. That was before I had pursued another year and a half of law school without realizing I still didn't know where I was going. That was before Liz split. Now, with less than a semester to go until the end of law school, Leslie would bring sun and rain to fertile soil. Widening cracks in my self-confidence ran in all directions after Liz left. Until then, I had reassured myself that once I learned enough, my path in life would become obvious. I would know what to do to make the world a better place. But it hadn't worked out that way. Socrates said, "The unexamined life is not worth living." He might have added that the *over-examined* life could be very frustrating in its complications and unresolved questions. Perhaps that didn't occur to him. I had to be sure, whatever I did, because if I had learned anything from all of the corruption and wrongdoing in the 1960s and 1970s, doing the right thing was most important. And I couldn't be sure. Despite the fact that my ego told me I could do anything, my inability to decide what to do had me stuck in place like an insect in amber. Indecision had paralyzed me. I needed something, anything that would enable me to move forward, decisively. I hadn't gone to the party looking for that something, at least not consciously, but I found it anyway.

Leslie and I hit it off right from the start in my soon-to-be-well-lubricated state. Although I didn't know it at the time, what I perceived was the life-condition of a Buddha. I had no interest in talking further with any of the other partygoers. Compared to Leslie, they were semi-somnambulant. She wound up in my lap, where we blissfully exchanged kisses, heedless of the party continuing around but apart from us. The experience was nothing like what I supposed an orthodox introduction to Buddhism *should be*, but it was an effective one nonetheless. At the conclusion of the evening, in my intoxicated state, I couldn't find a pen and paper to write down her phone number.

"I'll remember your number," I said, repeating it several times to ensure success.

"I'll remember your kisses," she replied, with a happy smile promising more.

It could only have been through a concerted act of will that I did remember the number. I called her the next day. I had to know why she had such a self-confident zest for life. More importantly, I had to know how I could get one. Recognizing my intellectual bent, Leslie gave me a thick book to read the very next time we were together, *The Toynbee-Ikeda Dialogue*. The book was a compilation of an extensive discussion between the noted historian Arnold Toynbee and Daisaku Ikeda, the leader of an international Buddhist lay organization (the Soka Gakkai). I read it quickly, ravenously. Three things running through the dialogue impressed me: pragmatism, humanism and hope.

Ikeda's Buddhist perspective offered a different worldview than the Western philosophical tradition I had studied in college. He asserted a duality of self and environment that agreed well with the ecology movement that had flourished in the 1970s. He asserted a duality of mind and body that made sense. Underlying all else, he had a great respect for life, human and otherwise. Integrating and synthesizing values I shared, Ikeda's worldview offered holistic explanations and solutions to the issues of war, racism, pollution and poverty. Even the name of the organization he led, the Soka Gakkai, translated into English meant value creation. That was what I wanted to do, create value. It was what I had always wanted to do, even as a spoiled and troubled child, I just could not focus on that back then.

Ikeda argued that solving issues like war and poverty required achieving a more humanistic world, a world in which people shared a fundamental respect for life. That made sense to me, but changing so many hearts and minds seemed a nearly impossible task. He didn't think this impossible. He was not merely hopeful but actually confident it could be done. Despite my doubts, I wanted to hear more.

My college education confirmed the common knowledge that, over thousands of years of so-called civilization, people around the world have fought and killed each other. Political systems of all sorts have come and gone without making a lasting impact on civilization, stopping bloodshed or ensuring the wealth and happiness of their populace. Economic systems promised financial fairness to all and fell far short of the mark. America, champion of democracy, allied itself with despots when it suited our economic or political interest. Perhaps America has been better than the rest, but we've still had great difficulty reaching, not to mention maintaining, the noble and virtuous nation our founding fathers described. For some, there is no hope on Earth; they await the rapture. Ikeda said Buddhism promised better things here and now. I had concluded that a solution to the world's problems lay not in devising an effective system, but in reforming the behavior of people. That is what Ikeda was saying as well. *But would Buddhism really do that any better than the other systems of religious belief, politics or economics?*

Leslie took me to discussion meetings, held in people's homes, to see the practical application of Buddhist concepts in day-to-day life. There seemed to be something of a disconnect between the rich philosophical discussion of issues facing humanity around the globe and the discussion taking place at these meetings. The personal experiences that people related about their Buddhist practice didn't concern changing the world. What they talked about was overcoming personal difficulties. They attributed success in doing so to the strange practice of chanting. Leslie's fellow Buddhists rapidly recited unintelligible phrases from a liturgy book (portions of the Lotus Sutra, I was told) and then repeatedly chanted the words "Nam-myoho-renge-kyo." That was the mumbo jumbo the person had told me about in Springfield Mall, that Leslie's presence had brought back into my consciousness. They called the entire ceremony gongyo, which translated into English means "assiduous prayer." If not attending a meeting of fellow Buddhists, each of the members performed the gongyo ritual twice daily in their own homes, once in the morning and once in the evening. Together, the two observances could take as much as an hour, or even more if the practitioner felt the need to chant more. That seemed as much arduous as assiduous to me.

The people in attendance at the meetings were happily earnest, very hopeful and manifestly sincere in their belief, that the Buddhist practice was enabling them to overcome their problems and attain their goals. I found it quite difficult at first, to fathom how the chanting of strange syllables to a scroll with Chinese characters could accomplish the beneficial results the people claimed. Nor was it apparent how achieving personal goals would make the world a more humanistic place. Since the people all seemed so happy and sincere, I kept my doubts to myself and asked only simple questions lest I burst any misplaced bubbles of optimism these people had. Hah.

"This scroll is called a Gohonzon. *Go* is an honorific prefix that means great and *honzon* means object of devotion," explained Jeff Kaye, a local leader in the Buddhist organization.

"Down the center, in Chinese characters (except for the Sanskrit character *Nam*) is written Nam-myoho-renge-kyo followed by Nichiren. This mandala was first inscribed by Nichiren Daishonin, a Buddhist scholar and priest living in Japan," Jeff went on to explain.

"So what does all that mean? What does chanting the words have to do with changing your life?" I asked.

"Good question. Let's start with the first part. Nam-myoho-renge-kyo is the ultimate law of the universe. We chant this mantra to fuse our lives with the Gohonzon and attain enlightenment. Dick, can you explain Nam-myoho-renge-kyo?" Jeff replied.

"Uh, sure. Nam means devotion. Myoho is the mystic law of life and death. Renge is the Japanese name for the lotus flower, and symbolizes the simultaneity of cause and effect. Kyo is sound or teaching. So chanting Nam-myoho-renge-kyo means we are devoting ourselves to the mystic law of cause and effect." Dick said.

"Great, Dick. Myoho-renge-kyo is also the Japanese name for the Lotus Sutra, the highest teaching of Buddhism revealed by the historical Buddha, Shakyamuni or Siddhartha," Jeff added.

"But what does that have to do with enlightenment, or changing your life?" I persisted.

"I was just getting to that," Jeff quickly added. "When Shakyamuni preached the Lotus Sutra 2,500 years ago, he predicted that in the future, the faith and practices he was teaching then, would lose value. At that time, a time called the Latter Day, another Buddha would come along to reveal the teaching that would be of use from that time on. Nichiren Daishonin is that Buddha. Nichiren taught that reciting the name of the Lotus Sutra would be the essential practice for the Latter Day. He also explained that we all equally possess the nature of the Buddha and myoho-renge-kyo. By chanting to the Gohonzon, we bring forth our Buddha nature, attain enlightenment and can reduce or eradicate our negative karma."

Oh sure, I thought. I had taken plenty of philosophy classes in college, but none on Eastern philosophy in general or Buddhism in particular, so this was all new to me. Although I had done many other strange things during college, this was like nothing I had ever done or encountered before. I had read plenty of self-improvement books. I had read Carlos Castaneda and thought he was cool, but never was tempted to try his vision of Yaqui sorcery. Then again, these people weren't suggesting I ingest any hallucinogenic drugs, just do the chant. And none of those other books with intriguing beliefs had provided a simple methodology to actualize their purported benefits. I was far from convinced that the practice of chanting to a scroll had any functional benefit or purpose, yet I couldn't see any harm in it. Unless Leslie and her friends were totally crazy, which they did not seem to be, their confidence inspired me. If chanting strange words could give me the power I needed to get my life moving, then I would at least give it a try.

Odd as the chanting might be, it got me moving way more rapidly than I had any reason to expect. The end of law school loomed ahead. A maze of conflicting emotions toward Liz pulled me this way and that. Soon I was back at the proverbial square on the chessboard with Alice and the Red Queen, brought there by a confluence of events in February 1977. This time, however, I was looking at them over my shoulder as I raced on by. I was running very fast indeed, certain of getting not somewhere but exactly where I needed to go. Encountering the vibrant Leslie and the life-affirming powers of Buddhism put rockets on my feet.

I was on the phone or out at all hours of the day or night with Leslie. She had something I wanted—her mind, her power, her discipline and self-control. I wanted her body too, but I couldn't have it. She was trying to remain *objective* about the decision she had to make—would she be marrying this other guy or not. That didn't keep us from getting very intense or me from trying for more.

At the same time, despite our separation and ended relationship, there were meetings and conversations with Liz. I had recovered from the shock of the separation and the pain of hearing the voice of intimacy she used with another man so quickly after she left me. I suggested that we attempt to be friends—after all, we had several years of shared times together that to me held value. Liz was suspicious that it was a ploy to get her back and resisted affirming any such proposals. Nonetheless, since she had no car and didn't even know how to drive, whenever she needed transportation she called on me. So either we were friends of a sort, or she was using me; sometimes I thought it was one and sometimes the other.

For reasons that escape me now, I kept notes of my busy social life on a small calendar during the first few months of 1977. The notes show me on the phone or out with Leslie several days a week for much of February and March. In between, I spent time on Liz. At the same time, the final semester of law school wore on. I had a major research paper to write in family law class. I also had motions to write and arguments to present in a practice course, a class intended to prepare the law school graduate to navigate the shoals of courtroom protocol and procedure.

If this wasn't enough to keep me busy, buoyed by the hope and confidence of the Buddhists I had met, I took on the additional challenge of a creative writing class. It was an adult/community education course offered at the Department of Agriculture building on Independence Avenue in Washington, DC. With the end of law school near, I thought I should get a head start in reclaiming my writing dream. By now, it had become quite specific. It would be a book about Vietnam. It would incorporate typical literary themes, such as rites of passage, loss of innocence and man's inhumanity to man. The overall focus, of course, would be the evils of the Vietnam War and the betrayals of the American public by their leaders.

It wasn't just because of jargon or legal terminology that there had to be a movement to write contracts and other documents in "Plain English." Compound, complex, dependent phrases and clauses were the norm, not the exception. Three years of legal writing had profoundly damaged my ability to write simple narrative sentences or supply imagery. I really needed a writing class if I hoped to reach any readers. But I couldn't finish the writing course that spring. The demands of law school and of Liz and Leslie were too much. Besides, as I would come to learn, it really wasn't the right time yet. All the events were still too close in time, too fresh in mind. More to the point, there were still experiences I needed to have that hadn't happened yet. Meaning and purpose needed more time to reveal themselves.

In addition to the calendar annotations, for the only time in my life (a sad confession for a would-be writer, that), I was keeping nearly daily notes on the events of the day. Or perhaps more accurately, I should say the introspection of the day. I deposited the thoughts and realizations racing through my head onto my trusty legal pad.

2/28/77—Can two people ever really feel the same way about one another—see the relationship identically? Of course not! As individuals, they each see and feel not just with a sense of now before them but with the instruction of what has gone before. Yet it is the task to make the unique entity that is the confluence of two identities capable of comprehension and communication. To create a common language, a common vision; yet to bring forth the new, to share of the product from the individuals.

And—

Is it really a change in the color of your perceptual lens from gray to rose?

3/1/77—The big news: Leslie cannot handle more than a casual friendship because she must be able to clarify her relationship with Michael. She thinks it won't turn out in the end but she wants to be objective. She feels she owes him that much respect.

The name of the game between us is now called honesty. Also no sex.

3/2/77—What a curious state of affairs; I love two women yet may have sex with neither! But I'll settle for two birds in the bush in the absence of one in the hand.

And—

It is truly exhilarating to perceive the prospect of finally leaving the womb and entering the world. A rite of passage nears and it inducts the spirit of joy into the coming challenge. Change will be abounding; in change there is growth.

3/20/77—Think not what the universe can do for you (but do appreciate what it does) but what you can do for it. (Maybe that is why I have residual good feelings after I have been busy doing other-directed acts rather than when I have just been satisfying my self).

3/24/77—Here I tell Liz I think I am going to give up on dope for awhile and then I go ahead and buy another ounce rather than leaving [a friend] hanging after he gratuitously bought some for me when getting some for himself. I have to cut back on it even if it's in my possession. How? Maybe chanting will do it.

Actually, chanting did do it. A neighbor, with whom I had often exchanged grass, was very impressed with the power of Buddhism when I declined his offer to get high, explaining to him that I needed to be straight to emcee a discussion meeting. What a change had come over me, to have so much concern and a sense of responsibility. I had made progress since the time I had spent $900 to replace the motor in the old green telephone van.

By now, I had realized that Liz made the right decision when she didn't return to our moribund marriage the previous fall and I didn't resent her imposing on me for transportation. Actually, I enjoyed her company again. I briefly entertained the notion that reconciliation might be possible between us, despite my designs on Leslie. Liz knew all about those designs.

After attending a Buddhist study meeting with Leslie on March 31, we stopped for drinks at Coco's, a bar on Columbia Pike in Arlington. The next night, I went with Liz to a Fools Party. *How apropos.* There were no singles at the party. It was all couples, whose common thread was wives working the same place as Liz. While there, Liz made a remark of some sort to which I jokingly said, "You can be replaced."

"I already have, by Leslie," she retorted.

The following night, as typical as it had become, Leslie called me at 1:30 a.m. and we stayed on the phone until 3:30.

In between time spent on Leslie and Liz, school, clerking 20 hours a week at the law firm and the odd hours devoted to sleep, I managed to continue going to Buddhist meetings. Despite its foreign philosophical flavor, I was surprised to see how familiar Buddhism's concept of cause and effect seemed to me. Driving in Minnesota winters many years before, I had learned and accepted the unstated principle that one should always stop and help another motorist whose car got stuck in a snow bank. As I learned more about Buddhism, it became apparent why this happened. While this might appear to be a simple matter of being a Good Samaritan, it's really more than that. It's part of the interrelationship of self and others. It's an example of cause and effect, of karma at work at the simplest level.

Buddhism says the effects we see in life come from the causes we make. In a person's life, the aggregate of cause and effect is karma. While nobody I know in Minnesota ever called it karma or cause and effect, their understanding of why you need to stop and help the other guy stuck in a snow bank illustrates their belief in it. This action (cause) is a deposit in the bank of goodwill (karma) essential to ensuring a similar result (effect) when one's own car becomes stuck (almost inevitable in snowy environs). A bit oversimplified, but that is the general principle.

Since the people I met while attending Buddhist meetings seemed so sincere and otherwise not self-righteous, I continued to resist asking any questions that I thought might pop any bubbles of misplaced faith they had. I hoped I would not be too obviously condescending in my intellectual conceit. Their beliefs were a lot to swallow, that simply by reciting a portion of the Lotus Sutra and chanting the words Nam-myoho-renge-kyo to the scroll, the potential Buddha within becomes actual. Not only that, but by changing myself, I could change the world. The world of Buddhists definitely seemed different from the rest. I attended a few larger meetings of the organization at a community center on Eastern Avenue, a street dividing Washington, DC from Maryland. The people in attendance were the most diverse group of worshippers I had ever seen. There were people of virtually every race or ethnic background, from teenagers through senior citizens, from poor to moderately well-off and gay as well as straight. Despite obvious differences, no one looked askance at anyone else. They greeted each other warmly, with genuine friendship. So maybe they could change the world. I kept studying more of the material supplied by the members and attending meetings, although I wasn't ready to accept it wholeheartedly.

I was quite comfortable with applying Sly Stone's lyrical expression of relativism, "different strokes for different folks," to religious belief and practice. So I wasn't too troubled as much as I was dubious about their claim that this form of the religion was the *true* Buddhism which needed to be practiced during the times in which we lived and indeed, the only way to truly attain enlightenment. Buddhism, like Christianity, has an abundance of sects—many of which claim an inside track on the truth. Having now become interested in Buddhism, how did I know that this particular form or practice of Buddhism was better than any other was?

Like the long-term student I was, I embarked on my own research about Buddhism at the main campus of Georgetown University. As a Jesuit-run institution, I expected Georgetown would have an extensive library on religions of the world. I was not disappointed, finding a vast quantity of books on the various sects of Buddhism. I soon realized that this would be an epistemological task requiring more time than I could reasonably afford to devote. I explained my predicament, cautiously, to one of the persons I met at a Buddhist meeting. He explained that there were three types of proof of a religion: theoretical, documentary and actual. Of those three, actual proof was most important. He offered this shaggy dog story-like example:

"A man comes into a room, where he sees this other man rotating his arm in the air as if turning an imaginary crank. As he extends his other hand out, palm up and underneath the other moving hand, dollar bills begin dropping onto his palm. 'Wow, that's a great trick. How did you do that?' The observer asks.

'Oh, it's no trick. Anybody can do it, you just turn the crank on the money machine and the bills drop in your hand,' the man replied.

'Oh sure,' the skeptical observer snorts.

'No, really,' the money man says, walking out the door. After he is gone, the puzzled observer looks around to make sure no one else is looking, before holding out his hand and beginning to turn the imaginary crank."

"Beginning to practice Buddhism is like that, accepting on faith that something will work despite the appearance of a magic trick. But getting benefit from the practice of Buddhism is not magic or a parlor trick. Chanting to the Gohonzon is connecting your life with the fundamental law of cause and effect, resonating throughout the universe. Gravity is not a trick. Throw a ball in the air and it comes down. You try this practice and see if it works. If it doesn't, you will soon stop, regardless of what you learn in the library." I was already seeing the benefit of the practice, from the initial efforts I had made. Yet I continued to procrastinate about accepting the Gohonzon, the formal name for the scroll. That would be a decision fully committing to this religion, a decision that I wasn't quite ready to make.

Meanwhile, I proceeded toward the end of law school riding the crest of one very high wave after another on my metaphorical surfboard. I pressed to complete papers and crammed for exams, while alternating evenings of calls or visits with Leslie and Liz. While challenging and frustrating at times, this period in my life was mostly exhilarating. On April 23, I went with Liz to see *Annie Hall*. In Buddhism, I would learn, there is no such thing as coincidence.

On May 29, 1977, Georgetown awarded my Juris Doctor degree. Liz insisted I invite her to the ceremonies. She said she had it coming. After all, she had contributed financially and emotionally for *most* of the way to the completion of law school. Besides, she didn't want to miss the splendor. Georgetown being the kind of institution it was, the ceremonies and reception would not be humdrum. Law school graduates didn't wear mortarboards. Instead, they wore velvet caps like those worn to court in the Renaissance period. They served champagne and balled melons on the Healy lawn, a cut above my college graduation. Afterwards, we had a relaxed dinner at the Magic Pan Créperie, reprising the ending scene from *Annie Hall*. As Diane Keaton [Annie Hall] departs, Woody Allen so oddly but aptly concludes with, "Guy goes in to see his psychiatrist and says, 'Doc, my brother's crazy. He thinks he's a chicken.'

'Why don't you turn him in?' The psychiatrist asks.

'I would, but we need the eggs.' I guess that's pretty much how I feel about relationships—they're totally irrational and absurd but we keep going through it because most of us need the eggs."

It became clear that there would be no reconciliation with Liz. I was all right with that, but like Woody's character, I still needed the eggs. It would be a little while before I went looking for any. When I did, it would be with a different intent and a sharper eye.

With graduation over, studying for the bar exam started almost immediately. I had crammed an enormous amount of information into my brain over the course of three years of study. Having invested that much time, I invested an additional six weeks and a few hundred dollars more to take a bar review course. To do otherwise would be foolhardy at best. The Virginia Bar exam would be in Roanoke on July 26th and 27 th; a two-day test of three years worth of education. Four weeks into the review, I was getting nervous. Can I remember all this stuff? Can I pass?

Doubt, desperation and my innate pragmatism exerted a pull on me. Even without the Gohonzon, I had been able to stay on top of the waves of work during the last five months instead of being crushed into the sand under the heavy surf breaking over me. I didn't have the luxury of becoming a student of comparative religion. I needed to make a decision now. So I accepted the Gohonzon on July 17, 1977. With the help of my Buddhist prayer and determination to "remember the answers to the questions asked" on the bar exam, I passed it on the first try.

I still needed a job. I wasn't *too* disappointed to find out that the firm I had been clerking for was unable to offer me an associate position. They said there was not enough work to justify hiring another attorney. They were kind enough to try and get me connected with something else, like working as a staff attorney at the Montana Public Utilities Commission (PUC). Whew, that would have been a change of pace, going from Arlington, Virginia to Helena, Montana. The PUC flew me out for an interview. I hobbled onto the plane in crutches, having sprained an ankle playing softball a couple days before the flight. It was an inauspicious way to start an interview, feeling like a klutz on crutches, but it did break the ice. It didn't break enough ice, though, since they didn't offer me the job. I probably wasn't cut out to be a Big Sky cowboy attorney anyway.

I didn't make the cut at the Federal Trade Commission either. Nor at any other federal agencies that interested me. Jobs in public interest law paid too poorly, if at all, and were equally difficult to land. Ralph Nader's Public Citizen Organization, for example, offered graduating law students a starting salary of $8,000 in 1977. That's how much the Post Office paid me for sorting mail seven years earlier, when I only had a high school education. After four years of college and three years of law school, I *couldn't* take a job at that salary. Having lived in poverty for so many years, a desire to earn at least a modestly secure income outweighed my desire to do good. With no offers of employment in sight, I thoroughly explored the potential of solo practice, the proverbial "hanging out the shingle."

A healthy wad of startup capital would have been helpful for setting up my own legal practice, but I had no stack of cash. A wife to bring in the bacon for the short run would have been helpful too, but I didn't have one of those anymore either. Solo practice would be a tough nut to crack. Still, the author of *How to Start a Solo Practice Without Missing a Meal* assured the novice lawyer that it could be done. I kept the option alive, even discussing with a Small Business Administration official whether starting up a solo practice law firm would qualify for a small business loan. But I had reservations about the whole idea. Although passing the bar exam was my immediate motive in fully committing to the practice of Buddhism, the core purpose was to overcome indecision and procrastination. I had not succeeded yet in that challenge.

In between efforts to find a job, create a job and to escape from the impending financial pressure of not having a job, I happened to read an article in a Buddhist publication that described the author's experience working for John Crystal. Crystal coauthored, with Nelson Bolles, a book called *Where Do I Go From Here With My Life.* Bolles is better known for writing *What Color is Your Parachute.* These books were just what I needed at this point, providing a road map for self-inventory. How strange, after all this time to find a tool like this when looking at a Buddhist publication. But I would need an income while going down this path of discovery and I did not have one. Not only had the admin law firm I had worked for not offered me an associate position, they told me they didn't need my services as a clerk anymore either. They objected to my request for unemployment compensation, but the District of Columbia granted it to me anyway.

Having that check coming in allowed me to devote the time I needed, or most of it anyway, to deciding what next to do. Buddhism confirmed my quest to do the right thing. I had to have a means of income, but it had to entail creating value, acting ethically and humanistically. I didn't care so much WHAT I did but HOW I did it. Of course, that was the essential problem; I did need to focus on *something* specific. I had already invested seven years in this quest, taking a little more time to integrate my newfound Buddhist perspective with the Bolles/Crystal methodology seemed time well spent. At least the time would be well spent if I weren't just kidding myself, making another excuse for continuing my bad habit of procrastinating.

So, what *should* I do with the rest of my life? Lots of interests, lots of objectives appeared over the next several months. Perhaps I could write political satire, legal commentary for laypersons or fiction. Yes, I could do that, but not without a financial backup, that day-job Clifford Simak assured me most writers needed in order to live comfortably or at least survive. Could I work at reforming the political/regulatory morass? Well, maybe I could, but not right now. There were no current openings for short-resumé reformers.

Why not teach legal topics to undergraduates considering a career in law? I could do that, as an adjunct professor, but that too would likely require experiential credentials in the work world first before any school would hire me. Not to mention that there were a glut of such people in the Washington, DC metropolitan area who already had such credentials.

In the end, it came down to a choice between making a solo legal practice work somehow, or being in the consumer protection field—even if it had to be in a non-legal capacity. One didn't have to be a lawyer to be involved in consumer protection, at the state or local level. Almost everyone working at the Federal Trade Commission in consumer protection was an attorney, of course. I would have liked to work there, but I couldn't even get an interview. When my unemployment compensation ran out in February, nothing had panned out at all. Thereafter, I made do on short-term stints at the law school proctoring exams, a few legal tasks for friends at little or no cost and even using the old telephone van to haul things for a few friends. It wasn't bringing in much money. Along with food and rent, payments on my loans for college and law school would be starting soon. I had to decide.

How could I even consider a non-legal job? After three years of my time, money and the mental challenges spent on law school, how could I now give it up? I had even passed the bar exam. But I wondered whether I was up for the financial struggle of solo practice. I wondered whether I could find enough ways to make a difference in the world working alone. Laws don't change people's hearts or minds, they just provide the means to settle disputes, enforce agreements or resolve grievances. If everybody behaved virtuously, there wouldn't be a need for so many laws. But that would be a long time coming. I talked about it with one of local leaders in the Buddhist organization. He encouraged me, "chant to make the right decision. Once you've made the decision, keep chanting to make it correct." Seemed tautological, but it worked, eventually.

Working in consumer protection or consumer education was not what I expected to be doing when I first began my academic quest. Somehow, doing this made sense, though. I had progressed from the dirty deeds of selling encyclopedias door-to-door through completing a curriculum for consumer education in Minneapolis. From there it was on to law school to learn federal consumer protection first hand from the former head of the Bureau of Consumer Protection at the FTC. Protecting or educating consumers wouldn't dramatically change the world or open people's minds, but it seemed to be a good first step for me to take at this time. There were plenty of crooks and scoundrels willing and able to take advantage of those who could least afford it. Preventing that abuse would satisfy my goal of a job creating value and of doing the right thing. It was not the only alternative, just the first step, on the way to a final destination.

Meanwhile, Liz and soon Leslie too were out of the romantic picture. It seemed that a break from serious relationships was past due. With a nearly fatal affair bracketed by two failed marriages, I knew I needed to be more careful. I needed to forget about trying to get somebody in bed and forget about getting in her head. I had been chasing intimacy as a substitute for happiness, through someone else. I had been worshipping the womb, insistent on a communion of souls through the offerings I left there. I needed to find happiness first within myself. Then I could share my happiness with someone else rather than expecting that someone to supply it to me. The wisdom of the Buddha was coming through. Buddhism had returned to me, control over my own life. My future was up to me. I would no longer be reliant on somebody else to make me happy, to confirm my self-worth.

What should a successful relationship look like? What could I offer to someone else? What did I want from them? In a very relaxed frame of mind, I set out to find out. I went on dates with perhaps a dozen women over the next 12 months. I went to bed with none of them. I just enjoyed conversation and company for a while. It's amazing how far a little self-confidence and no ulterior motives will take you in getting dates!

Finally, the job seeking strategy was bearing fruit. In April 1978, I had a wonderful interview for a job with Fairfax County, Virginia's Department of Consumer Affairs. At least I thought it was wonderful. I answered their questions well. My qualifications matched their requirements. But I failed to get the job. They told me they would keep me in mind for future jobs. *Yeah, right,* I thought.

In early June, in fact, they did call me in for another interview. This job paid 25% more than the one I didn't get in April. I had an even better interview for this one. Still, my time and money were running out. At the end of the month, I had enough money to pay just half of the July rent on my apartment. Having heard nothing about a decision on the job, I paid 50% of the rent due, leaving my bank balance at $2 and some odd cents. I told the resident manager to take the rest of the rent out of my security deposit and that I would move out at the end of July. I didn't know where I would be living if the job didn't come through soon, but it didn't worry me. I had absolute confidence that the job was mine. No one else could possibly have been better qualified or had a better interview than I had. The power of Nam-myoho-renge-kyo could not fail to move the universe. I just waited for their call and continued chanting.

While waiting for their call, I left home long enough one day to have lunch with Leslie. She was happy to hear that I was at last looking forward to getting the job I sought. At the ceremony enshrining my Gohonzon, the year before, she had given me a postcard commemorating the occasion. On it, she had written an excerpt from one of the letters Nichiren wrote to his disciples. In pertinent part, it says, "Be diligent in developing your faith until the last moment of your life. Otherwise you will have regrets. For example, the journey from Kamakura to Kyoto takes twelve days. If you travel for eleven but stop on the twelfth, how can you admire the moon over the capital?" So it was no surprise when the call came early in July, asking if I could report for work on the 17th—which of course I did. The job began exactly one year from the date I received my Gohonzon.

Chapter 18—Human Revolution

WITH A PAYCHECK COMING IN, my financial fortune began changing. At first, it was difficult to spend money since I had been tightfisted so long. I found it challenging shopping for something as inexpensive as a couple pairs of socks, my first non-food purchase in quite some time. Only with a great act of will was my right hand able to pry open my wallet from the secure grip of my uncooperative left hand. A few months later, my hands and mind began working in unison again. I had earned enough money to leave the roaches behind, moving from the efficiency in Rosslyn to a much nicer two-bedroom apartment in Falls Church. Thanks to cheap and simple decorating tips from *Apartment Life,* I decorated the bedroom walls and ceiling with sheets matching the linens on my bed. The arrival of a roommate even allowed me to *save* money. That was something I hadn't done for more than a week or two since a brief period in high school while living with my brother Bill. Although a better quality roommate than the six-legged ones I had become accustomed to, my roommate had the annoying habit of starting his day out gyrating to Bohannon or some other loud disco music.

At a Halloween party a few months later, I finally found someone with whom I could get more seriously involved. Like everyone else there, Juanita was a fellow Buddhist, and the woman whose father would later threaten our death. I had already known her for over a year, having first met her at a meeting in the spring of 1977. She was an attractive woman, trim at 5'6", with relaxed hair falling around her café-au-lait face. She had not been one of the many women I had casually dated. Now we hit it off dancing. I came to the party in a caftan, carrying a six-foot stick serving as a staff. I was Gully Foyle, Bester's protagonist from *The Stars My Destination*, with his Maori tiger-face painted on mine, NOMAD and all. She was a silver-skinned alien, of uncertain origin.

The next time we met, at a gathering of friends, I was under the weather. We had just returned from a midnight showing of the *Rocky Horror Picture Show* at the Key Theatre in Georgetown. To top off the evening, we smoked a little dope. Which led inevitably to the munchies, some forgettable assortment of brownies, cookies and chips augmented by the pseudo healthy veggies and dip. The munchies, in turn, led to the cheap wine. "Whoa, man, skip me on this round," I said to whoever was pushing the produce, "I'm green enough already." Juanita was warmly sympathetic, compassionately comforting me in my discomfited state.

"That's OK, John, just sit back and relax for a few minutes," she said, stroking my cheek. "Do you want some Alka Seltzer or Mylanta?"

"Nah. I just need to sit still for a little while."

"All right."

Nobody had been so felicitous to me in a long time. *Maybe she cares about me.* It had to be time to go for the eggs—she even liked SF! Soon enough we were an item, going together to one party or another, to the movies and to the local science fiction convention, Disclave.

Then came the incident at her house in northeast DC, in early January 1979. We had a party to go to in Virginia. I came early to pick her up, parking the old phone van (with its $900 engine) I still drove at the curb next to her house. We had time to relax before leaving. So we smoked a joint while filling her large bathtub with a gallon of milk and some hot water. We got undressed, but before we could slide into the milk-bath, we heard a knock on the front door. Without time to think whom it could be, the door opened and a voice boomed upstairs to the bedroom, "Juanita, what the hell's going on? Who you got in here?"

"Nobody, Daddy," she lied, as I ducked into the closet—where I was quickly discovered.

"Get your clothes on and get the hell outta here," he said to me. I scrambled into my clothes and quickly departed.

I had seen scenes like this in the movies, but had never experienced one in real life. I went on to the party we were both supposed to attend. I called her from there, concerned about the aftermath. Her father was still there so she couldn't talk. Eventually she called to say he had left, very angry. At 29, she was a full decade beyond her teenage years and no longer living at home. Nonetheless, her father exerted a control over her still. She had reason to fear him, she said, based on things he had done over the years. From then on, we were more circumspect. I continued to see her at Buddhist activities, but I never went to her house again. Instead, she came to my apartment in Falls Church, after Buddhist meetings in Arlington.

I had found a measure of happiness in myself since I had begun practicing Buddhism. Having endured a self-imposed period of celibacy to calibrate my non-sexual perceptions, I felt confident that I had learned what kind of person I wanted to be involved with. I felt confident that Juanita was that person and I refused to allow the incident with her father to keep us apart. Over the next several months, she and I went out on a regular basis. We attended movies and concerts, went to museums and drove far away from the city. The more things we did, the more things we found we had in common, despite our very different backgrounds. We both liked the outdoors, hiking the trails along Skyline Drive in Shenandoah National Park or stopping to watch waterfalls cascade into the valley below. We both liked *Star Trek* and other science fiction TV shows or movies. Taken together with the intimate times we spent together, these common interests enriched and helped fuel the love that continued to grow.

Eventually, certain that we were each happy in our own right and not dependent on each other, we bought wedding and engagement rings shortly before Juanita's birthday, in November 1979. The likelihood that others might find our interracial relationship objectionable did not escape us. Nor did it deter us. It was an obstacle we expected to face and would deal with when it happened. We had no problems with acceptance among our fellow Buddhists because the group was more diverse than any other group with which we were associated. I expected the same would not be true in the rest of society. The chief objection would come from her father. As I now know, of course, it had to.

The week before Thanksgiving, when I called George Harrison to announce our wedding plans, I quickly realized we had a problem. The conversation had not gone well. "Oh yeah, I remember you! Why are you calling here? I got nothing to talk about with you." Those were his first words to me, before I could even tell him why I was calling.

"Well, I know we met under awkward circumstances, but I want to put that behind us. I was calling to let you know that your daughter Juanita and I are planning to get married next year." For a brief moment, I held out a faint hope he would hear me out. Then he yelled into the phone.

"Married? You say you gonna marry *my* daughter! Don't you think I got something to say about that?"

"Well…sure, that's why I was calling you. But she is 30 years old. I was calling as a courtesy, out of respect to you as her father."

"Respect! You don't respect me. You don't know nothing about respect!" he snorted.

"I'm sorry you feel that way." I backpedaled, with no sensible response coming to mind.

"You're sorry all right! You stay away from my daughter and don't you be calling back here again," he said, slamming down the phone.

Only two more days after my call, time enough for him to imagine the union of his daughter and me, his anger reached its full force. It was then that Juanita overheard her father telling her brother, "If the two of them get married or I find the two of them together, I'll kill the both of them."

To my knowledge, no one had ever felt that strongly about me before. Juanita convinced me to take him at his word. She believed that if the two of us got married or he found both of us together, we could die. We had to make sure that didn't happen. Death could come at any time, at any place he could find me. Thankfully, he didn't know where I worked. I told my roommate to warn me if he saw a black Chevy station wagon, like her father's, drive by the apartment.

Juanita had said, quite correctly, that we needed to chant about this. When I called George Harrison to tell him our wedding plans, I had been practicing Buddhism for almost two and a half years. For the first 18 months, I was fairly consistent in my practice, as new members go. I tried to keep following the admonition from Nichiren, quoted on Leslie's card to me two years before. The quote read, in part: "Be diligent in developing your faith until the last moment of your life. Otherwise you will have regrets." But as time passed, I had become complacent. I had passed the bar. I had gotten the job I wanted. I had been out with all sorts of women and had now found one worthy of marriage. Laziness had reasserted itself. Now I often missed doing gongyo, skipping either the morning or the evening prayers once or twice each week. On most days, I chanted only a few minutes of daimoku (Nam-myoho-renge-kyo). George Harrison's threat changed all that. Terror proved such a great stimulus to my practice that I began chanting two hours of daimoku every day and didn't miss another gongyo for the next three years.

Juanita's father was right about one thing—I didn't respect him. I had grown up spoiled with little respect for authority. Three years in the military had convinced me that few so-called superior officers were worthy of any respect. Finally, given all the jerks, assholes and incompetent fools I had worked for as a civilian left me no capacity for respecting someone based only on their position of authority. I didn't care whom you were or what position you occupied, you had to earn my respect by your words and deeds. Slowly, however, I was beginning to absorb Buddhist teachings, principles that lightened my arrogance and offered a different perspective on the shortcomings of others, including even those in positions of power.

One of the allegorical personas of Buddhism, called Bodhisattva Never Despising, would bow to every person he met and say, "I deeply respect you. I would not dare despise you or be arrogant for you will practice the bodhisattva way and surely attain Buddhahood." In response to this humble behavior, people would beat him with sticks and stones, because they failed to see their own potential for Buddhahood or understand his appreciation of it. While I still had a little ways to go in modeling the conduct of this Bodhisattva, I did understand the need to move myself in that direction. I needed to be able to overlook a person's bad behavior and to respect a person not for the deeds they had already done but those they might do in the future. Most of all, I needed to see the potential Buddha in every human being.

After hearing her father's death threat, Juanita and I couldn't go on as if nothing had happened. We would still see each other at Buddhist activities, but we had to curtail our amorous adventures for the time being. We needed to discuss our feelings, to discuss why this was happening. More importantly, we had to come up with a solution to this death cloud hanging over our heads. We met at well-lit but out of the way places, where we could be sure her father hadn't followed her.

"I understand that your father has good reason to not like or even to hate white people. But I'm not like those other people. My mother raised me to be against racism."

"It doesn't matter. You're still white. Plus, he found you in my house high on dope and with your pants off."

"But killing us! Isn't that too extreme?"

"I don't know. For you, maybe, but not to him. It doesn't really matter why he wants to kill us does it? If that's what he has in mind, we need to figure out what to do."

"Yeah, you're right. I'm going to keep chanting two hours a day until I do."

Up until I learned of George Harrison's plans, I thought that I had made great strides in my problem with relationships. I no longer looked at marriage as a refuge. I no longer needed someone else to make me happy. Buddhism had done that much for me. Should I just give her up and find somebody else? I was never one to cave into authority, which had caused me all kinds of grief in the Army and elsewhere, even before I was a Buddhist. I wasn't about to do that now—death threat or not. Maybe we should we run far away, to another country perhaps, where her father couldn't find us? Nah, probably not, since we would always be looking over our shoulders, expecting him to pursue us. Plus, we both had jobs here and would have to start over. That was not much better than simply splitting up. Should I just set a trap and blow him away first, setting up a claim of self-defense to keep me out of jail? If I couldn't kill Stubby, I certainly couldn't kill Juanita's father. What then?

Other Buddhists we sought advice from confirmed that we could not run away or hide from our karma. Like a shadow, karma accompanies you wherever you go. We had heard it all before, but needed to hear it again. "Quitting your job to escape a boss who's a jerk might seem sensible, but if it's your karma to have a jerk for a boss, the jerk will reappear with a different face in any new job you get. To eliminate the jerk you have to eradicate the karma. You can't change your boss directly, you must change yourself." That is what they told us. Like other elements of the Buddhist practice, it was a radical concept, difficult for many people to accept. But to me, it made more sense than any of our other options did. To remedy the relationship with Juanita's father so we could survive together, I needed to change myself. I recalled an odd incident from several months before, proving this point to me.

As I came into an apartment where a discussion meeting would soon begin, a woman who I knew barely at all caught my eye. She gave me a withering glare before turning away. I was flabbergasted, totally unaware of what might have prompted the look. So far as I knew, I had done absolutely nothing to deserve this. I had recently learned about the Buddhist concept of apology, which, according to the translations available at that time, entailed a three-part prayer. I jumped right on it during the gongyo at the outset of the meeting. I silently accepted responsibility for the situation, determined to change it, and silently expressed my gratitude at having this opportunity to change my karma. It was very different from any kind of apology I had previously encountered. After gongyo concluded, the discussion part of the meeting began. To my surprise, the first time I spoke up during the meeting, the woman who had glared at my arrival was now beaming brightly at me! Incredible, I thought, that this Buddhist prayer should work so well.

So that is what I had to do with George Harrison. I had little hope that such speedy results would follow. But I prayed for his happiness on a daily basis, in the same fashion as I had for the woman during the discussion meeting. At first, it was very difficult to do. A glare was one thing, but a death threat? Nonetheless, as I continued chanting this way, my life became happier, stronger and more peaceful. Things went well at work. I breezed through the traffic on congested Northern Virginia streets. When confronted with a bad case of bronchitis, I used the illness to help me accomplish giving up cigarettes, a goal that had eluded me up until then. Buddhists call this turning poison into medicine. Thanks to his threat, my Buddhist practice grew stronger, my faith deeper and my life more powerful. It became easier and easier to pray sincerely for his happiness—if it were not for him, I would not have been able to make so many valuable changes in my life a through my Buddhist practice.

Assuming we did succeed in avoiding death, after marriage, I was looking ahead to the prospect of having children. Perhaps, I thought, I should give up smoking dope for a while, to clean the cannabis out of my system before we try having kids. Here, in the summer of 1980, I was still smoking dope recreationally. Mary Jane had been a very seductive mistress in my life, seemingly harmless and always promising a good time. But when facing challenging tasks needing completion, she was an evil escape, sapping my will and clouding my mind. With her gracious assistance, I had played a fool for Juanita's father. But Buddhism has no prohibitions comparable to the Ten Commandments of Judeo-Christian belief. The only precept is to chant Nam-myoho-renge-kyo. Experiencing the effects, good or bad, from causes one makes should be sufficient to control one's behavior. Indeed, I did now control my behavior, including smoking dope. I still enjoyed smoking it but didn't use it as a crutch or an escape anymore. While I was unaware of any studies linking cannabis in a man's bloodstream to birth defects, I didn't want to take any chances.

I didn't expect stopping would be easy. While I had given up dope for an entire year after coming back from Vietnam, marijuana had been a regular part of my life for over ten years since I had started up again in Minneapolis. So I assumed giving it up now would be much more difficult than was giving up cigarettes. It took three weeks of a hacking cough to quit smoking tobacco. Surprisingly, the change came easily with nothing so unpleasant as bronchitis needed to assist me. Instead, a midnight Gohonzon conferral provided all the impetus I needed. The occasion was such a happy one for me, that while driving home totally straight, I experienced the same high that I got from marijuana! So impressed was I by this unexpected phenomenon, I simply gave up smoking marijuana from that point on, without any difficulty at all.

Confident that we could hold off the dark forces of George Harrison's heart, Juanita and I got married in October of 1980. Co-workers from her office and mine, our friends and fellow Buddhists were there. None of her family could come to the wedding because of her father, but at least her father didn't come gunning for us. During the course of the next year, her sisters kept her up to date on what was happening. She talked to her mother on the phone while her father was at work. He wouldn't talk to her. We were safe, but her father had disowned her. We needed to do more to change the situation.

In November 1981, we went on a pilgrimage to Japan to see the original Gohonzon inscribed by Nichiren Daishonin in 1279. While there, I determined that within a year, Juanita would have our baby and her father would shake my hand. This represented two major challenges. According to her OB/GYN, getting pregnant would be unlikely at best. One of her Fallopian tubes was completely blocked while the other was partially blocked. Nonetheless, within three months of our return, she was pregnant. Richard was born November 10, 1982, one year after the encouragement we received from a leader in Japan. Her father came to her hospital room the very next day.

"Congratulations," he said, shaking my hand, a broad smile on his face.

"Thank you," I replied simply.

"If Juanita and the baby are doin' OK, we'd like you all to come to Thanksgiving dinner," he added.

"Well sure. It's two weeks away. We should be doing fine by then." I was almost in shock. All I could do was smile back.

I don't know that I could say Juanita was completely fine in just 14 days, but two weeks later, we bundled up Richard for our first family visit to the Harrison house in northwest Washington. The 45-minute car trip from the small rambler we bought in Annandale, Virginia early in 1981, gave us more time to wonder what awaited us. When we arrived for dinner, George Harrison took me aside, saying,

"C'mon John, let's go downstairs."

"OK," I said. As we descended the stairs, I briefly doubted whether our prayers had been successful after all. Perhaps his invitation had all been a ruse. Once we got downstairs, he would shoot me. My doubts were soon dispelled. I first heard, and then saw the TV.

"Let the womenfolk take care of the kitchen, John. We can watch Dallas get their butts kicked."

"Yeah, all right," I said, the confidence in my prayers restored. He too, was a Redskins fan. No matter who played the Cowboys, Redskins fans always rooted for the other team to beat Dallas.

The man who had wanted me dead had invited me to Thanksgiving dinner. Next, he had us over for Christmas. Later on, he invited us to a Harrison family reunion in Columbia, South Carolina. There my white face stood out in stark contrast to those of the 700 or so other attendees, all of whom, along with Juanita's father, welcomed me into the family. Eventually he began telling me, "Just call me Dad." His heart changed because mine changed. Of course, I can't take all the credit. The change in Juanita's father and the birth of Richard were due to our combined prayers and determinations. I have never doubted the power of my prayers since.

All through college and then law school, I had looked in vain for a lever to change the hearts and minds of people who didn't see things correctly, the way that I saw them. But did I really know best? I knew the war in Vietnam was wrong. I knew Nixon was a crook. I knew Kissinger was at best an amoralist. I knew there were plenty of avaricious lawyers around to work as hired legal guns for the highest bidder. I knew there were plenty of anarchists, radicals and other malcontents who simply wanted to tear down the system. There were also plenty of apolitical people who cared nothing about the burning issues of the day and just wanted to be winners in life by "dying with the most toys."

Despite pursuing my noble quest of realizing those abstract and romantic ideals I had held since childhood, I could never connect one-on-one, with any of those persons whom the ideals were supposed to serve. The people I saw around me were an uncomfortable reminder of a reality that didn't match my idealized worldview. While I might be sympathetic to the plight of people like the shell-shocked son of my Mankato landlady, I could not get too close to these tangible trees lest I lose sight of the forest on which I focused my attention.

I looked for escape in the pleasures of marijuana, secluding myself in psychedelic sounds, progressive rock and fusion jazz. With dope and without, I also sought a refuge from the stresses of daily life through communing with the uber womb. I looked for happiness in the security of on-demand sex, most easily achieved through serial monogamy. Upon my return to the quest, the questions always remained. How could people be so greedy, so willing to step on others to get ahead? Why didn't people care whether things worked efficiently, cost-effectively? How could the American people have been so stupid as to reelect Richard Nixon? Why would the world around me not resolve itself into the form it should be in? Why could I not find a path to the place of peace and harmony I could see only dimly in my mind?

The answers finally came, once I began studying the teachings of Buddhism. I learned that my thoughts and actions were those of delusion. I had been separating my inner world from the world outside me, separating myself from others. The human, social environment around me was an inescapable part of my own inner reality, reflecting my own self. A Buddha is simply a common mortal who is no longer deluded. Someone who has become aware of his or her true nature and thereby able to see things the way they really are.

George Harrison had threatened my life because many years before, I had fantasized killing MSgt. Seagram. During my year in Vietnam and for a time thereafter, I thought Stubby was symptomatic of the evils war and the career military bring into the world. Then came Nixon and the Watergate conspiracy to darken my thoughts and deepen my cynicism. Yet without those people and experiences, I would not have quested for the knowledge and wisdom to defeat the evils I saw. Without that quest, I wouldn't have been prepared to accept what would have seemed preposterous notions about the religious practices of Buddhism. Without that acceptance, I wouldn't have been able transform the heart of George Harrison by changing myself for the better, nor found the means to reclaim my ideals.

Buddhism finally gave me the lever I sought. I learned that to change the world, I first needed to change myself. Once I stopped blaming others and took responsibility for my own happiness, everything moved forward. I didn't need sex or drugs as a refuge anymore. I found a woman with whom I could enjoy life, even amidst great challenges. Juanita and I overcame her father's opposition to our marriage. Without any medical intervention, she overcame physical impediments that should have prevented conception, enabling us to raise two children of our own.

It's hard work being your own person, but far more rewarding than the alternative. Godot never will come and even if Westmoreland eventually does come, after all the waiting, the answers he gives will probably be wrong. It seems patriotic and certainly *convenient* to have someone else on whom to rely, like a president. We as citizens *should* be able to rely on the presidents we elect, but as we eventually find out, our reliance is all too often misplaced. Presidents lie. They tell not just little white lies but big whoppers that result in the death or suffering of thousands or even millions of civilians and soldiers around the world. So it is also *convenient* to have someone to blame, like a president. There is always someone to point at, to identify as the source of our personal problems, like a boss, a coworker or that illegal immigrant standing outside the convenience store. There is always someone on whom frustration can be released, like the cashier in the store, the driver of the car in front of us, that handicapped child disrupting the classroom, or even our spouse. Sometimes the culprit in our suffering can be difficult to find, but if we look long and hard, we can find them. It's better than looking at ourselves, isn't it? That is what I used to think. Now I know better.

Thank you, indeed, Mr. Harrison, for threatening my life. Thank you, Master Sergeant Seagram, for so aggravating me that I wanted to kill you. Thank you Richard Nixon and Henry Kissinger too, for showing me how *not* to behave while working in government. Your bad examples were always available to me when considering a course of conduct. Despite my personal opinion of your behavior as human beings, I have come to realize and accept that a Buddha nature exists within you as well. The respect Bodhisattva Never Despising has for others depends on neither their conduct nor their rank or status. That respect is for their potential Buddhahood. I understand and appreciate that now.

"A great human revolution in just a single individual will help achieve a change in the destiny of a nation, and further, will enable a change in the destiny of humankind." — Daisaku Ikeda[4]

Everyone has the potential to see things the way they really are. Everyone has the potential to treat others with the dignity and respect they would like to be treated with themselves. Everyone great or small has the capacity to influence profoundly the course of human events. It happens incrementally, as one human heart changes another. It happens as one person after another accepts responsibility for his or own life. No longer waiting for Westmoreland or Godot to tell them what to do or think. Neither blaming nor blindly supporting political leaders for success or failure. Restoring or creating a sense of value in human life, kindness and compassion.

---

[4] Ikeda, Daisaku, *The Human Revolution,* Book One, p. viii, World Tribune Press, 2004.

Epilogue

WHILE WE OCCASIONALLY PUT SOME effort into landscaping, neither Juanita nor I spend much time on fruit or flowers. Nonetheless, just as Candide eventually did, we spend our time "cultivating our garden." Max Weber, the father of sociology, wrote about the Calvinist-derived Protestant "work ethic." For me, the work ethic is as much at the core of Buddhism as it is in Calvinism, but in a happier and more humane fashion. In other words, we are putting our ideals into practice on a daily basis. We are setting goals and striving to accomplish them confidently and diligently.

Juanita and I continue enjoying the many interests we have in common, while developing separate pursuits we have more time for as we share our retirement from successful careers. We look forward to many more years of success, no matter what further challenges we may face. In more than 27 years of marriage, we have never experienced any overt or covert racism directed at us as a couple. Evidently, when we overcame the situation with her father, we took care of that issue as well.

My children have never experienced hardships like those I faced during the nine years between the deaths of my father and mother. We kept our promise to fund their college expenses yet both Juanita and I were able to retire at age 55 with no further employment necessary. I can now pursue my childhood dream of writing without needing a day job. Juanita is busy pursuing her dream of crafting quilts.

In my childhood, I was a spoiled brat. In my youth, I was lazy and irresponsible. During my time in the Army, I held superiors in what I viewed then as justified contempt. During the 25 years I spent working for Fairfax County, my Buddhist practice enabled me to change those negative elements of my character. Having chosen to create value by working in consumer affairs for 14 years, I educated thousands of consumers. I wrote booklets and spoke to groups on the process of buying homes and cars, renting apartments, resolving disputes through small claims court and a variety of other topics, including managing homeowner associations. Along the way, I served both as president and as a public sector representative on the board of the Washington Chapter of the Community Association Institute. There, my experience in working with the exceptionally diverse group of people who practice Buddhism, helped me bring together the competing interests (property managers, homeowner and condominium association members, builders and developers, government and the various professionals or businesses providing services to associations) who belong to the association community.

Having tired of consumer issues and managerial shortcomings in the department, I was happy to leave when a reduction-in-force took me from consumer affairs into public works. Nonetheless, working there had provided me with great practical knowledge for my own benefit as I researched the topics to educate others. That sort of incidental benefit continued in public works. From grade school through college, I had always hated and done poorly at math. So it came as a surprise and challenge when they made me a budget analyst in my new agency. In the process, I added an education in financial matters, using spreadsheets to forecast revenues and expenditures. That became valuable knowledge for managing my own family finances. At the same time, the working environment was much improved over my former office.

A few years before I retired, the County instituted a "pay-for-performance" evaluation system. I wasn't worried; I was no longer lazy and irresponsible. I assured those coworkers who feared their future salaries were at risk that the best defense they had against a poor rating was to do a good job. I made out well under the new system, always getting the highest available increase.

Human revolution is an unceasing process. Indicative of how my character had changed from my pre-Buddhist days was the relationship I had with the division director of my agency. Before working for Fairfax County, he had spent 30 years in the Army, retiring as a full Colonel. Although we never dwelled on it or discussed it at length, he knew of my Vietnam experiences and perspective on the military. Nonetheless, we got along well and respected each other. At my retirement reception, the director said, "whenever I needed something done, done right and done on time, I always knew who to give it to—John."

Retired from work but not from life, the revolution continues. Juanita and I eagerly await fresh challenges.

For more information about Nichiren Buddhism, including locations where activities are conducted nearest you, go online to www.SGI.org or www.SGI-USA.org. For books about Nichiren Buddhism, look for titles by Middleway Press at your nearest library, bookstore or online. Of course, for the sake of comparative study, libraries and bookstores will also have materials about many other forms or sects of Buddhism as well its history and development throughout the world.